Scrum

FOR

DUMMIES®

A Wiley Brand

Scrum
FOR
DUMMIES®
A Wiley Brand

by Mark C. Layton

FOR
DUMMIES®
A Wiley Brand

Scrum For Dummies®

Published by: **John Wiley & Sons, Inc.,** 111 River Street, Hoboken, NJ 07030-5774, www.wiley.com

Copyright © 2015 by John Wiley & Sons, Inc., Hoboken, New Jersey

Media and software compilation copyright © 2015 by John Wiley & Sons, Inc. All rights reserved.

Published simultaneously in Canada

For general information on our other products and services, please contact our Customer Care Department within the U.S. at 877-762-2974, outside the U.S. at 317-572-3993, or fax 317-572-4002. For technical support, please visit www.wiley.com/techsupport.

Wiley publishes in a variety of print and electronic formats and by print-on-demand. Some material included with standard print versions of this book may not be included in e-books or in print-on-demand. If this book refers to media such as a CD or DVD that is not included in the version you purchased, you may download this material at http://booksupport.wiley.com. For more information about Wiley products, visit www.wiley.com.

Library of Congress Control Number: 2014958355

ISBN 978-1-119-0575-3 (pbk); ISBN 978-1-118-90583-8; (epub); 978-1-118-90577-7 (epdf)

Manufactured in the United States of America

10 9 8 7 6 5 4 3 2 1

Contents at a Glance

Table of Contents

Introduction

Welcome to *Scrum For Dummies*. Scrum is an agile project-management framework with proven results in decreasing time to market 30 to 40 percent, improving product quality, and heightening customer satisfaction — all this while lowering costs from 30 to 70 percent. Scrum accomplishes all this through integration of business and development talent, improved communication models, increased performance visibility, regular customer and stakeholder feedback, and an empirically based inspect-and-adapt mentality. Even the most complex project can be managed more effectively using scrum to increase your bottom line.

About This Book

My goal is to demonstrate explicitly how scrum can be used for any project — not just software development. As with my *Agile Project Management For Dummies* (published by John Wiley & Sons, Inc.), this book is intended to be a field manual for the application of scrum in real-world situations. While I cover scrum fundamentals in detail, this book also delves into how to actually get out and experience its amazing benefits.

Scrum itself is easy to explain, but often the application is difficult. Old habits and organizational mind-sets need to be shifted, and new ways embraced. For this reason, I've included success stories so that you can see how scrum can fit into your unique situation.

The main thrust of understanding scrum lies in the three roles, three artifacts, and five events that form its foundation. While I cover these thoroughly, I also include common practices from myself and others in the field. From there you can choose what will work best for your project.

Several books on scrum already exist, but the one you hold in your hands differs in its practicality. I have over a decade of experience with agile methods and scrum, and I bring this to you in a practical guide. You don't need to be a rocket scientist or a whiz programmer; all you need is a project and a passion to get it done in the best way possible. I give you examples from Fortune 100 companies all the way down to a family organizing their vacation.

I focus on the steps necessary to get scrum's magic working for you. My audience ranges from code programmers to sales professionals to product manufacturers to executives to mid-tier management — and to stay-at-home moms who want a more organized household.

If you're in the IT industry, you have probably heard the terms *agile* and/ or *scrum.* Maybe you've even worked within a scrum environment but want to improve your skills in this area and bring others in your firm along with you. If you are not in IT, you might have heard that scrum is a great way to run projects. You are right! Perhaps it's all new and you're just searching for a way to make your project more accessible; or you have a great idea burning inside and just don't know how to bring it to fruition. Whoever you are, an easy way exists to run your project, and it's called scrum. Within these pages, I show you how.

Foolish Assumptions

Scrum itself isn't technical. In fact, its basic tenets are common sense. However, in many cases, I've wrapped this information within the world of technology and have used technical terms to help explain this. Where useful, I've defined these.

I also cover common practices from scrum experts throughout the world. You can learn so much from others who use this framework in a seemingly limitless spectrum of projects.

Scrum falls under an umbrella of project management called agile project management. Neither scrum nor agile practices is a proper noun. Scrum is a framework for organizing your work, while agile is an adjective used to describe a wide variety of practices that conform to the values of the Agile Manifesto and to the 12 Agile Principles. Scrum and agile are not identical or interchangeable, but you frequently see them written in many sources, especially online, interchangeably. In this book, you will see terminology from both descriptions, because scrum is a frequently used subset of agile practices.

Conventions Used in This Book

If you do an online search, you will see the words *agile* and *scrum,* different roles, meetings, and documents; and various agile methodologies and frameworks, including scrum, capitalized. I shied away from this practice for a couple of reasons.

To start, none of these items are really proper nouns. *Agile* is an adjective that describes a number of items in project management: agile projects, agile teams, agile processes, and so on. But it is not a proper noun, and except in chapter or section titles, you will not see me use it that way.

For readability, I did not capitalize agile-related roles, meetings, and documents. Such terms include agile project, product owner, scrum master, development team, user stories, product backlog, and more. You may, however, see these terms capitalized in places other than this book.

Some exceptions exist. The Agile Manifesto and the Agile Principles are copyrighted material. The Agile Alliance, Scrum Alliance, and Project Management Institute are professional organizations. A Certified ScrumMaster and a PMI-Agile Certified Practitioner are professional titles.

Scrum For Dummies has six parts. Each part focuses on a different aspect of scrum and utilizing scrum in project management:

- ✔ **In Part I,** I show you the basics of scrum and its origin. I define concepts and important terminology as well as introduce the difference between scrum and common practices in scrum.

- ✔ **In Part II,** I show you how to get a project started using scrum. You get a look into how the three roles, three artifacts, and five events are broken down and get introduced to some common successful practices. You will discover release and sprint planning and find out how to estimate requirements.

- ✔ **In Part III,** I tell you how scrum is applied in industries such as software, manufacturing, construction, healthcare, and education and give concrete examples of success. You find out how scrum can address challenges specific to each industry.

- ✔ **In Part IV,** I show you how scrum is helping transform the business world. You see how scrum is used in large-scale organizations. You see how scrum is not just an individual unit or only in one company department but how using scrum can be incorporated across an entire organization from human resources to finance to business development and to customer service.

- ✔ **In Part V,** I help you to identify the universality of scrum outside of the business world and applied to daily life. You discover how scrum can be used to find love and for families, as well as how to use the framework of scrum for life goals.

- ✔ **In Part VI,** I introduce you to proven tips, metrics, and resources for making a successful transition to scrum and describe useful information to continue your journey in implementing scrum.

Icons Used in This Book

The following icons in the margins indicate highlighted material that I thought would be of interest to you. Next, I describe the meaning of each icon that is used in this book.

Tips are ideas that I would like you to take note of. This is usually practical advice that you can apply for that given topic.

This icon is less common than the others in this book. The intent is to save you time by bringing to your attention some common pitfalls that you are better off avoiding.

If you don't care too much about the technical stuff, you can easily skip these paragraphs and you won't miss much. If the technical stuff is your thing, you may find these sections fascinating.

This is something that I would like you to take a special note of. This is a concept or idea that I thought was important for you know and remember. An example of this would be a best practice that I think is noteworthy.

Beyond the Book

A lot of extra content that is not in this book is available at www.dummies. com. Go online to find the following:

✔ **Online articles covering additional topics at**

> http://www.dummies.com/extras/scrum

Here you will find articles, blogs, and other information regarding the implementation and experience of scrum.

✔ **The Cheat Sheet for this book is at**

> www.dummies.com/cheatsheet/scrum

Here you'll find the major highlights for understanding the scrum framework.

✔ **Updates to this book, if any, are also available at**

> http://www.dummies.com/extras/scrum

Where to Go from Here

To start getting scrum working for you, you can begin applying scrum on smaller projects to get the feel, and before you know it, you'll be handling your most important ones in the same way. This book is applicable to a diverse set of readers and is organized in a way that will allow you to navigate it by finding specific areas of interest that are relevant to you. Each chapter can be a reference to you at any time you have a technical question or want to see an example of scrum in real life.

- If you are new to scrum, begin with Chapter 1 to understand introductory concepts and terminology; then work your way through Chapter 6 to find out about the entire framework. Then, as you continue on past Chapter 6, you'll see how to apply scrum in any situation.

- If you are already familiar with scrum and want to find out more about how it applies to many industries, check out Chapters 7 through 10 and read about scrum being practiced in a variety of industries.

- If you are a product owner, scrum master, or business leader and want to know more about scrum on a larger scale, start by reading Chapter 12 and all of Part VI for valuable resources.

- If you are familiar with scrum and want to know how it can help you address daily life, read Chapters 16 and 17 to get inspiration and examples.

Part I
Getting Started with Scrum

In this part . . .

- ✔ Connecting scrum with the principles of agile project management.

- ✔ Using constant feedback through transparency and quantification to elevate success rates of projects.

- ✔ Becoming tactically flexible to create strategic stability.

- ✔ Visit www.dummies.com for great Dummies content online.

Chapter 1

The Basics of Scrum

In This Chapter

▶ Seeing essential scrum principles

▶ Identifying useful scrum values and structure

At its barest, scrum is an empirical exposure model, which means knowledge is gained from real-life experience, and decisions are made based on that experience. It's a way of organizing your project — whether it be releasing a new smartphone or coordinating your daughter's fifth-grade birthday party — to expose whether your approach is generating intended results in reality. If you need to get it done, scrum provides a structure for increased efficiency and faster results.

Within scrum, common sense reigns. You focus on what can be done today, with an eye toward breaking future work into manageable pieces. You can immediately see how well your development methodology is working, and when you find inefficiencies in your approach, scrum allows you to act on them by making adjustments with clarity and speed.

While *empirical exposure modeling* goes back to the beginning of time in the arts — in sculpting, for example, you chisel away, check the results, make any adaptations necessary, and chisel away some more — its modern-day usage stems from computer modeling. The empirical exposure model means observing or experiencing actual results, rather than simulating them based on research or a mathematical formula. You then make decisions based on these experiences. In scrum, you break down your project into actionable chunks and then observe your results every step of the way. This allows you to immediately make the changes necessary to keep you on the best track possible.

The Bird's Eye Basics

Scrum is not a methodology. It isn't a paint by the numbers and end up with a product approach; it's a simple framework for clearly defining roles and organizing your actionable work so you are more effective in prioritizing work and more efficient in completing work selected. Frameworks are less pre-scriptive than methodologies and provide appropriate amounts of flexibility for additional processes, structures, and tools that complement them. When this approach is used, you can clearly observe and adopt complementary methods and practices and quickly determine whether you are making real, tangible progress. You create tested, usable results within weeks, days, or in some cases, hours.

Like building a house brick by brick, scrum is an iterative, incremental approach. It gives you early empirical evidence of performance and quality. Roles are distinct and self-ruling, with individuals and teams being given the freedom and tools to get the job done. Lengthy progress reports, redundant meetings, and bloated management layers are nonexistent. If you just plain want to get the job done, scrum is the approach to use.

Scrum is a term from the rough and tumble game of rugby. Huddles or scrums are formed with the forwards from one side interlocking their arms, heads down, and pushing against the forwards from the opposing team, also inter-locking arms, heads down. The ball is then thrown into the midst of this tightly condensed group of athletes. Although each team member plays a unique position, all play both attacking and defending roles, and work as a team to move the ball down the field of play. Like rugby, scrum also relies on talented people with varying responsibilities and domains working closely together in teams toward a common goal.

I want to emphasize, and have written two-thirds of this book on, an over-looked concept of scrum — its absolute versatility. For those who know of scrum, they commonly think it's customized for software, IT, tech stuff. But that's the tip of the scrumberg. Absolutely any project — large, small, tech, artistic, social, personal — all can be productively placed within the scrum framework. In Chapters 7–17, I show you how.

A roadmap to value

Throughout this book, I discuss techniques that I and other scrum practitio-ners apply as common practice extensions to scrum. These complement, not replace, the scrum framework. I point out the differences when they occur. Each common practice I include has been tried and tested by me and others and are those I can recommend — but always with the clear understanding that these are outside of scrum and choices for you to make in your own situation.

As a model, I call this aggregation of scrum and vetted common practices the "roadmap to value." It consists of seven stages that walk you through the vision stage of your project all the way through to the task level and back again in a continual process of inspection and adaptation. In other words, the stages help you see what it is you want to achieve, and then have you progressively break it down into pieces through an efficient cycle that leads to real results every day, week, and month.

You know that billion-dollar idea that's been lurking in the back of your head for years? Follow the seven stages. They'll show you the feasibility and fallacy of it and where to make your improvements — step by step, piece by piece.

Figure 1-1 is a holistic view of the roadmap to value.

From this chart you can easily see how you begin with the vision, work through planning, and then enter the cyclical world of sprints, reviews, and retrospectives.

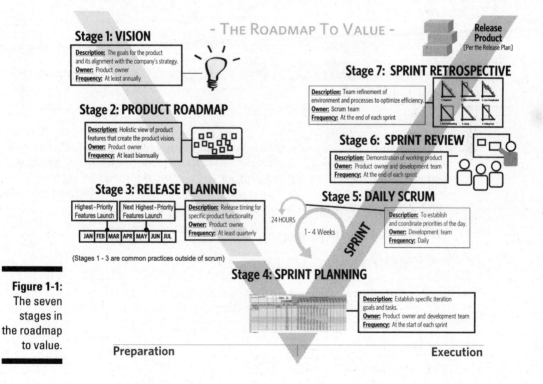

Figure 1-1:
The seven stages in the roadmap to value.

A simplified scrum overview

The process of scrum is simple and circular, with a constant element of inspection and adaptation:

- A ruthlessly ordered to-do list — called a product backlog — is created and maintained.
- Top-priority items are selected for a fixed, regular, time box — called a sprint — within which the scrum team strives for a predetermined and mutually agreed upon goal.

Figure 1-2 gives a visual depiction of scrum.

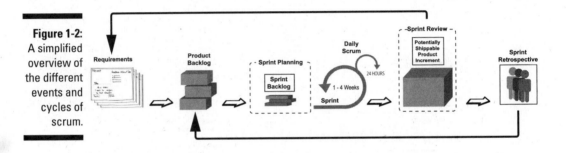

Figure 1-2:
A simplified overview of the different events and cycles of scrum.

The scrum process allows you to adapt quickly to changing market forces, technological constraints, regulations, new innovations, and most anything else you can think of. It's the ongoing process of working on the highest-priority items to completion that holds the key. Each of these highest-priority items gets fully developed and tested through the following steps:

- Requirement elaboration
- Design
- Development
- Comprehensive testing
- Integration
- Documentation
- Approval

The seven steps to fully build the scope of each requirement is done with every single item. Every requirement taken on during a sprint, no matter how small or large, is fully built out, tested, and approved or rejected.

When a requirement is accepted and therefore deemed "shippable," you will know that it works. Hope and guesswork are taken out of the equation and replaced with reality. You tangibly build your product, increment by increment, and showcase these tangible increments to stakeholders for feedback. This feedback generates new requirements that are placed in the product backlog and prioritized against existing known work.

TIP
What's more important, efficiency or effectiveness? Hands down, it's effectiveness. Don't worry about efficiency until you've figured out how to be effective. A very efficient development team working on the wrong things is a waste of time. However, a super-effective development team can easily learn efficiency. Always work on the *right* things first.

TIP
"There is nothing so useless as doing efficiently that which should not be done at all." —Peter F. Drucker

The scrum cycle is run again and again. With the constant flow of feedback and emphasis on only developing those items of the highest priority, you not only better reflect what your customers are looking for, but you also deliver it to them faster and with higher quality.

Scrum teams

No matter the scope of your scrum project, your scrum team will have similar characteristics. The size of the development team will vary somewhat, but the roles remain the same. I go over each specific role in detail throughout this book. Figure 1-3 gives a visual representation of the scrum team.

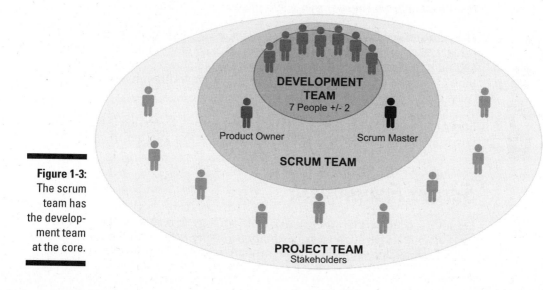

DEVELOPMENT TEAM
7 People +/- 2

Product Owner   Scrum Master

SCRUM TEAM

PROJECT TEAM
Stakeholders

Figure 1-3:
The scrum team has the development team at the core.

The heart of the scrum team is the development team. These are the folks who work together to create the product itself. They work directly with a product owner and scrum master. Although I go over both of those roles in detail, suffice it to say that their jobs are to help align business and development priorities for the organization and to eliminate distractions for the development team so that they can focus on their job — developing!

Stakeholders are not scrum roles, but I include them because they impact your project even though their necks aren't on the line. They can be internal or external. Marketing, legal, infrastructure team and especially customers are examples. But the scrum team itself holds the ultimate level of accountability. As a team, they figure out how to achieve their objectives within the environment that they find themselves.

Governance

Scrum has three roles, and each is equal in status yet separate and independent in function. Each of these three roles has a defined purpose directly designed to enhance the productivity of the team as a whole:

- ✔ Product owner: the *what* and the *when* (not *how much)*
- ✔ Development team: the *how* and the *how much*
- ✔ Scrum master: the *process*

The creators of scrum didn't happen on these roles by chance, but rather through years of experience working with all kinds of project teams. They've seen the good, the bad, and the ugly combinations and found that the best results came from these three pillars of success.

I prefer each scrum role full-time and dedicated solely to the scrum team's project. No thrashing your team members across several different projects, and no part-time players. How many major league football teams have part-time players or those who play for more than one football team at once? None that are successful.

In scrum, no single person or role is above another. Everyone is a peer; no one is a boss or underling. "We" is the operative word rather than "I."

Scrum Framework

Scrum is a framework rather than a methodology. It provides clarity of responsibilities through roles, visibility through artifacts, and opportunities for inspection and adaptation through its events. Within this structure, scrum is a container for other processes and tools that are appropriate for meeting the specific needs of a team, organization or product.

Basically, a scrum project has a 3-3-5 project framework:

✔ Three roles

✔ Three artifacts

✔ Five events

Each of these framework elements fits within the scrum process, which is iterative and incremental. You will incrementally create and improve your product, and you will incrementally improve your process with this basic framework. As you can see, the framework is incredibly simple:

✔ Roles:

  • Product owner

  • Development team

  • Scrum master

✔ Artifacts:

  • Product backlog

  • Sprint backlog

  • Product increment

✔ Events:

  • Sprint

  • Sprint planning

  • Daily scrum

  • Sprint review

  • Sprint retrospective

In the scrum world, *artifacts* refer to either lists of the work to be done or a work product that has been done and is deemed "shippable." Unlike archeological artifacts, the scrum artifacts aren't set in stone. Rather, the scrum process requires a constant review and assessment of artifacts to make sure that you're digging in the right direction.

Each role, artifact, and event in scrum has a set purpose. This framework, moving through the seven stages of the roadmap to value, will be what you place your project within. But the actual tools and techniques for accomplishing your goals will be your own. Scrum doesn't tell you how to achieve your goal; it provides a framework within which you clearly see what you are doing.

In concept, scrum is simple. In practice, scrum can be complicated to implement. It's much like getting into shape physically. In concept, you need to exercise more and take in fewer calories. However, it can be more complex in practice.

To help in this process of application, I recommend some common practices to complement scrum. Throughout the years, I've seen incredible success with this model (my extra elements are in italics):

- ✔ Roles:
  - Product owner
  - Development team
  - Scrum master
  - *Stakeholders*
  - *Scrum mentor*
- ✔ Artifacts:
  - *Vision*
  - *Product roadmap*
  - Product backlog
  - *Release plan*
  - Sprint backlog
  - Product increment
- ✔ Events:
  - *Project planning*
  - *Release planning*
  - Sprint
  - Sprint planning
  - Daily scrum
  - Sprint review
  - Sprint retrospective

Here, I've switched the framework to a 5-6-7 formula. It's still simple, but with additional roles, artifacts, and events designed to smooth the process. I go through each of these in detail throughout the book.

The Feedback Feast

One of the clear advantages that scrum holds over other project management frameworks is the feedback loop generated. You find out early on and continuously what's working, what's not, what's missing, and what's extraordinary.

Feedback is generated regularly from scrum team members, stakeholders, and end-use customers. It goes something like this:

- ✒ Daily feedback between development team members as they go about developing each project requirement.

- ✒ Direct and daily interaction between the product owner and the development team for on-the-spot question answering and feedback.

- ✒ Direct feedback from the product owner as they literally accept or reject every requirement completed.

- ✒ At the end of each sprint, feedback is received from internal stakeholders.

- ✒ At the end of every release, feedback is received from the external marketplace.

You will get more from the scrum model than from traditional project management models because the emphasis is on product development rather than artifact development — delivery of tangible, tested products rather than tomes of reports on what's theoretically possible. You will have received regular feedback along the way, enabling you to incrementally get your product to market as fast as possible.

Therefore, at the end of the project, which is actually a series of sprints within a series of market releases, you're not left wondering whether you've produced what your customers want. You've been communicating and receiving feedback from them all along the way. The inspection and adaptation process has been at work on your behalf, and you're delivering what your customers have actually asked for.

Agile Roots

To understand scrum, it makes sense to dip for a few pages into the broader world of agile techniques. Agile is the umbrella under which scrum resides. (For a thorough and entertaining look at broader agile techniques, see my book *Agile Project Management For Dummies,* published by John Wiley & Sons, Inc.)

Agile is a descriptor of approaches that align to the values of the Agile Manifesto and the 12 agile principles, which I outline here. Scrum is one agile approach, and you can find many more. So to get a better idea of scrum itself, I first look at its godfather.

Watch out! Scrum is such an addictive framework that you'll be using it to coach your kid's soccer, plan your Neighborhood Watch, and even ratchet up your exercise routine.

Three pillars of improvement

The empirical process control model sits securely on three pillars. These apply to agile and scrum:

- ✔ Transparency
- ✔ Inspection
- ✔ Adaptation

Transparency

One of the distinguishing features of scrum, and agile techniques in general, is their unfettered transparency. Through clear and accessible channels of communication, information is radiated throughout. The entire organization is able to know what's been done, what's being worked on, and what's left to go. Right from the start, you are producing real results that are tested and either approved or immediately sent back for adjustments. The lag time between the start date and usable results is now days, not months.

But transparency isn't just about quickly seeing the work and results. Everyone needs to be looking through the same lens. A common framework — scrum in our case — is shared along with an agreed upon definition of done. Observers and participants can see what is being accomplished and can interpret the results through a common language.

Inspection

As you discover in the following chapters, agile projects are broken down into the smallest actionable chunks possible (commonly captured as user stories; see Chapter 3). Goals are set within fixed time frames — the sprint, the release, and the project. As each item is accomplished, it is then inspected to make sure that it actually works and does what the customer wants.

These inspections are done by people closest to the job — both those who do the work and those who represent the customer. This eliminates the time lag for an outside person to complete this task, and it also means that any adjustments can be done quickly and with the required knowledge at hand, literally.

Adaptation

If the above inspection shows inaccuracies and/or inefficiencies — that is, the feature doesn't work right — an adaptation needs to be made. The adaptation should be done as soon as possible and before moving onto the next actionable item on the to-do list. In other words, before you move on, you know that everything behind you is functioning properly.

Scrum also allows inspections and adaptations to be accomplished immediately on the team and project level in the form of reviews, retrospectives, and the daily scrum. I get into these more in Chapter 6.

One Agile Manifesto

If scrum is an approach that aligns with the Agile Manifesto, it's best that you understand the remarkableness of this short paragraph containing four key sentences.

Scrum is a framework, not a by-the-numbers methodology. You still need to think and make choices. Part of the scrum framework's benefit is that it allows you to make discretionary decisions that are the best ones for you, based on the reality in which you find yourself.

In 2001, 17 software and project experts, successful in each of their own divergent processes, agreed upon four main values for their programming methodologies.

We are uncovering better ways of developing software by doing it and helping others do it. Through this work we have come to value:

- ✔ **Individuals and interactions** over processes and tools
- ✔ **Working software** over comprehensive documentation
- ✔ **Customer collaboration** over contract negotiation
- ✔ **Responding to change** over following a plan

That is, while there is value in the items on the right, we value the items on the left more.

Agile Manifesto Copyright © 2001: Kent Beck, Mike Beedle, Arie van Bennekum, Alistair Cockburn, Ward Cunningham, Martin Fowler, James Grenning, Jim Highsmith, Andrew Hunt, Ron Jeffries, Jon Kern, Brian Marick, Robert C. Martin, Steve Mellor, Ken Schwaber, Jeff Sutherland, Dave Thomas

© 2001, the above authors

This declaration may be freely copied in any form,

but only in its entirety through this notice.

Even though the Agile Manifesto and principles were written by and for software experts, the values remain valid for whatever scrum project you embark upon. Just like GPS was designed by and for the military, it doesn't mean that we can't benefit from it when we sit in the car and head for a new part of town.

The bolding of the first part of the four values is intentional and in the original manifesto. These bolded concepts were the emphasis, but their unbolded counterparts still have value. The final sentence is stabilizing, in that everything has value, but the weighting of that value has changed and attained a new relevancy.

For more information on the history of the agile manifesto and its founders, visit `http://agilemanifesto.org`.

Twelve agile principles

But the founders didn't stop at just values. They also agreed upon 12 principles to expand on those impactful values. Within your scrum project, you can use these principles to check that your framework is true to agile goals:

1. Our highest priority is to satisfy the customer through early and continuous delivery of valuable software.

2. Welcome changing requirements, even late in development. Agile processes harness change for the customer's competitive advantage.

3. Deliver working software frequently, from a couple of weeks to a couple of months, with a preference to the shorter timescale.

4. Business people and developers must work together daily throughout the project.

5. Build projects around motivated individuals. Give them the environment and support they need, and trust them to get the job done.

6. The most efficient and effective method of conveying information to and within a development team is face-to-face conversation.

7. Working software is the primary measure of progress.

8. Agile processes promote sustainable development. The sponsors, developers, and users should be able to maintain a constant pace indefinitely.

9. Continuous attention to technical excellence and good design enhances agility.

10. Simplicity — the art of maximizing the amount of work not done — is essential.

11. The best architectures, requirements, and designs emerge from self-organizing teams.

12. At regular intervals, the team reflects on how to become more effective, then tunes and adjusts its behavior accordingly.

The principles don't change, but the tools and techniques to achieve them can.

Some of the principles will be easier to implement than others. Consider, for example, principle 2. Maybe your company (or group or family) is open to change and new ideas. For them, scrum is natural and they're ready to get started. But on the other hand, some may be more resistant to change.

How about principle 6? Is working face-to-face possible in your project? With the Internet and globalization of workforces, you may have team members from Mumbai to Moscow to Miami. But rather than letting this stop you, how can you find a solution? Skype? Google Hangouts? Teleconferencing regularly? None of these are the intention of principle 6 and none are as good as face-to-face communication, but we deal with the reality of today while trying to improve tomorrow.

You are bound to have unique challenges. Don't let a hiccup or less-than-perfect scenario stop your project cold or even let it limp along. Part of the fun in using scrum — is to work through issues and get to the results. The same goes with the 12 principles. Stick with them and your projects will get quality results faster.

Three platinum principles

I've worked with agile and scrum projects for over a decade, and have personally consulted with dozens of companies, businesses, and altruistic non-profits. I know how well these principles work and have seen their value as I assisted in their implementation.

The Marshmallow Challenge

In 2010, Tom Wujec gave a remarkable TED talk called The Marshmallow Challenge. (TED stands for "Technology, Entertainment and Design," and "is a nonprofit devoted to spreading ideas, usually in the form of short, powerful talks. . .") He discussed an interesting design exercise devised by Peter Skillman. In this exercise, small groups of participants were given 18 minutes to build a freestanding structure with strange and minimal tools: 20 sticks of spaghetti, one yard of tape, one yard of string, and one . . . marshmallow.

Wujec began giving this test and studying the results. Most groups struggled to create anything high or reliable. They would discuss options, plan one final design, and then within the last minute or so, put it all together to find out they'd left out some crucial aspect and it wouldn't stand.

The groups who performed the worst? Recent graduates of business schools (ouch, I have two MBAs). The groups who performed the best? Kindergarteners. They consistently produced higher and more creative structures.

The reason? Wujec believes it's because when business students work on an idea, they believe that only one "correct" solution exists and spend much of their time contemplating and planning for that approach, while the children started right off by playing with the tools. They learned what didn't work and changed it, and then figured out what did work and kept it. They built prototypes all along the way.

A takeaway in the context of scrum is that our natural state is that of inspect and adapt. It's what we want to do, but somewhere along the way, we get trained out of it. We discover that planning and coming up with one solution is the correct way of doing things. But kindergarteners can remind us of how wrong this way of thinking is.

Through this experience, I've identified three additional principles that have consistently improved the performance of teams we've helped:

- ✔ Resist formality
- ✔ Think and act as a team
- ✔ Visualize rather than write

These principles can be applied to absolutely any project, not just software development. That's part of the beauty of agile techniques — you can use them for anything.

Resisting formality

Have you ever seen a knockout PowerPoint presentation and wondered how much time someone spent putting it together?

Don't even think about doing it for a scrum project. You can scribble it on a flip chart in 1/1000th of the time, stick it up on a wall where people will actually look at it, and then get back to creating value? Or if it requires discussion, walk over to the concerned parties and ask them in the moment, and as it comes up. Focus your valuable time and effort on the product instead of prepared presentations.

Atos Origin produced independent research showing that the average corporate employee spends an amazing 40 percent of his or her working day on internal emails *that add no business value whatsoever.* That means the real workweek doesn't start until Wednesday. (Guardian Professional, Dec. 17, 2012, *40% of staff time is wasted on internal emails,* by Nick Atkin.)

Pageantry is too often mistaken for professionalism and progress. In scrum projects, you're encouraged to communicate immediately, directly, and informally whenever you have a question and to work closely with your team members to increase efficiency and save time.

Avoid these unproductive traps:

- ✔ Fancy, time-consuming presentations
- ✔ Long and/or unfocused meetings
- ✔ Tomes of documentation

Emphasize these productivity builders:

- ✔ Being barely sufficient. In all things, the work should be barely sufficient to accomplish the goal. (Don't mistake this for mediocre. Sufficient is sufficient. More is wasteful, and problems often arise in that bloat. See agile principle 10 above.)
- ✔ Frequent communication with all parties to reduce the need for extensive updates.
- ✔ Simplicity and direct communication. If you can walk over and speak to someone instead, do it.

Figure out the simplest way to get what you need, always with the goal of delivering the highest-quality product.

Before long, your projects will evolve a scrum culture. As people become educated on the process and see the improved results, their buy-in for barely sufficient will increase accordingly. So bear through any initial push back with education, patience, and consistency.

Think and act as a team

The heart of scrum is working as a team. However, the team environment can at first be unsettling, because in U.S. corporate culture, we encourage the opposite — the mind-set of the individual. "How well can I succeed in this environment so that I stand out and get the next promotion?"

In scrum, the project survives or dies at the team level. Through leveraging the individual's talent to that of a team, you take the road from average to hyper-productive. According to Aristotle, "The whole is greater than the sum of its parts."

How do you create this team culture? The scrum framework itself empha- sizes the team. Physical space, common goals, and collective ownership all scream team. Then add the following to your scrum frame:

- ✔ Eliminate work titles. No one "owns" areas of development. Status is established by skills and contribution.
- ✔ Pair team members to enhance cross-functionality and front-load quality assurance, then switch the pairings often.
- ✔ Always report with team metrics, not individual or pairing metrics.

Visualize rather than write

On the whole, people are visual. They think pictorially and remember picto- rially. For those of you old enough to remember encyclopedias, which part did you like best? Most kids like the pictures — the visual illustrations of the text. As adults, we're no different. We are still more likely to read a magazine flipping first through images, and then sometimes going back for articles that piqued our interest (if at all).

Pictures, diagrams, and graphs relay information instantly. However, if you write out a report, buy-in drops as the length of the report grows.

Twitter was interested in studying the effectiveness of tweets with photos versus those that were text only. It conducted a study using SHIFT Media Manager and came up with some interesting results. Users engaged five times more frequently when tweets included photos as opposed to text- only tweets. And the rate of retweets and replies with photos was doubled. However, the cost per engagement of photo tweets was half that of text-only tweets. (Shift Newsroom, January 17, 2014.)

When possible, encourage your team to present information visually, even if that means sketching a diagram on a white board. If anybody doesn't understand it, they can ask and changes can be made, right there and then. Also, with technology today, simple graphs, charts, and models are at your fingertips.

Scrum's origins

Although there have been almost 100 years of building toward the agile frameworks we use today, the first scrum team was created by Jeff Sutherland in 1993 after applying the concepts outlined in a 1986 Harvard Business Review article called "The New New Product Development Game." With co-scrum creator Ken Schwaber, Jeff formalized the scrum framework at OOPSLA'95 (International Conference on Object-Oriented Programming, Systems, Languages, and Applications).

The Five Scrum Values

Scrum is founded on five values that each member of the team uses to guide his decision making. These aren't rocket science. Instead, they fall into that familiar category of common sense. Yet they're critical to the successful implementation of scrum, so they deserve discussion here:

- Commitment
- Focus
- Openness
- Respect
- Courage

I look at each of these values more closely and see how vital they are within your scrum project.

Commitment

Scrum team members must be committed to success and be willing to create realistic goals and stick to them. You must participate. It's an "all in" situation where you're part of a team, and your job is to work together to meet your commitments. Fortunately, the scrum model ensures that you have the authority and freedom to do just that.

At the core of scrum is an event called a sprint. I get into that in Chapter 5. The point here is that the sprint requires clear goals set within fixed time boxes. The good news is, in this model, you break down those goals into the smallest chunks of work possible so that you know what you're getting into. You'll know what "realistic" is, so you can set appropriate goals and meet your commitments.

Focus

Part of the magic of scrum is that it's built around the very concept of focus. Focus on a few things at a time. You will have a clear role and clear goals within that role. Your job then is to do just that use your role to contribute to achieving the goal!

You've made your goals and commitments earlier. Focus on those goals and nothing else. I even provide you with tools and techniques for getting rid of common distractions that you can certainly live without in Chapter 2.

Don't worry, contribute your best, be happy.

Openness

Everything in your project, and everyone else's project, is transparent and available for inspection and improvement. Gone are the days of six-month-down-the-road surprises.

Fortunately, the very basis of scrum is the agile pillars of empiricism — transparency, inspection, and adaptation. Information radiators (big, visible charts) and real-time intelligence allow for unfettered action. The thing is, we're not used to this level of exposure. But after your organization catches on, it won't have it any other way.

You, your boss, your employees, your in-laws — everyone's goals and progress are open and visible. You're famous!

Respect

Each team member is selected for his or her strengths; along with these come weaknesses and opportunities to learn and grow. Each participant must respect everyone else. It's the golden rule within scrum.

Harmony is created by each role syncing and thereby creating a development rhythm as the project progresses. If one or another person is out of tune for a bit, because you're held accountable as a team, it's in your best interest to help that person.

People want to do good work; it's in our wiring. If you seek the positive, you'll find the positive. Just as if you seek the negative, you'll find the negative. Respect is the burning ember of positivity.

Courage

Scrum is all about change. Scrum is about honesty, and every idea you have will in a scrum model get challenged. Is every procedure justified by "we've always done it this way"? Say good-bye to procedures done by habit and say hello to a process that is built on what the team finds to be successful.

"It is important that students bring a certain ragamuffin, barefoot irreverence to their studies; they are not here to worship what is known, but to question it." — Jacob Bronowski

Fiefdoms will be challenged. Rules will be tested. Routines will be broken. Improvements will happen. Change can be hard. Change takes courage.

Scrum takes courage.

Part II
Running a Scrum Project

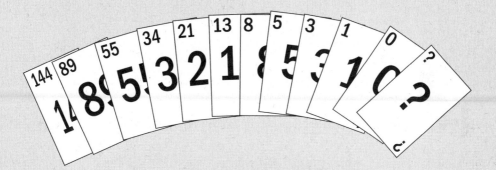

In this part . . .

- ✔ Running a scrum project.
- ✔ Complementing scrum with commonly used agile practices.
- ✔ Moving projects from broad scope vision to executable tasks.
- ✔ Planning releases and sprints.
- ✔ Optimizing sprint results.
- ✔ Visit www.dummies.com/extras/scrum for great Dummies content online.

Chapter 2

The First Steps

"Work expands so as to fill the time available for its completion."

— Parkinson's Law

*U*nderstanding scrum is simple in concept yet often difficult in application. Changing 70 years of product development paradigm is going to be challenging. Still, 30–40 percent time-to-market increase and 30–70 percent cost savings are realistic. Jeff Sutherland has documented 1,000 percent performance improvements by using scrum. Given that potential, it's worth it to disrupt your comfort zone, and start dealing with the organizational dysfunctions that are holding you back.

If the number-one trend in IT is converting to scrum and associated agile engineering approaches (such as eXtreme Programming), it is possible for your organization to make the transition. Many companies are doing it and doing it well. It just takes an open mind — something that's good for all of us. By the end of this chapter, you'll be up and running with your project and ready to take the next scrum steps.

Getting Your Scrum On

Two factors come into play as you convert to scrum:

- ✔ **The nature of the project**

  It's easy to find out whether the nature of a project fits scrum because the fact is, scrum is for everyone. Any project where you want early, empirical evidence of performance and quality can, and should be, done using a scrum framework.

- ✔ **The social culture within which the project resides**

  Social culture is more complex because people are complex. Changing processes can be easy; changing people is not. Every individual and every group of individuals have their own sets of idiosyncrasies. As entertaining as these are at a BBQ, they can be a hurdle to overcome when teaching new project management techniques.

It's natural for people to resist change, and different individuals will resist in different degrees and ways. "There is nothing more difficult to take in hand, more perilous to conduct, or more uncertain in its success, than to take the lead in the introduction of a new order of things." —Machiavelli

However, when people understand how the changes will benefit them directly, the conversion is faster and easier.

As you'll see in Parts III–V of this book, billion-dollar companies benefit, as do everyday folks. A colleague of mine used it to plan, day by day, a recent vacation. He and his wife agreed that because it allowed the right combination of structure with freedom, it was the best vacation they ever had. (Chapter 17 tells their story.)

I now look at some common benefits of scrum — the WIIFM (What's In It For Me) Principle.

Show me the money

Consider Net Present Value 101: A dollar today is, literally, more valuable than a dollar six months from now. The biggest problem in organizations is not the efficiency of the tactical execution teams; it's poor portfolio management. Executives fail to show the leadership necessary to make the tough prioritization calls, resulting in too many projects being pushed down to a level that lacks the power to fight back (see Chapter 12 for more on this dynamic).

This dysfunction is then masked by thrashing people across multiple projects so that each business unit is getting something. It takes considerably longer to get anything done, but management for each project is placated by getting binders of documents telling them how great their product is going to be when they eventually get it.

Scrum is the opposite. You focus, you produce deliverable tangible results, and then you increment forward. The product backlog (described in detail in Chapter 3) forces you to be effective before worrying about efficiency.

You might be a billion-dollar company, or you might be a mom-and-pop store struggling to get your great idea to market. Maybe you're one of a gazillion employees, but you've been given this one project to prove yourself with. In each case, disciplined prioritization, increased efficiency, and incremental, tested progress can help you survive.

Because of this prioritization within scrum, you're working exclusively on the highest-value features. You're not perfecting a third-tier widget instead of a higher value feature. You're going for the meat each and every time. As a result, what you produce during each sprint is what's the most important, practical, and immediately desirable. In every release, you have something valued by the marketplace. That's scrum. That's showing you the money.

REMEMBER

When your back is against the wall, everyone reverts to agile techniques, whether you realize it or not. If your company had 60 days of cash left on hand, nobody would worry about your status report having the right cover sheet. Bureaucracy is the luxury of the financially bloated. It's a luxury that can change overnight in today's economy.

TIP

In my seminars, I teach "It's better to do all of something than a little bit of everything." If you wait for everything to be ready, chances are that nothing will get done. Rather, take those tangible steps of progress that you achieve through scrum, get them out to market, get feedback, and let the revenue flow in.

TIP

Using my practice of doing something before doing everything, a client of mine agreed to put a product out to market with only one way for the customer to purchase it. Instead of making sure that every credit card on earth was tied in, that PayPal was set up, and even personal checks could be processed with speed, the client decided to chance raising early funds with only one credit card payment option. The result? Between October and January, he brought in over 1 million dollars in sales. Now the site can process multiple credit cards, PayPal, and several other payment options — each of which was rolled out one sprint at a time *after* it was actively generating revenue.

Fortunately, the very nature of scrum is built around delivering tested, usable results early and often. You don't wait to see results. You see them after every single sprint.

Scrum may still be a fresh concept to many, but its usage is growing by leaps and bounds. In 2008, I was thrilled to learn that more organizations were using agile techniques than waterfall techniques for software development. By 2012, Forrester estimated at least 80 percent of organizations would be using agile techniques for software development. In May 2012, SimplyHired.com showed 20,000 jobs requiring scrum knowledge, and by May 2013, this had increased to 670,000 jobs. We have crossed the chasm.

I want it now

Ever heard that? And not from a three-year-old, but from a boss, colleague, or even that inner voice within your own head? Our scrum projects regularly see less than a 30–40 percent time-to-market increase. But how?

It's simple: by starting development early and thus ending development early. You're creating "shippable" products from the start. You don't wait for months, or in some cases years, for results that may have passed their technological sell-by date. You quickly plan, create, inspect, adapt, ship, and benefit. In this process, you churn out value early and continuously.

In science as in business, we've discovered it's not survival of the fittest after all. Rather, it's survival of the fastest. Whoever could crawl into safety fastest missed being snatched up by the pterodactyl. In business, innovations are released to market at exponentially increasing speeds. Brands are created and killed overnight. You simply can't afford to be late.

But that's not the only reason you experience increased speed to market. As you create your product backlog (the project to-do list), you also order and prioritize the items. In prioritization, you take two things into consideration:

- ✔ Items with the highest value
- ✔ Items with the highest risk

Both factors get them to the top of the list.

We're not sure what we want

Most people don't know what they want, at least not until they interact with it. The vast majority of people, companies, and organizations only realize what they want when they interact with the product or service directly. The gap in those two things is the difference between waterfall (seeing it in documents) and scrum (using it in reality).

In your roadmap to value (see Chapter 1), you begin with a vision of what you want your end product to be. This vision acts as a beacon for your team, the way any established destination acts as a beacon. The roadmap allows for the natural progression of decision making — from large, fuzzy generalities down to small, specific operationalization of that goal. So the vision provides the outer boundary of what can change. If it deviates from the vision, it's a different project.

Your vision might be to develop a website where people can order organic, allergy-specific restaurant food for home delivery. How about constructing an Alzheimer's patient residence with individual-specific, on-site monitoring; alerts; and security? Or selling Grandma's donut recipe that you're convinced will be the next Krispy Kreme? How can you build out a successful business, whatever it may be?

How these ideas would pan out in reality is yet to be determined. The good news is you will develop the most effective path of progress through the scrum framework. The process of tangible creation, inspection, and adaptation gives you the tools to create the product that's actually needed.

Is that bug a problem?

Each item that the development team completes is tested and integrated to ensure that it works. The product owner is responsible for either accepting or rejecting each completed requirement, as it's completed. In other words, if it doesn't work, it doesn't make it out of the sprint.

Of course, issues can come up with enterprise integration, load limits, and so on after a product makes it into production. But the feedback cycle is so strong during development that as soon as a defect or process inefficiency is spotted, it can immediately be corrected. It's either fixed in that sprint or it's placed back in the product backlog to be prioritized against future work.

Your company's culture

When people see the success and value of scrum, using it becomes easier. Employees learn how scrum improves communication and collaboration, creates a team esprit de corps striving for excellence, has a natural life cycle, develops an honest and transparent environment, and increases ownership and self-empowerment. This all directly impacts company culture in a hugely positive way.

The level of resistance to change varies from company culture to culture. The solution, as with so many things, is through tangible success. (Remember: You'll find no defense against demonstrated success!) Find what the key individuals need — increased profits, higher product quality, faster delivery, or improved talent retention — and show them how the scrum model delivers.

In any group of people, you'll find the influencers. They're the ones with clout and can get change rolling. Maybe that's you, and maybe it's someone else. But get them on board and your job will be easier. Sometimes this means going to higher management, but not always.

Involvement begets commitment. You want to build a team to move the gears of change.

The Power in the Product Owner

Key to moving the gears of change is the product owner. The product owner's primary job is to take care of the business side of the project. They are responsible for maximizing product value by delivering the return on investment (ROI) to the organization. The product owner is only one person, not a committee, and is a full-time, dedicated member of the scrum team. They don't literally own the product, but they take ownership of the business-side duties, representing the stakeholders and customers.

Some of the primary responsibilities of the product owner are as follows:

- ✓ Setting the goals and vision for the product, including writing the vision statement
- ✓ Creating and maintaining the product roadmap, which is a broad view of the scope of the product and the initial product backlog
- ✓ Making in-the-moment priority and trade-off decisions
- ✓ Ensuring visibility of the product backlog
- ✓ Optimizing the work done by the development team
- ✓ Taking full ownership and responsibility for the product backlog
- ✓ Accepting proposed requirements and ordering them by priority in the product backlog
- ✓ Setting release and sprint goals
- ✓ Determining which product backlog items go into the next sprint

- Handling business aspects of the project, including ROI and business risk, and interfacing with business stakeholders and customers

- Being available throughout the day to work directly with development team members, thereby increasing efficiency through clear and immediate communication

- Accepting or rejecting work results throughout the sprint, ideally the same day they are completed

I'm often shocked that organizations that are planning to plow millions of dollars into a project "don't have the resources" for a dedicated product owner to ensure that the business and technical priorities align, and ensuring that the product created is the product needed. Yet many of these organizations have a project manager to direct the project. Because the project manager role does not exist in scrum (relevant duties are part of the three scrum roles), the money for product owners can be taken from there.

Product owners clarify, prioritize, and set an environment for focus. They ensure that the scrum team is effective. The product owner determines what requirements are pursued and when work shifts to those requirements, that is, the "what and when" but not the "how or how much." The "how and how much" is the responsibility of the development team.

Imagine that your passion is building something. In scrum, you would be a member of the development team. The product owner for you is a gift. They excel at portfolio management because they are empowered to make decisions, clarify, prioritize, and fight to ensure that team members are focused on one project at a time. Because of effective product owners, development team members are freed from outside distractions and can spend more of their attention on getting their jobs done.

Both the product owner and the scrum master work to create the best environment possible for the development team to do the highest quality work they can. The product owner handles and deflects business concerns and noise, and the scrum master ensures that other organizational interruptions don't impact the development team.

The abstraction layer created by the product owner and scrum master doesn't mean less business noise. It means that, for the most part, it's not the development team that has to deal with the noise.

On the other hand, a development team member can contact stakeholders or other team or nonteam individuals directly when they need clarification on something they are working on. This model of filtering prioritization but not clarification is like the membrane of a cell that's designed to let certain fluids travel in one direction but not the other.

The end result is that the development team is protected from outside interferences, but they're not hindered in their quest for knowledge. These boundaries are important and integral to the successful functioning of the development team.

Why Product Owners Love Scrum

Product owners love scrum for the following reasons:

✔ Development and business are now aligned and held accountable as a single unit, rather than being at odds as in historical methodologies.

✔ Schedules and costs are empirically forecasted, and you have daily clarity on progress.

✔ After every sprint, product owners know that they'll have the highest-priority items fully functioning and shippable.

✔ Customer feedback is early and continuous.

✔ The earliest possible tangible measurement on ROI is available, that is, after every single sprint.

✔ Systematic support for changing business needs, thus allowing continuing flexibility to adapt to market realities.

✔ Reduced product and process waste through an emphasis on prioritized product development over process artifact development (usually documents).

The product owner's number-one characteristic should be *decisiveness*. They will make tough, pragmatic, and uncomfortable decisions every hour of every day. They need to be able to create an environment of trust and pivot when changes are needed. They must begin by doing what they think is right and then change based on empirical evidence.

The product owner agent option

In today's world of globalization, it's not always possible to have an on-site product owner. You may be headquartered in California, yet be running projects out of a facility in Hyderabad, India. In my own consulting practice, we've found a controversial but workable solution to be the *product owner agent* role. This is an on-site individual who is responsible for day-to-day communication and decision making. The agent is the physical representation of the product owner, speaking and acting on behalf of the product owner, who is not on-site.

We view the product owner agent as the following:

✔ Product owner agents are not scrum.

✔ While we don't recommend product owner agents, we've used them with success in certain situations while the organization matures.

✔ The goal is to have the role of the agent be temporary, like an apprenticeship, while the person proves their ability to be a true product owner.

With the product owner agent, you're able to provide the quick clarifications and decision making that scrum requires. However, much like a real estate broker takes final responsibility for any real estate agent's decisions and actions, so the headquartered product owner is responsible for the agent's decisions. The liability remains singular.

Rather than having one foot in each place and getting marginal results, a better choice is to take action and embed a product owner onsite. The up-front cost seems high, but if you take into account the increased speed and quality of the result, your true project costs are actually lowered.

The scrum product owner's role is much different than a traditional project manager's role. Imagine telling a golfer to hit the ball 400 yards and straight into the hole. If he doesn't succeed, hit him with his club. That's how the traditional IT world works. With scrum, the golfer hits the ball, assesses the results, and adapts around that reality to achieve the goal in the best possible way given where he is, not where he "should be."

Small, colocated, cross-functional teams are cheaper than dislocated teams when the total cost of ownership is viewed, rather than singular per-person costs.

The Company Goal and Strategy — Stage 1

Vision statements aren't part of the scrum model. However, the concept of a vision statement is useful and widely adopted. Companies, nonprofits, and individuals on personal journeys of intent often use vision statements.

When I coach my clients, I always have them create a vision statement so that their goal is right in front of them. I'm looking for an elevator pitch — crisp, concise, clear — that can be conveyed during the ground-to-fourth-floor ride.

Vision statements are so useful that I've made them Stage 1 in our roadmap to value. See Figure 2-1. Think of your vision statement as a destination with a beacon. You might have 100 ways to get there, and it doesn't matter which way you take; the point is to end there. With this beacon of a statement, you always know where you're headed — you have the end goal in sight. From this stable, strategic destination, you have limitless tactical flexibility.

A common agile practice.

Figure 2-1:
The vision statement is Stage 1 in the roadmap to value.

Stage 1: VISION

Description: The goals for the product and its alignment with the company's strategy.
Owner: Product owner
Frequency: At least annually

A vision statement is

- ✓ Internally focused, with no marketing fluff.
- ✓ Fine-tuned to the goals of the marketplace and the end-customer needs.
- ✓ Strategic in nature. Show what, rather than how.
- ✓ Reviewed annually on multiyear projects.
- ✓ Owned by the product owner.

Your vision statement must be communicated throughout the organization or group of people you're working with. Whether you're designing a new model of sports car or planning a wedding, everyone needs to clearly understand the end goal. It sets expectations and the tone of the project.

Structuring your vision

In Geoffrey Moore's excellent book *Crossing the Chasm* (published by HarperBusiness), he recommends an effective method for creating your vision statement. I use this model often with first-rate results:

- ✓ The entire statement should be no longer than two or three sentences.
- ✓ Geoffrey Moore recommends this model:
  - For *<target customer>*

- who *<statement of the need>*
- the *<product name>*
- is a *<product category>*
- that *<product key benefit, compelling reason to buy>*
- Unlike *<primary competitive alternative>*
- our product *<final statement of product differentiation>*

✔ I recommend adding this conclusion:

- which supports our strategy to *<company strategy>*

These are examples of what this format looks like in real life:

✔ Tankless water heater:

- **For** home owners **who** desire continuous hot water flow and better conservation of energy, **the** Acme Tankless Water Heater **is a** "demand," "point-of-use," or "instantaneous" water heater **that** efficiently heats water as you use it. **Unlike** tank-type water heaters, **our product** provides continuous flow at consistent temperatures with lower operating costs at 94 percent efficiency,

- **which supports our strategy to** provide for tomorrow's generation by reducing the waste of natural resources today.

✔ Hawaiian vacation:

- **For** my spouse and me, **who** are stressed out of our minds, **the** Hawaii or Bust 2015 **is a** spontaneous, last-minute getaway **that** will remove us from our hectic lives long enough to provide new experiences. **Unlike** family vacations or structured itineraries, **our product** provides complete flexibility without expectations,

- **which supports our strategy to** make the most of each moment together.

The vision statement itself is functional. However, the addition of business strategy is emotional. Bring purpose to your project in the form of a company strategy that makes people's lives better. It's never your company strategy to make money; it's to do something of such value that it can be monetized.

When I work with clients, I ask them to have their vision statement done before I first meet with them. I then spend one hour with the people responsible for it honing it down to something we can work with. It doesn't take long to create this invaluable artifact.

Finding the crosshairs

The vision statement is created and owned by the product owner and is integral to the business side of the project. However, one mind is just that — only one mind. The product owner may own this statement, but they will surely have better luck creating and refining it by using collective intelligence. To this end, the product owner can choose to receive input from development team members, the scrum master, external or internal stakeholders, and even end users themselves. It's the product owner's choice and the product owner's responsibility.

By being open to this input, nuances, features, and market angles may be revealed that one person alone wouldn't think of. The product owner might be wise to take feedback and then carefully filter this through his own understanding of the project itself.

The Scrum Master

In *The One Minute Manager,* by Ken Blanchard (published by William Morrow), the author discusses how sometimes the most effective managers he studied lacked the technical skills that their employees had. Funny enough, they also had a lot of time on their hands. So if they couldn't do the job themselves, what were these managers good at?

The managers were able to clear the path so that their employees could get the work done. This is the role of the scrum master. Whereas the product owner is a directing role, the scrum master is an enabling role. The scrum master is responsible for the environment for success.

The scrum master's most important trait, after deep expertise in scrum, is clout. Diplomacy, communication skills, and the ability to manage up are all good, but the scrum master needs to have the respect and clout to get difficult situations resolved. Clout is something you have or you don't have. Where the clout comes from doesn't matter — expertise, longevity, charisma, association — it all works in the scrum master role.

As a servant leader, the scrum master teaches, encourages, removes tactical impediments, and most importantly, removes strategic impediments so that the tactical ones don't reappear. As with every other role, the scrum master is best full-time and solely dedicated to the scrum master job, especially with new teams, projects, and organizations.

If the product owner is the quarterback calling the plays and the development team is the running back getting the yards, the scrum master is the front line. Yet, they're all peers with a common goal.

In my experience, developers who double as scrum masters and scrum masters thrashed across multiple teams throw off a team's ability to extrapolate past performance to future capability. This introduces availability variation and delivers inferior protection to a development team. This rarely makes sense quantitatively, because a minor improvement in a scrum team's velocity (I talk about this in Chapter 4) often has a huge impact on the bottom line. If your team is able to schedule its organizational interruptions and is so mature that it can't improve further, contact me; I want to write a book about you.

A development team is ideally five to nine people, Accordingly, one scrum master improves the performance of up to nine people. Likewise, even a minor reduction in performance is also 9x.

In addition to coaching the scrum team on how to optimally play scrum, the scrum master facilitates the events in scrum — sprint planning meetings, daily scrums, sprint reviews, and sprint retrospectives. Think about it: You have a bunch of intelligent, engaged team members with a high degree of ownership in the work that they're doing. Put these folks in a meeting together and the creative energy might cause them to explode, or at least go off on a lot of tangents. It's the scrum master's role to focus this energy.

The concept of *servant leader* dates back to around 500 BCE, from China's Lao-Tzu, thought to be the author of the Tao Te Ching. Yet it is also mentioned in every major religion and is popular with modern-day corporate leadership models. That's staying power.

The servant leader puts others first so that they can do their jobs. The leader enables people rather than presenting the solution on a silver plate. If someone says, "I'm hungry,"the servant leader doesn't hand them a fish. Rather, the leader says, "How can I help you so that you're not hungry today, tomorrow, or next year." The scrum master helps the person build skills and find the solution that best works for the individual, whether the answer lies inside or outside the project itself.

If you're making decisions as a scrum master, you're not doing the right job. A development team will never become self-organizing if they're not making their own decisions. Scrum masters extract themselves from day-to-day decisions and instead ensure a conducive environment while shielding the team from interference.

The interference issue

Three types of interference prevail in the workplace.

Personal interruptions are email flashes, phone calls from Aunt Martha, and text messages with links to cat videos. Discipline is the solution. Turn off your technology to tune in to your job. Check out the Pomodoro technique, discussed later in this chapter.

Team interruptions are those from your workmates. The key here is first to identify collaboration time versus concentration time. These times should be balanced based on team dynamics and project needs:

✔ Collaboration time is when it's okay to interrupt, talk, and exchange ideas in any way. This is healthy and productive time and should be the bulk of your day.

✔ Concentration time can be delineated by physical indicators: noise-canceling headsets, Do Not Disturb signs, and so on. These help you get to a deep level of concentration and crank out product.

External interruptions are the scrum master's domain. These interruptions can happen anytime, all day every day, and the scrum master is there to shield these from team members.

Where do most interruptions come from? The higher-ups who pass tactical emergencies to the team responsible for creating quality products. This is part of the reason why the scrum master's role should be full-time, and they should have plenty of organizational clout.

The scrum master's influence extends to everyone involved, including stakeholders impacting the project and the product owner. The scrum master is a coach to everyone, because everyone needs ongoing education and smooth facilitation in scrum.

Studies have shown that it takes 15 minutes to get to the right level of concentration for peak productivity — often called "being in the zone." Yet it only takes a 2.3-second interruption to burst that bubble, requiring another 15 minutes to reestablish that focus. A 4.4-second interruption *triples* the amount of mistakes made on a sequencing task.

As the scrum master shields the development team from external interference, the velocity of the team increases dramatically. Think about how well you work when the door's shut, the phone's off, and everybody's away or asleep versus when you're fielding constant interruptions from colleagues, family members, and even the dog?

See my webinar "It's Your Fault" for a fun explanation of why most organizational performance problems are caused by the executives who, ironically, are the ones demanding improved performance.

TIP

The Pomodoro technique

The Pomodoro technique for time management was developed in the late 1980s by Francesco Cirillo. It entails running personal work sprints of 25 minutes (though you can customize) to get your own stuff done:

1. Create your to-do list and prioritize the highest-value items.

2. Work on the top-priority item for 25 minutes.

3. Take a 5-minute break.

4. Go back to the same highest-priority item until it is completely done, and then move on to the next-highest-priority item.

After four Pomodoros, take a longer break of 15 to 30 minutes to reset your concentration ability.

Do this throughout the day to ensure that every day you accomplish your most important items.

Even when outside interference is kept to a minimum, because social density is higher in scrum, it's not unusual for conflict to also be higher. The intrinsic pressure to get working products in short sprint windows with people who are *right there* can be wearing. So the scrum master's job entails managing conflict to just the right level:

- Task conflict is healthy (being willing to fight for what you think is right).

- Personal conflict is not healthy (when conflict boils over from challenging someone's idea into challenging them personally).

Why Scrum Masters Love Scrum

Scrum masters love scrum for many reasons:

- They focus on having quantifiable impact rather than administrative responsibilities — a rising velocity has a direct tie to additional value that the scrum team can deliver.

- They coach people rather than serve as check-the-box managers.

- They get to enable people rather than direct them.

- They are involved with fewer meetings, and the meetings they are involved with are shorter in duration.

✔ They facilitate building empowered, self-motivated teams that think for themselves and act with authority.

✔ Performance accountability isn't outsourced to them (for example, "Hey Joe, what's the status of the tasks Nancy is working on?"); instead, accountability is sourced directly to the person doing the work.

A good scrum master motto is Never Lunch Alone. Always be creating and developing relationships. Influence is the currency that you operate from, so make sure that you create an environment where you can easily pick up the phone, or walk to their desk, and get results.

Cool Common Roles Outside of Scrum

The product owner and scrum master are scrum roles. They were created by the founders of scrum and are integral to any scrum project. The third role is, of course, the development team themselves. I go further into the development team in Chapter 4. But like all good things, project management is evolving and growing. Scrum remains a solid framework and foundation. Some common and proven practices can add value.

In my years of hands-on scrum work, I've added some common practices and I've also learned from others. So while the following two roles aren't scrum, I've found that they add enormous value and clarity when approached properly.

Consider the following two roles for your project; they may bring more value to your regular scrum endeavor.

Stakeholders

Stakeholders can be internal or external and are people who impact or are impacted by your project:

✔ Internal stakeholders are from within your company or organization.

✔ They could be from legal, sales and marketing, functional management, procurement, or any other department, arm, branch, or division of your group.

✔ External stakeholders could be investors or end users.

While scrum prescribes only scrum team members, the role of stakeholder explicitly interfaces with scrum teams, and we prefer to acknowledge it explicitly so that we can manage it explicitly.

The product owner is the business interface for the scrum team, so stakeholders should work with the development team *through* the product owner. Stakeholders may communicate directly with the development team during sprint reviews or when a development team member contacts them directly for clarification, but stakeholders generally work through the product owner.

Who deals with stakeholders?

- If they're on the business side (for example, customers, sales teams, or marketing), the product owner is usually responsible.

- If they're on the nonbusiness side (for example, vendors or contractors), it's usually the scrum master's role.

The key is to recognize their influence and leverage it, yet shield any associated interference from the development team.

Swinging to success

Years ago, I took up golf for business and in the process caught the golf bug. I loved it, worked at it, and improved my game. However, I always struggled with inconsistency. While some days I was unstoppable, at other times, I was like an escaped zoo ape. I couldn't hit a clean shot to save my life.

So I did what many people do: I hired a golf coach. Admittedly, I was suspect of this man who earned hundreds of dollars an hour and claimed to be able to cure my golf woes. If I'd practiced for years and wasn't making progress, what could someone who never even saw me play do?

On my first session, he teed up a ball and I hit it. One swing, that's all, and he said, "I know what your problem is." I laughed. How could he possibly know what I was doing wrong by watching one swing? I knew my money was down the drain. Then he said, "You used to play baseball, didn't you?" Oops. Yes, I'd played baseball for years. He could tell with one golf swing.

My golf swing was, in fact, my baseball swing — a habit I'd carried from years of one sport right into this newer sport. When you convert to scrum, you too will be carrying habits, ones that you don't even realize you have from a lifetime of managing your projects differently, often from a waterfall methodology.

Scrum mentor

I want to illustrate exactly what I mean when I say that scrum is a simple framework in concept, but more complex in practice. The same can be said for the game of golf. Theoretically, you whack a motionless, white ball into a hole, using a stick, in the fewest strokes possible. Yet it isn't easy. The reason is because golf, like scrum, is a game of nuance. Small factors make an enormous difference in performance.

A scrum mentor's benefit is that they are not focused on getting product out the door. Their glasses aren't tinted with organizational politics. Instead, like the golf coach, they are able to objectively step back and see what you're doing mechanically. They can identify not only old habits, but they can also put the brakes on "modifications" to scrum that are simply ways to give an old dog back its old tricks.

You'll have the greatest ease and success with scrum if you stick to it in its truest form. A scrum mentor's job is to help you do just that — keep good form. Like a golf coach, they can stand aside; see your old, unproductive habits; and structurally help you form the new habits that will make you successful.

Chapter 3

Planning Your Project

• •

• •

*W*illiam of Ockham, a 14th century logician and Franciscan friar, was quoted as saying, "Entities should not be multiplied unnecessarily." In simpler, modern-day terms, this is now known as Occam's Razor: "When you have two competing theories that make exactly the same predictions, the simpler one is the better."

In other words, Keep It Simple Smarty. This mantra can be applied again and again when managing your project with scrum. It's all about common sense. If it doesn't feel right, it probably isn't. In this chapter, you'll see that this applies to a technique that I use to enhance scrum projects — called the product roadmap — as well as to decompose your product's features into the smallest requirements possible.

Keep. It. Simple.

The Product Roadmap — A Common Practice, Stage 2

In the seven roadmap to value stages I outline in Chapter 1, you begin with the end in mind by creating your vision statement (a common agile practice that works well). The next step is to create a map toward achieving that vision. See Figure 3-1.

A best practice outside of core Scrum

Figure 3-1:
The product
roadmap is
Stage 2 in
the roadmap
to value.

Stage 2: PRODUCT ROADMAP

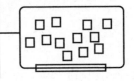

Description: Holistic view of product
features that create the product vision.
Owner: Product Owner
Frequency: At least biannually

Although neither the vision statement nor the product roadmap are formal
aspects of scrum, they are common practices within the agile industry.

Creating a product roadmap is common sense. If you're heading out of town
on vacation with the family — including kids, neighbor's kids, and dog, you
would want a clue as to where you're going so that you don't waste days wan-
dering aimlessly with all that cacophony in the car. The same holds true with
most any project:

✔ Decide where you want to go (vision).

✔ Figure out how to get there (product roadmap).

The product roadmap can change. But it gives you something tangible to
start with, thereby increasing efficiency.

Take the long view

The product roadmap is a holistic, high-level view of the features necessary to achieve the product goal that you outlined in your vision statement.
Natural project affinities are established (if we do this, we should logically do
that), and gaps in features are made readily visible (hey, where is . . . ?).

The product roadmap is the initial product backlog (your master to-do list),
and as the likelihood of product backlog items being developed increases,
items are increasingly broken down (progressive elaboration). The product
backlog expands to include items that are

✔ Small (imminently developable — often referred to as user stories)

✔ Midsized (midrange developable — often referred to as epics)

✔ Conceptual (clear but lacking details — often referred to as features)

The details on these follow.

The product roadmap isn't fixed in stone and fully paved. It too is a living, dynamic artifact. I review and update these roadmaps at least twice a year, although this will vary depending on your individual project.

While the vision statement is fully owned by the product owner, the development team will need to be part of the roadmap–building process. They're the technological experts who will be doing the work, and only they can provide technical constraints and effort estimates. If the development team hasn't been chosen yet, include the functional managers after the initial product roadmap has been created. These managers can help identify the skills that will be necessary and get the development team assembled as quickly as possible so that high-level effort estimates can be given.

When creating your product roadmap, use the simplest tools possible. I prefer a whiteboard and sticky notes. Each product feature fits onto the sticky note, and the notes can be created, swapped, and crumpled up and thrown away with ease. This is simplicity in true working form.

Human brains were not created in the digital age. Studies have proven that electronics have a dulling effect on our minds. In fact, it takes less brain-wave function to watch TV than it does to watch paint dry — literally! Yet using the simple system of sticky notes? It's physically and mentally engaging, and using them fosters an environment of change and creativity.

In Figure 3-2, you have a real-life example of a product roadmap that we helped create with a client. The project itself was worth almost half a billion dollars, and we put this roadmap together in under three hours. The items on the left are the highest priority. The map background was simply a convenient place for the sticky notes to stick (keep it simple) and had no relevancy to the project.

Throughout this book, I'm incorporating common practices that I and other scrum trainers successfully use. While totally optional and not officially scrum itself, I recommend that you give them a try. They just might make your project transition and completion that much more successful, too.

When I first begin working with a client, both the vision statement and the product roadmap are created on Day 1. I sit down with the business stakeholders, the product owner, the development team, and the scrum master and begin the process. We finish on Day 1 so that the actual development begins on Day 2.

Figure 3-2:
Sticky notes
and a wall
or white-
board to
stick them
on are all
you need
to build a
product
roadmap.

Steps to creating your product roadmap

Seven easy, common-sense steps can build your product roadmap. Do these on Day 1 of initiating your project. It should take no longer than a few hours at most. For smaller projects, you'll get it done over morning coffee. The product owner completes the steps with the rest of the project team (the entire scrum team and the business stakeholders).

Using sticky notes, colored flags, and a whiteboard, follow these steps to build your product roadmap:

1. **Write down one product requirement per sticky note.**

   Think of as many product requirements as you can.

2. **If appropriate and synergistic, arrange some requirements into related categories or groups.**

3. **Prioritize the requirements on the roadmap.**

   At the macro level, the highest are on the left and the lowest are on the right. At the micro level, highest-priority requirements are at the top and lowest are at the bottom. So, the highest priority items would be top-left, and the lowest would be bottom-right.

4. **Identify business dependencies (noted by flags on the sticky note).**

5. **Have the development team identify technical dependencies (noted by alternative color flags).**

6. **Have the development team provide order-of-magnitude relative estimates for the sticky notes.**

7. **Adjust ordering based on dependencies and estimates as appropriate.**

For estimation methods that your development team can use, check out Chapter 4.

Incremental funding is quickly becoming a common practice preferred over up-front funding for the entire project. Whereas traditionally you made hypothetical projections of return on investment (ROI) once at the start and had funding for the entire project (and ROI was rarely looked at again because the funding organization wasn't recovering the sunk cost anyway), incremental funding enables the entire project team to inspect and adapt not only with the requirements of the project but also with the funding of the project.

For example, if $3 million is allocated to your project, you might be funded initially with $500,000 to see how you do with the first release of working functionality. If you are way off on your ROI projections for the initial requirements, the company might reconsider the viability of the project. With scrum, you know early on whether you are delivering value and therefore can determine sooner how to optimize your limited talent, infrastructure, and time. For more on incremental funding, see Chapter 13.

Ideally, you want to release tested, approved product after every sprint, or better yet, several times during a sprint (continuous delivery). Occasionally, when I am working with clients, we create high-level product releases (for framing the requirements, not for timeline commitment) so that we can see how those releases would align with other product releases, budgetary cycles, holiday cycles, and so on.

Figure 3-3 shows an example of quarterly product releases (we often do this with our publically traded clients) using the pen-pencil model discussed in Chapter 5. The first release reflects our initial release planning and has a level of commitment to it. Everything after that is for understanding how outside influences might impact our project.

If your time frame is shorter than this or isn't relevant for your project, consider what your project's time frame is, and break that down into the initial logical groups, going no further out than necessary (usually no more than a year):

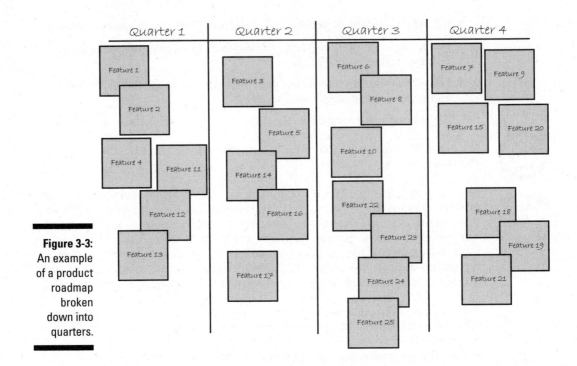

Figure 3-3:
An example
of a product
roadmap
broken
down into
quarters.

✔ Create the initial groups' worth of features, starting with the highest-priority requirements and moving down.

✔ Assume at each product release that you will deliver tested, approved, "shippable" results.

✔ Above each release, write its conceptual theme.

✔ Adjust as necessary.

The nature of your product will determine the quantity and timing of your product releases. I suggest a minimum of once per quarter; however, the pace of innovation is speeding things up. I have two clients who push to production every single day. Several massive social media and Internet firms push twice a day or more.

The product roadmap and product backlog are excellent for scope control. In traditional project management models, every new idea had to be justified. With scrum, if the idea brings you closer to the project vision, you can add it to the list. Its level of prioritization will determine whether it actually gets completed. Sometimes only the highest-priority items get done, and sometimes every single requirement gets done. It depends on the budget and the organizational drag on the scrum team.

It won't take you long to notice that one product requirement can be broken down into several different pieces. Chances are, those pieces can be broken down further. And those pieces, I'm willing to bet, can be peeled apart, too. How do you manage this decomposition process? Read on.

When to Break It Down

With the product roadmap, you begin with the largest pieces of your project. It's truly an eagle's-eye view and is based on what makes sense according to business value and/or risk elimination. These pieces (requirements) are then prioritized by the product owner. What is most important to get out to that customer first? Which of them logically belong together in groups?

As these requirements are prioritized, they become part of the product backlog. The key is to be working on the smallest set of highest-priority items necessary to generate value, not just anything scoped for the project, which is why scrum projects release functionality faster.

Take two things into consideration as you prioritize: business value and risk. Business value is easy. If it has high value, it gets high prioritization. But you also want to take on the highest-risk requirements first.

These are the four reasons to take on the highest risk first:

✔ At the beginning, you have the simplest system to work with.

You want to take on your highest-risk developments within the simplest system (see Occam's Razor, earlier in this chapter).

✔ You have the greatest amount of money at the beginning.

If you are going to take on something of high risk, you should do so with the greatest resources at your disposal.

✔ Because you have the greatest amount of money, you can fund the development team for the longest amount of time.

If you are going to take on a high-risk item, do so with the benefit of the longest runway possible.

✔ If you're going to fail, fail early and cheap.

If a fundamental flaw exists, you want to know this as early as possible. The highest-risk requirements are where the hidden land mines are lurking.

The product roadmap creates your first cut of dependencies. "I don't need to worry about having to 'submit application' functionality until I have a website to house that functionality," for example. Critical dependencies are revealed early on and help with prioritization of the product backlog by the product owner. You will begin working on Day 2 (not on Day 120) on those highest-priority items. Before I go into product backlog details, I first check out the different stages of decomposition that need to occur.

Decomposition Definitions

In looking at the process of decomposing your requirements into smaller and smaller pieces, the key is to do as little as possible. In fact, I want you to become an expert at doing the bare minimum, progressively elaborating requirements as the likelihood of bringing them into a sprint grows. Gone are the days of spending endless hours working on defining and refining requirements that never see the light of day. Figure 3-4 depicts the different layers of requirement decomposition.

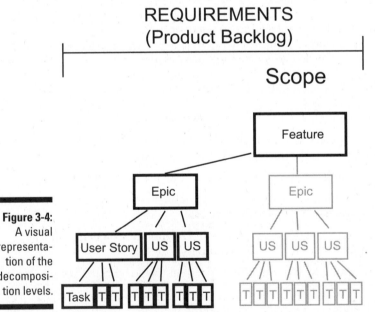

Figure 3-4: A visual representation of the decomposition levels.

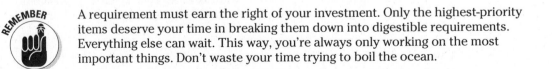

A requirement must earn the right of your investment. Only the highest-priority items deserve your time in breaking them down into digestible requirements. Everything else can wait. This way, you're always only working on the most important things. Don't waste your time trying to boil the ocean.

The following terms relating to product roadmaps and product backlogs have been developed by scrum experts over the years. They aren't scrum; rather they're part of a collection of common practices that many of us use in the field:

- ✔ *Themes* are logical groups of the features that you created in your product roadmap.

  If a feature is a new capability that a customer will have, a theme is the logical grouping of these features. The ability to purchase items from your website would be an example of a theme. Your product roadmap usually identifies and/or groups features as part of a theme.

- ✔ *Features* are capabilities that your end customer will have that they didn't have before.

  For example, purchasing items online via your mobile phone would be a feature. Your product roadmap usually consists of feature-level requirements.

- ✔ *Epics* are the next stage in breaking down a feature into an actionable requirement.

  They are a series of actions related to the feature. The ability to purchase an item via your mobile phone from the shopping cart using a credit card would be an epic. It's smaller than a feature (purchasing an item online), but yet it is bigger than the individual credit card integrations that singularly enable an item to be purchased. We don't allow requirements larger than epics into a release plan.

- ✔ *User stories* are the smallest forms of requirements that can still stand on their own. A user story consists of one action of value or one integration of value.

  For example, purchasing an item via your mobile phone from the shopping cart using a Visa card would be a user story. Purchasing an item using a MasterCard could be a different integration and thus a different user story. User stories are small enough to add to sprints and begin developing. I go into user stories in detail in the sections that follow.

- ✔ *Tasks* are the internal steps needed to implement the user story.

  During sprint planning, a user story is broken down into tasks. While requirements are things that the end user does, tasks are what the development team does to make the requirement work.

Each requirement goes through seven steps to fully build out its scope. At the end of these seven steps, you will know that each requirement works, can be integrated, and has been approved by the product owner. You are tangibly building products to showcase to stakeholders and thereby garner feedback. This feedback is then used to refine and create new requirements that make the product better reflect stakeholder needs, and the cycle is run again. You incrementally improve the product based on reality.

The seven steps for building each requirement are

1. Requirement elaboration
2. Design
3. Development
4. Comprehensive testing
5. Integration
6. Documentation
7. Approval

Your Product Backlog

The product backlog is a true scrum artifact and the master to-do list for the entire project. All scrum projects have product backlogs, and they are owned and maintained by the product owner.

The requirements from the product roadmap initially create the product backlog, and the highest-priority ones are broken down into user stories on Day 1 (I describe how below). Figure 3-5 depicts a sample product backlog.

PRODUCT BACKLOG

Order	ID	Item	Type	Status	Estimate
1	121	As an Administrator, I want to link accounts to profiles, so that customers can access new accounts.	Requirement	Not Started	5
2	113	Update requirements traceability matrix	Overhead	Not Started	2
3	403	As a Customer, I want to transfer money between my active accounts, so that I can adjust each account's balance.	Improvement	Not Started	3
4	97	Refactor Login Class	Maintenance	Not Started	8
5	68	As a Site Visitor, I want to find locations, so that I can use bank services.	Requirement	Not Started	8

Figure 3-5: The product backlog is your project's ordered to-do list.

In traditional project management frameworks, change was viewed as a reflection of poor planning. If something had to be changed, it was because someone messed up. In scrum, we see change as a sign of growth. As you discover your product more deeply, you will identify changes that need to be made. In scrum, if you're not changing, you're not learning, and that's a problem. It's a lack of change that is a sign of failure. Every day you need to learn something and that causes change.

Each item in the product backlog has the following elements:

- ✔ Specific order number (priority slot in the product backlog; although product backlog items may be similar in priority, they cannot be worked on at exactly the same time).
- ✔ Description.
- ✔ Estimate of the effort required to complete.
- ✔ ID number (optional).
- ✔ Status (optional).
- ✔ Type of item (optional). This could be a requirement, overhead, maintenance, or improvement (see the following section).

Highest-priority requirements get broken down into the smallest actionable requirements possible in the product backlog. However, a small requirement doesn't automatically make it a high-priority item. Many small requirements of low priority will likely never see production.

The dynamic to-do list

The product backlog never goes away while the project is active. It's never signed off on, marked complete, and stuck in a drawer. If you have a project, you have a product backlog, and it's always changing. As larger requirements are broken down into smaller requirements, it changes. As client feedback is received, the backlog changes. As your competitors bring new offerings to market, it might change again.

Keep your product IDs simple. You don't need to be able to track every item back to its more generic origin; you just need to give it a numerical name, like 123, not like 10.8.A.14. Practice maximizing the amount of work you don't do by ridding your project of intellectually gratifying time-wasters so that you can focus on the important things.

The product owner doesn't just prioritize items in the product backlog. They also order them in a logical sequence. This way, the next sprint can be quickly and efficiently organized from these ordered items.

All changes to the product backlog are made by the product owner. At any point, if anyone (product owner, developer, stakeholder) identifies a new requirement or design idea, it's given to the product owner. It will get prioritized along with everything else. With scrum, *change* is no longer something you crawl under your desk and hide from. Change is good. Change is life. Change is scrum.

Product backlog refinement

Product backlog refinement is how the scrum team advances its understanding of the items in the product backlog and prepares them for upcoming sprints. It is a continuous process of breaking down and preparing the feedback and responses to change for future development. It is owned by the product owner and performed with the help of the development team, who ask clarifying questions and provide estimates based on the best information available at that time. The scrum team as a whole will spend up to 10 percent of their active sprint time in this process. As with scrum events, the scrum master usually facilitates product backlog refinement activities to keep the group focused and on task.

The target outcomes of product backlog refinement are

- ✔ **Clarity:** All developers and the product owner are clear and in consensus on the scope of the product backlog items discussed.
- ✔ **Acceptance criteria:** All requirements (that is, user stories) include sufficient acceptance criteria.
- ✔ **Risks identified and mitigated to the best extent possible:** Other known risks should be documented and accepted by the team as necessary.
- ✔ **Sizing:** Requirements are estimated and broken down sufficiently to be accomplished within a sprint.

Anyone can write out a product feature or requirement. An idea or concern can be sparked by a business stakeholder, a member of the development team, the scrum master, the product owner, and even the company barista. Ideas are expected from any and all. However, only the product owner has the power to accept or reject a requirement into the product backlog, based on whether it supports the vision for the product. The product owner is the full owner of this artifact. If accepted, they will then number, refine, prioritize, and order that new requirement.

Backlog refinement should be a regular occurrence, but scrum does not prescribe how formal or frequent refinement discussions should take place, nor does it prescribe a specific agenda. Here are suggestions that have worked very well for us and our clients:

- ✔ **Format:** The product owner presents one requirement to the team at a time. For each requirement in turn, the team asks questions, challenges assumptions, explores implementation strategies, and uses a whiteboard for drawing and clarification until they have consensus on the details and scope of the requirement. The development team then uses estimation poker or affinity estimating to assign a relative estimation.

  For requirements that move up in priority, the estimation serves as an indicator of when it has been broken down small enough to fit into a sprint.

- ✔ **Time:** Scrum teams, on average, spend about 10 percent of a sprint in refining the backlog in preparation for the next sprint.

- ✔ **Frequency:** Backlog refinement is a progressive activity. Requirements get refined gradually, just in time, with those closer to delivery being made "ready" for sprints.

  Teams may prefer conducting backlog refinement with one of these schedules:

  - Daily, at the end of each day. This also acts as a demobilization exercise for the development team to transition into going home for the day (for 15–30 minutes)

  - Daily, at some other mutually agreed-upon time

  - Once per sprint during a regularly scheduled block of time

  - Once per week during a regularly scheduled block of time

  - Multiple times per week during a regularly scheduled block of time

  - As needed, determined, and scheduled by the team in each sprint

- ✔ **Activities:** Backlog refinement activities may consist of any or a combination of the following types of activities:

  - Entire team discussions, including whiteboard, modeling, Q&A, and design discussions

  - Individual team members researching items identified during team discussions

  - Interviewing subject matter experts or stakeholders to gain insights for determining scope and suggested solutions to requirements

  - Estimation poker or affinity estimation sessions (see Chapter 4 for more on estimating)

As the team discusses and refines the next-highest-priority requirement candidates, use as many of the following questions and guidelines as needed to guide the team through the refinement process. Not all of these will apply to every team and/or requirement:

✔ Breaking down large requirements

- Does the user story satisfy the INVEST criteria? (see "INVEST" section in this chapter)

- Can it be completed within one sprint or part of one sprint?

- Is the user story a single action of value or a series of actions?

- Is the scope barely sufficient?

- Has the product owner added technical tasks or other technical details that should be left to the development team to determine?

- Has the scrum team's definition of "done" (see Chapter 4) been considered before determining that the story is sufficiently broken down?

- What are the unknowns? Is more research required before the team can estimate?

✔ Clarifying and refining where needed

- Does the development team understand the business intent and/or value of the requirement?

- Is there shared understanding among the team? Have development team members tried paraphrasing the requirement to make sure that everyone is on the same page?

- Is the desired deliverable clear?

- When suggesting implementation approaches, does it make sense from both technical and business perspectives?

- Are we considering all the work that is needed to fully complete and deliver the story (get it to "done")?

- Does the team know the tasks that will be required?

- Will we be able to deliver a fully "done" increment of our product at the end of this sprint?

✔ Ensuring adequate acceptance criteria

- If needed, have personas been identified? (See later in this chapter.)

- Is the acceptance criteria adequate? Are any criteria missing that should be included?

- Have test-oriented development team members weighed in on whether the criteria is sufficient?

✔ Addressing potential issues and risks

- Can it stand alone, or are there dependencies?
- What conflicts may arise during implementation?
- What technical debt might this requirement introduce?

✔ Assigning high-level estimates

- Has the scrum team decided on a consistent estimation method? Estimation poker (Fibonacci numbers)? Affinity (T-shirt sizes)? (See Chapter 4.)
- Has the team agreed on how to reach consensus? Fist of Five? Thumbs Up/Down? (See Chapter 4.)
- Have estimations revealed that any of the requirements are still too big?

  If estimations bring up additional points that need clarification, use these guidelines to further refine them before reestimating.

You need to watch a few factors in this process:

✔ Only development team members estimate requirements, because they're the ones doing the work.

✔ The product owner provides immediate clarifications to developers' questions by being actively involved in the refinement discussions.

✔ The frequency and duration of refinement activities will vary by team and project, and even from sprint to sprint.

Other possible backlog items

When I coach clients in building their product backlog, I encourage them to identify a "type" of backlog item. Refer back to Figure 3-5.

I use four different types to help clarify the nature of the item to be completed. All of these items are things that can be done or not done at the product owner's discretion, as each has opportunity cost against the others:

✔ **Requirement:** This is mainly what I've been writing about. What functionality needs to be developed for the end user? "The customer will be able to do . . ."

✔ **Maintenance:** Design improvements for the code, such as fundamentally rethinking a login class that can't be tactically tweaked anymore. Maintenance items reduce the technical debt of the project.

✔ **Improvements:** Based on results from the sprint retrospective, what can be done differently in the process? For example, "Expand automated testing skills."

✔ **Overhead:** Companies often have overhead items that they just like to see, such as a requirement traceability matrix, and most companies don't add the matrix into the equation. They assume that it's free, but it costs time and money. I like to make that cost obvious.

These additional types aren't required, but they're a common practice for you to consider using in your own situation. The more proven ideas I can feed you, the more likely you are to achieve success.

Product Backlog Common Practices

Agile techniques are practiced by thousands of companies and organizations throughout the world. As a natural result, common agile practices abound. Some of these I incorporate into my own consulting business; others I use and find they don't work for me, so I discard them. I recommend that you do the same. No one set of universal best practices exists. Rather, tried and tested outside-of-scrum techniques are available that work for some and not for others. User stories are one such common practice.

User stories

User stories are a format used to gather end-customer requirements. They are also a common term for requirements small enough to be brought into the sprint and broken down into tasks. User stories are one action of value that an end user will achieve: "As a shopper, I want to be able to scan a product bar code with my phone so that I can compare and find the lowest price of the same product at multiple stores."

Working with the highest-priority requirements to completion isn't just convenient, but it also saves money and is part of why scrum projects can come in at a 30–70 percent cost savings. If your project runs out of money 80 percent of the way through, you can say without a doubt that you have 80 percent of the highest-priority items completed, functioning, and accepted. The remaining 20 percent? If they were such a low priority, many times you can live without them anyway.

Multiple user stories go into every sprint, and each are of the highest priority at that time. On average, you might have six to ten user stories per sprint.

Therefore, at the end of each sprint, if the development team concentrates on completing one requirement at a time (swarming, described further in Chapter 6), you will always have something to show for your work. Tangible progress every sprint. That's scrum.

I use 3x5 index cards to write out each user story. Even with these small cards, because we use a "Card ⇨ Conversation ⇨ Confirmation" model, you'll get richer requirement clarity before development starts than ever before. User stories aren't the only way to describe what needs to be done, but I've found them to be incredibly effective. Figure 3-6 shows the front and back of 3x5 index card user stories.

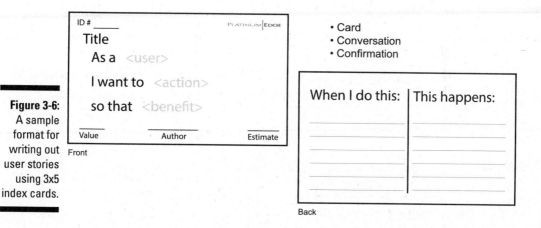

Figure 3-6: A sample format for writing out user stories using 3x5 index cards.

The use of 3x5 index cards is optional. I find them easy, sufficient, and efficient. If you have a different solution that suits your situation, such as needing electronic cards for distributed teams, go for it.

In the "Card ⇨ Conversation ⇨ Confirmation" model, the product owner uses the 3x5 card as a reminder of the requirement — a reminder that a conversation must take place to refine and clarify it. It enables the immensely valuable activity of conversing with the development team and answering the specific questions they have, supported by an explicit description of what success looks like on the back of the card. Compare this simple, expedient, and vastly more efficient process to its historical predecessor. Previously, we developed tomes of documents prior to having a development team in an attempt to answer all the questions we thought that team might have — an endeavor we invariably failed at.

Don't use technical jargon in your user stories. You're writing these with the end user in mind. Keep them direct, customer focused, and simple.

Sometimes it's easier to work with *personas*. These are fictional characters who are amalgams of the target qualities that your clients will have. For example, consider a 35-year-old single male, professionally employed; living in Portland, Oregon; and looking for his future significant other. Give him a name, George, and then use that persona to ensure that your project meets the needs of George, your target customer.

The user story description is simple, yet focused. You will clearly describe the user, the action, and the benefit. With each card, fill in the following lines:

✔ An ID that is the same as in the product backlog and is given by the product owner when they accept an item into the product backlog

✔ A shorthand title, for example, *email capability*

✔ As a: *<describe the user, such as your persona "George" or a brief description: "single, 35-year-old man">*

✔ I want to: *<describe the action, such as "email a specific individual from findmytruestoftruelove.com">*

✔ So that: *<describe the benefit, such as "I can initiate contact">*

Critical to the user story is what's written on the flip side of the card — the acceptance criteria. This is how you know that the user story has been successfully implemented:

✔ When I do this: *<describe the action, such as "email potential dates">* this happens *<describe the results: "I can see the sent emails in my Sent folder">*

Each user story is written in the first-person point of view: "When *I* do this, *I* get this." This is intentional as it sets the author into the shoes of the end user or customer.

The person submitting the user story writes out the user story on the card and gives it to the product owner to share directly with the development team. Oftentimes, the stakeholder also participates in the conversation phase. By this, I mean that they actually sit down together with the product owner and development team and goes over each and every card. This act of direct communication is vital to a thorough understanding of the tasks necessary to achieve the result desired. As a result, communication is clearer and mistakes are fewer, and your project quality and delivery speed are increased.

INVEST

INVEST is an acronym for qualities that you want to look for in your user stories. (Bill Wake first created the INVEST mnemonic for user stories.) These letters will help you write focused, clear, and precise user stories:

- ✔ **I**ndependent (to the best degree possible): The story does not need other stories to implement it or for the user to interact with it.

- ✔ **N**egotiable: The product owner and the development team must discuss and expand on the story's nuances and details. The value of a user story is in the conversation, not the card.

- ✔ **V**aluable: The story shows product value to the customer, not the technical steps (tasks) that the developer will use to enable the story.

- ✔ **E**stimable: It is refined enough for developers to estimate the amount of effort required to create the functionality.

- ✔ **S**mall: An executable size. A rule of thumb is to bring between six and ten user stories into each sprint.

- ✔ **T**estable: The story needs to be testable so that the development team knows definitively that the story has been done correctly. "It needs to be fast" or "It needs to be intuitive" is not testable. "I need to get a response from the application in less than a second" or "I need to complete the action in three clicks or less" is testable.

Break it down even more

Development team effort determines whether a requirement needs to be broken down further to progress on to the product roadmap, into the release plan, or into the sprint (see Chapter 5 for details). Especially at the beginning, as you find out how to apply user stories within your scrum framework, you may find the ones that you write are too big to fit into a sprint.

While most user stories have multiple steps, some are bigger than practical and can (and should) be broken down into more granular requirements. This is part of the discovery process and part of the benefit of using user stories.

You also may find additional requirements that need to be placed in the product backlog during the user story elaboration discussion. Excellent! It's these discoveries that help you gain a deeper understanding of what the customer and/or end user will actually need.

Chapter 4

The Talent and the Timing

"Talent wins games. But teamwork and intelligence wins championships."

— Michael Jordan

The development team sits at the core of scrum projects. The product owner and the scrum master revolve around making sure that the environment is as ideal as possible for the development team to reach maximum productivity. In this chapter, you find out how a development team is organized and therefore able to best contribute to the scrum team.

After you have your team roles, vision, and roadmap in place, the next step is to begin to estimate the amount of work for each requirement. The development team begins by estimating the effort involved in high-level requirements. Here you create a starting point for future reference. You establish the numerator (product backlog total)/denominator (average velocity) relationship that gives you the estimated number of sprints necessary to complete all, or a target portion of, items in the product backlog. I show you how these high-level estimates can be achieved quickly and accurately.

The Development Team

In Hollywood, actors and singers are referred to as "the talent." They're the ones who get on stage and do the job. Everyone else facilitates this process, because when the talent is successful, everyone is successful. Think of the development team as the talent.

The development team is the talent responsible for creating and developing the actual product. They drive the how and the how much. In other words, they determine how they will develop the requirements and how many they can do in any one sprint. They are solely dedicated to one project at a time, cross-functional, self-organizing, and self-managing.

The development team is intentionally size-limited to around seven members, plus or minus two. This size allows for a self-sufficient and self-organizing group with a diversity of skills, yet it's not too big and unwieldy. Remember, for each new member, the lines of communication increase geometrically. With more than nine development team members, you can't have a self-organizing team. Under a waterfall model, this issue is masked with a project manager, who is responsible for coordinating all that communication. Scrum doesn't have the overhead cost of too many lines of communication, nor a project manager.

While seven people, plus or minus two, is a manageable and efficient size, the key factor is self-encapsulation. Is the team able to elaborate the requirements, design them, develop them, test them, integrate them, document them, and have them approved? Have single points of failure been eliminated (that is, at least two people can do any one skill)? Is the total size no more than nine people? If all three answers are "yes," you have a good-sized, cross-functional development team. Whereas a product owner must be decisive and a scrum master must have clout, a development team member must be versatile and intellectually curious, and have a predisposition for sharing. No prima donnas allowed. Their fires are lit with building and creating.

The uniqueness of scrum development teams

In many ways, the scrum development team is the opposite of a traditional team. In scrum, each development team member is going to develop cross-functional skills. They are part of the goal-setting process, and as a team, they have complete control over how they will do their developing. Additionally, credit is taken as a team.

Harvard psychologist Dan Gilbert conducted research that showed that people who bring in $5 million annually are not much happier than those who earn $50,000.

Creating a motivating environment

Daniel Pink writes about motivation in his excellent book *Drive: The Surprising Truth About What Motivates Us* (published by Riverhead Books). Here Pink dispels the myth that the way to motivate people is through more and more money. Surprisingly, Pink found that the higher the monetary incentive, the worse the results. Money is a factor, but only enough to take the subject of money off the table.

As he continued to dig, Pink found three specific factors that produced the environment for the best-quality results, whether at home or work: autonomy, mastery, and purpose. Let your people determine how they will do their work, give them the space and time to master current and new skills, and communicate a sense of purpose in what they're doing.

The scrum framework can enable this same environment that Pink discusses. The development team is designed to be self-organizing and autonomous in how it does the work. Cross-functionality and developing new skills are fundamental. Through the vision statement and direct communication with the product owner and stakeholders, the development team members are able to understand what they're working on and why.

Check out Pink's book or TED talks for more information on his research.

Dedicated teams and cross-functionality

As I mentioned previously, development team members are solely dedicated to one project at a time. No thrashing your development team. You want them to be focused each day on the current sprint's goal. Whether functional management chooses the team members or someone else does, a diversity of skills is sought after to be self-encapsulated. Which leads me to the next point — cross-functionality.

People don't necessarily start out being cross-functional; they grow into this state. Start with a team of diverse talents and then organically build that team toward being individually cross-functional. Ideally you want every developer to be able to do everything. This is not always possible, but you at least want every developer to be able to do more than one thing. Becoming cross-functional is a process.

Whatever your business or organization, the facts remain: People go on vacation, they get sick, they take on new roles and jobs. One day they're there next to you, and the next, they might be somewhere else. In traditional projects, when a key development team member goes on vacation, the project goes on vacation. You're forced into delays either from waiting for that person to return, or in the case of attrition, recruiting and mobilizing another.

In scrum, you strive for cross-functionality in your development team. In this way, you eliminate that single point of failure. If one development team member comes down with the flu, someone else can take his place and get the job done. Some additional benefits of cross-functionality are

✔ Allows for diverse input on development for optimal solutions.

✔ Enables the ability to do pair development to ensure higher quality.

✔ One of the best ways to increase your primary skill is to learn an associative skill, because this process exposes you to other ways of thinking about your primary skill.

✔ Allows people to work on various things and keeps the work interesting.

Several ways exist to create cross-functional individuals from cross-functional teams:

✔ **Don't use titles.** Encourage an equal playing field. I've found that this stimulates junior developers to get up to speed faster, and senior-level skills increase because senior people don't want to be outdone by young, hungry talent. A lack of titles also emphasizes skills over fixed hierarchy, thereby encouraging skill development. Informal status still exists, but now it's based on skills.

✔ **Do use pair programming.** Commonly used in software development practices such as eXtreme Programming, pair programming can be used by a development team to develop any type of product. Two developers work on the same piece of functionality together. Developer A is tactically developing (cutting code, for example), while Developer B is free to think strategically about the functionality (scalability, extensibility, risks, and so on). They switch these roles throughout the day. Because these developers are working so tightly together, they can quickly catch errors.

✔ **Do use shadowing.** Again, two developers are working together, but in this case, only one does the work while the other watches and learns.

Shadowing also increases product quality. Remember, visibility and performance are correlated — increase visibility and you will generally increase performance. The working developer doesn't want to take a lazy shortcut in front of the learning one, and the learning one will ask those smart "dumb questions." Explaining something improves your own knowledge of it, and vocalizing something uses a different part of your brain and improves functioning. Finally, ownership is reinforced if you're teaching and explaining.

The Hawthorne effect (or Observer effect) is based on studies showing that a worker's productivity increases when someone is watching them. It's named after Hawthorne Works, an electrical company outside of Chicago where the first experiments took place.

Rubber duck problem solving, rubber ducking, or the rubber duckie test are all terms used to describe an interesting phenomenon often used in software engineering. Programmers are told to explain their coding problem *out loud and in detail to a rubber duck*. I've seen it in action. Most of the time, before the programmer has even finished explaining it, the answer comes to them. The same phenomenon can be seen when a friend comes to you with a problem. Just the process of vocalizing the issue stimulates a different part of the brain so that answers can dislodge themselves and flow downstream.

The organizational structure of scrum development teams helps prevent bottlenecks in your work flow. Through cross-functionality, pair programming, colocation, and direct access between the requirement maker and the developer, communication lines are cleared and diversity in skills is expanded. This all leads to fewer plugs in the flow.

Self-organizing and self-managing

The key word here is *ownership*. Self-organizing and self-managing teams develop ownership in what they do. With a scrum development team, this is part of what creates such efficiency and success.

Pair programming

While pair programming at first may seem more expensive — employing two developers for the same job — when looked at holistically, it actually reduces costs. The development cost rises, but the quality assurance (QA) cost dramatically falls.

It's exponentially cheaper to prevent defects than to rip them out of a deployed system later, as described in these cases:

- If you catch the error on the spot, the cost to fix it is minimal.

- If the bug is found after committing the code, it costs 6.5 times more to remobilize, find, and fix it.

- If the bug escaped through testing and goes out to the production environment, finally being identified several days or weeks later, the mobilization time is much longer, the discovery time is longer, and the cost is about 15 times greater.

- If this same bug makes it into the marketplace and has to be corrected by a group that never developed the application — such as the production support group — the cost can be up to 100 times greater.

For every defect, the development team must find the bug, develop code to correct it, and hope that the correction for that specific defect doesn't cause another defect. Remember, for every two defects fixed, another one gets created in the process.

I sometimes get asked by clients how I can assure them that they'll get 100 percent from their development team. In response, I ask the client how they can assure me that a professional sports team will give 100 percent, because they would lose if they didn't. The visibility and acknowledgment of their hard work increases drive.

Visibility and performance are directly correlated. Increase performance by increasing visibility.

One technique sometimes used is to have two (or more) development teams. Synchronize their sprints so that the sprint reviews happen at the same time on the same day. Then, invite an executive to come to both sprint reviews randomly for a few minutes and have them ask at least one question before leaving. Each development team knows that their performance will have executive visibility, and they all want to look good. Historically, they might not even have been given credit for the work they did. Now they can produce a product that they can be proud of. They're on stage getting all the credit. This is hugely motivating and increases drive and buy-in.

Ownership and therefore accountability are increased in a scrum development team in the following ways:

- ✔ The development team is directly accountable for the deliverables that they create. This isn't always easy on them because visibility brings intrinsic pressure to perform, but this visibility also creates ownership.

- ✔ Cross-functionality creates ownership because there isn't any "my job versus your job." Everything is "our job."

- ✔ Because the whole scrum team is held accountable, individual performance is increased. Everyone wins as a team, and everyone contributes to the success of every sprint.

- ✔ The development team actively participates in creating the sprint goals and demonstrating the working functionality during the sprint review.

- ✔ The development team is responsible for tactical status reporting every single day. In less than one minute of administration per day (see burndown charts in Chapter 5), the organization will get a level of tactical status reporting that they've never had before.

Development teams perform best when they're stable. Feed them projects, and give them what they need to do their best possible work. Every time you have to switch members on your team, it takes time to stabilize again. Protect your development team to nurture good dynamics.

Cognitive Consistency Theory describes our tendency to seek out information, beliefs, and stimuli that are consistent with our current set of beliefs and attitudes. In scrum, if development team members have a voice, and if they have buy-in and control, they will strive harder to achieve their work-related goals. They will try to find consistency between the ownership that they have created and their future output.

Colocating or the nearest thing

Many people have forgotten what it's like to work with a colocated team and to experience the increased production involved. Most people appreciate the concept, but might not understand the underlying principles. Here are a few benefits of a colocated team:

- Increased speed and effectiveness of face-to-face communication, especially through kinetics, voice tonality, facial expressions, and so on.

  The value of face-to-face communication shouldn't be underestimated. Albert Mehrabian, Ph.D. and professor emeritus of psychology at UCLA, proved the following:

  - 55 percent of meaning is conveyed through body language and facial expressions.

  - 38 percent of meaning is *paralinguistic* (conveyed by the way we speak).

  - 7 percent of meaning is conveyed in the actual words spoken.

  These statistics alone are a whopping case for colocating your development team.

- Ease of using simple tools for planning and communicating — like whiteboards and sticky notes.

- Ease in immediate clarification of questions.

- Understanding what other members are working on.

- Ease in supporting other team members in their tasks.

- Cost savings due to decreased lag times and fewer misunderstandings that lead to defects or wasted work.

When colocated, your product owner and development team have access to each other all day every day. All sorts of banality gets exchanged, and it's tempting to think that this might be wasteful. However, I've found that this is when the really good work gets done. Little things aren't actually little — they are differentiators, and they are the things that matter. Quality needs input, and input needs access. When access is high, great things are possible.

Why development teams love scrum

Development teams love scrum for a variety of reasons, not least of which is that it's an empowering and motivating environment. When you allow people to contribute, they become part of the process and take ownership in the results. The effects snowball:

✔ Success is clearly defined with the sprint goal, the definition of done, and each requirement's listed success criteria.

✔ Members participate in creating the sprint goal, thereby increasing ownership.

✔ Acceptance criteria is clear with the requirements. The team clearly understands what success looks like.

✔ It's a *results-only work environment (ROWE)*. Work any way you like; just show results.

✔ Direct communication with product owners is available.

✔ Team recognition is given in the sprint reviews.

✔ Structured process improvement is achieved through the sprint retrospectives.

✔ Systematic knowledge is built through sprint retrospectives.

Sometimes outsourcing is the only viable solution for your company or organization. If this is the case, do it with both feet. Colocate the entire scrum team. Your development team needs an available product owner, so send one over to work directly with the remote scrum team. Or, develop a local product owner, even if they have to start as a product owner agent (see Chapter 2). The increase in quality and efficiency far outweighs the cost of the product owner.

Getting the Edge on Backlog Estimation

In the product roadmap stage (see Chapter 1), the development team does a high-level estimate of the amount of work entailed in the project. The practical value of this estimation process doesn't come in until the sprints start (see Chapter 5), but this initial estimation sets a mark from which future estimates may be calculated. The development team does the estimating because only the people who do the work should be estimating the effort of the work.

These backlog estimation techniques aren't requirements of scrum. They're common practices that scrum practitioners have found useful in the field.

The product roadmap is the start of the product backlog. What's on your roadmap is what you will begin developing. So how do you take all those items on your product backlog and with any degree of accuracy estimate the work involved? A few different common practices are used depending on the situation. Before I look at these estimating techniques individually, it's important to understand what you're actually trying to achieve.

Your Definition of Done

If you ask each member of a scrum team what they would expect to see when a requirement is "done," you would get as many answers as there are team members. So, before starting a project, scrum teams define what "done" means with a "definition of done." Until you have consensus on this definition, estimations will be based on bad data.

As described in Chapter 3, for each requirement within a sprint, you will complete the following stages of development:

- ✔ Requirement elaboration
- ✔ Design
- ✔ Development
- ✔ Comprehensive testing
- ✔ Integration
- ✔ Documentation
- ✔ Approval

This definition of done needs to be specific, refined, and focused about what it means to do these things to completion to achieve the level of quality that you're striving for in your project. Consider which environment the product or service needs to work within and at what level of integration to be considered done. "Works in the development environment," for example, is probably a bad, loose definition of done.

Consider these four factors in your definition of done:

- ✔ **Developed:** The product has been fully developed by the development team.
- ✔ **Tested:** The development team fully tested the product to make sure that it functions in the required environment without any glitches.

✔ **Integrated:** The product has been fully integrated within the product as a whole and any related systems.

✔ **Documented:** The development team created whatever documentation is needed. Just remember that the goal with all things agile is "barely sufficient."

When you've come up with your definition of done, write it out on a white poster board and tape it on the wall. You'll always have it right in front of the development team and product owner. I call it in-your-face documentation. No cover sheet, no table of contents. This is how I do documentation: What is the lowest-fidelity way that you can communicate the point?

Timebox is a term that refers to the allotted time for an event or activity. If your sprints last two weeks, the timebox is two weeks.

In your definition of done, consider not only the development but also the depth of testing and documentation that you might need. For example, you might consider which tests must pass:

✔ Unit

✔ Functional/System

✔ Performance/Load

✔ Security

✔ User acceptance

Also consider what documentation you'll need:

✔ Technical docs

✔ User docs

✔ Maintenance docs

Each of these testing and documentation points might differ between the sprint level and the release level, though I prefer that your sprint-level definition of done includes everything necessary to release. You also might have organizationally specific items that you want to include. It's your choice, and the point is to have a clear definition of done, defined by the scrum team for all to work by.

A *release* is when a set of marketable features are released outside of the scrum team. This could happen several times during a sprint, at the end of each sprint, or after a series of sprints. These requirements might be released into the market and to the end users, or they may go to internal or external stakeholders for real-world usage and feedback.

A regular sprint entails completing the development, testing, documentation, and approval of items in the sprint backlog. However, before you do a product release, other activities may be needed (such as performance and load testing) that the development team wouldn't have access to in a regular sprint. Therefore, sometimes scrum teams have a *release sprint* just before the release itself to allow these additional tests to be addressed. The key is at the end of every sprint, the requirements must work and be demonstrable. You can test and tune for scale in the release sprint, but the requirements must work every sprint.

Common Practices for Estimating the End

Estimating the effort involved in developing product backlog requirements is an ongoing process. (In Chapter 3, I discuss product backlog refinement.) For example, you could do estimations for 30 minutes at five o'clock every evening before team members go home. This way, at the end of the week, you've covered lots of ground and will be ready for each sprint start. Some teams don't like to develop on Friday afternoon and do product backlog refinement then. It's up to you — results-only work environment.

Teams will likely refine their estimates at three levels. This is part of the process of breaking the requirements down to be ready for sprint-level execution. Depending on your product, you might include more. Your estimate refinement will usually go in this order:

- ✔ Product roadmap
- ✔ Release planning
- ✔ Sprint planning

The development team is responsible for estimating the effort required to fully build the requirements. The scrum master can facilitate the process, and the product owner can provide clarification, but the end decision is made by developers doing the actual work.

I use relative estimating in lieu of precise (absolute) estimating, because in many situations, it's much more feasible. For example, if I ask you to look out the window and tell me how tall the neighboring building is, how precise would be your reply? Very — it's 950 feet. How accurate would be your reply? Not very. Why? Because you honestly have no idea; you gave it a wild guess. But if I ask you to look at two nearby buildings and tell me which one is taller, barring some vision problem, I can guarantee that you'll give me the right answer. I use this accuracy to my advantage.

Fibonacci numbers and story points

The Fibonacci sequence is an excellent sizing technique for relative estimating.

With Fibonacci, if something is bigger, you get an idea of how much bigger it is. The last two numbers in the sequence are added together to create the next number. It looks like this:

1, 2, 3, 5, 8, 13, 21, 34, 55, 89, 144, and so on

As the numbering progresses, the distance between the numbers increases. We use this to acknowledge the lesser degree of accuracy in predicting larger chunks of work.

REMEMBER

A *story point* is the Fibonacci number assigned to an individual requirement (that is, a user story).

Initial, high-level requirements are estimated at the product roadmap level:

- ✔ For scrum teams I work with, the development teams understands that requirements with Fibonacci number estimates from 1 through 8 can be brought into a sprint. This level of refinement usually results in a user story.

- ✔ Requirements with estimates numbered from 13 through 34 are those that you would let into a release but need to be broken down further before you would let them into a sprint. At this level of refinement, I call these epics.

- ✔ Requirements from 55 through 144 are too big for a release but are estimable at the order-of-magnitude product roadmap level. These requirements typically reflect features.

TECHNICAL STUFF

Who is this guy?

Leonardo Pisano Bigollo, also known as *Fibonacci*, lived near Pisa, Italy, from about 1170 to about 1250. Widely recognized as a brilliant mathematician, not only did he make famous the Fibonacci sequence, but he also instigated the spread of the Hindu-Arabic numeral system in Europe. Today this is the most common symbolic representation of numbers used in the world.

Requirements larger than 144 need to be broken down before the development team can give any semblance of an accurate estimate, so I don't estimate above 144. These may represent broader themes.

Whatever the Fibonacci number, only the highest-priority cards get broken down into sprint-level sizes (which I recommend shouldn't be more than an 8). So if you have a high-priority requirement with a 21 Fibonacci number assigned to it, it needs to be broken into smaller requirements before it can come into a sprint.

Many ways exist to break requirements down. See `https://platinumedge.com/blog` for a few white papers on breaking requirements into executable sizes.

With the sizes established, I can apply a few techniques to estimate requirements:

- When I have shorter lists of requirements, I begin with *estimation poker.*
- When I have hundreds of requirements, I begin with *affinity estimation* (discussed later in this chapter).

In the estimation process with smaller projects, I have the development team begin as follows. I have the team sit down with their stack of requirements written out on 3x5 cards. Then I ask them to pick a requirement that they can all agree has an effort level of 5. This creates a reference point.

I then have them pick another card, and based on the first one being a 5, ask them what number the next one would be. If it's greater than a 5, is it an 8? a 13? a 21? This process continues until a few representational sizes have been established. Now I'm ready for estimation poker.

Estimation poker

A popular way of estimating requirements is through a variation of poker.

You'll need a deck of estimation poker cards like the one shown in Figure 4-1. (You can find them on our website at `https://platinumedge.com/store/estimation-poker-cards`. And you can also download our poker estimation app for iPhone and/or Android by searching Platinum Edge Estimation Poker.) You can also make your own deck with index cards and a marker.

Figure 4-1:
Estimation
poker
cards for
estimating
the amount
of effort
required
in each
require-
ment.

Because only the development team decides how much it will take to develop a requirement, only the development team plays. The scrum master facilitates and the product owner reads the requirements and provides requirement details, but neither of those two gives estimates. It goes like this:

1. **The product owner reads a targeted requirement to the development team.**

2. **The development team asks any questions and gets any clarifications they need.**

3. **Each member of the development team picks from his deck a card with his estimate of the difficulty of the requirement.**

   The estimate is per the complete definition of done, not just to write code.

   Members don't show anyone else their cards because you don't want others being influenced.

4. **After everyone has picked a number, simultaneously the team members show their cards.**

   - If everyone has the same estimate, nothing is left to discuss. Assign the requirement that estimate and move on to the next requirement.

   - If differences exist in estimates, those with the highest and lowest estimates are asked to explain. Further clarification from the product owner is given as needed.

     With increased knowledge, everyone picks a new number for that requirement by repeating Steps 3–4.

I normally do up to three rounds of estimation poker for each requirement to get the core assumptions on the table and clarified and, at that point, usually have the estimates in a tighter cluster of numbers.

If all developers are in agreement on a single number after three rounds, I'm ready to move on to the next requirement. But you won't always have all developers in agreement on a single number after three rounds. At this point, I go on to a consensus-building technique called fist of five.

Fist of five

A fast and efficient method of reaching consensus, the fist of five can be used on its own or as an addendum for estimation poker. The purpose of the fist of five is to quickly find a consensus estimate that all team members can at least support. See Figure 4-2.

Figure 4-2: Fist of five is an efficient way of finding consensus in many situations.

5 = LOVE IT!
4 = Good idea.
3 = Yeah, I can support it.
2 = I have reservations, let's discuss further.
1 = Opposed. Do not move forward.

Perhaps some team members have given a requirement a 5, and others have given it an 8.

It begins with the scrum master holding up the requirement card in question and saying, for example, "How comfortable would you be with this as an 8?" Each development team member holds up the number of fingers associated with their level of comfort. If everyone is holding up three, four, or five fingers, it's settled.

If some developers are still holding up one or two fingers, similar to estimation poker, the outliers would be asked to explain, and further information would be garnered if necessary. The fist of five would be performed again. Continue with this process until all team members can give the number at least a 3 (that is, "I don't love it but I can support it").

With the fist of five completed and requirements estimated, I'm ready to move to release or sprint planning. They're covered in Chapter 5.

Affinity estimating

Estimation poker and fist of five are effective methods of establishing consensus in small projects. But what if you have several hundred requirements on the product backlog? It could take days to complete. This is where affinity estimating comes into play.

Instead of beginning with Fibonacci numbers, you begin with a more familiar concept — T-shirt sizes (for example, XS, S, M, L, XL).

With affinity estimating, you first create several areas marked with each size, and then you place each requirement in one of the size categories. It goes like this:

1. **Identify small tables to sort the cards.**

   Label a table as *clarify,* and label other small tables for each of these size categories:

   - Extra-small

   - Small

   - Medium

   - Large

   - Extra-large

   - Epic (too large to fit into the sprint, given that six to ten requirements are the target for each sprint; more on this in Chapter 5)

2. **For each size category, give your development team 60 seconds to pick a requirement from the overall stack of requirements and place it on the corresponding table.**

   This establishes the *representational anchor* for each size.

3. **Each member of the development team grabs a stack of requirements.**

4. **Each member places each card on the table that they feel reflect its size based on the representational anchor for that size.**

   As you can see, these are like T-shirt sizes. Each "size" will eventually correspond to a Fibonacci number:

   - Extra small equals 1

   - Small equals 2

   - Medium equals 3

   - Large equals 5

   - Extra large equals 8

Anything larger than an 8 needs to be broken down further before it can come into a sprint.

TIP

Don't let team members linger too long on their stack of requirements. Establish a timebox for them to work within, for example, 20 minutes for 20 cards.

Figure 4-3 shows what the relationship between size piles and Fibonacci numbers looks like.

	SIZE	POINTS
Figure 4-3: Affinity estimating uses T-shirt sizes for story sizes and gives each one a corresponding Fibonacci number.	XtraSmall (XS)	1 pt
	Small (S)	2 pts
	Medium (M)	3 pts
	Large (L)	5 pts
	XtraLarge (XL)	8 pts

5. **Have the development team members play "gallery" until all members agree on the sizes for each requirement.**

   In "gallery," the team members flip through all the cards on all the tables and provide feedback on only the cards that don't appear to be on the right table.

   If one team member wants to move a story from small to medium, for example, check that the original person who placed it there doesn't disagree. If the person disagrees, place that card on a separate Clarify table. Don't get into extensive discussions just yet.

6. **Invite the product owner to review for major disagreements:**

   • If the product owner sees a requirement on the medium table that they thought would be a small, don't waste any time discussing it. The development team ultimately gets to say the size of the requirement, and a one-size difference is not worth the time to discuss.

   • If you have greater than one table of difference between where development team members think a card should be placed and where the product owner thought it would be placed, put that card on the Clarify table. The development team may not have understood the product owner's explanation of the requirement.

   7. **For cards on the Clarify table, play estimation poker (as shown earlier in this chapter).**

Within a relatively short amount of time, you've now been able to reliably estimate the effort on hundreds of separate requirements. You're ready to plan your first release and/or your first sprint.

Velocity

After you have Fibonacci numbers assigned to your requirements, you now have story points to work from.

Chapter 5 shows how to plan both releases and sprints. In essence, to plan your first sprint, among those requirements that are between 1 and 8 story points, a scrum team determines a modest number of combined story points to work on. Then, at the end of the sprint, a scrum team looks at the requirements that were done to completion and adds their story points together. It might be 15 or 25 or 35 story points. This is the development team's velocity for the first sprint, and a starting input for a team determining how much they can accomplish in the next sprint.

Velocity is the combined number of story points that your development team completed in an individual sprint. It is a postsprint fact used for extrapolation, not a presprint goal.

To accurately determine velocity, you need more than one sprint to find an average. Velocity follows the law of large numbers — the more data points you have, the better. At a minimum, you will need three data points to establish an optimistic, pessimistic, and most likely extrapolation of how many requirements will be done during the project. After you have these, you can tell stakeholders optimistic, pessimistic, and most likely estimates for how many of the highest-priority requirements on the product backlog can be completed within a project. Giving stakeholders this type of estimation range provides the level of detail they're looking for while allowing some flexibility for the development team as they're still getting into a development rhythm.

In the first few sprints of a project, the team's velocity will usually vary greatly. It becomes more stable as the team gets into a development rhythm. Of course, changes in team members or sprint duration will introduce variability into the team's velocity.

Velocity is not a goal; it is a fact used for extrapolation. Higher numbers are not automatically better than lower numbers.

When story points are used, you'll find that some teams are pessimistic in their estimates. Their numbers always come in high. And other teams are optimistic. Their story point total comes in low.

Consider that an optimistic team's velocity is 15 and the estimates for the release total 150 points. It would take them ten sprints to complete the release.

If a pessimistic team's velocity were 30 and the estimates for the release total 300 points, it would take them ten sprints as well.

Optimistic or pessimistic doesn't really matter, because teams will generally be consistent one way or the other and therefore balance out in the end.

This is why you always value a team's velocity against itself, not against other teams.

In fact, don't even tell anyone what a team's velocity is. Consider it an extrapolation system, not a performance system.

When you have a clear method of estimating the effort required to complete each requirement, and you have an average velocity established for the development team, you're able to accurately predict the quantity of product that can be created within fixed cost and time constraints. You're harnessing in your variables.

Story points and velocity in real time

A real-world example of the value of story points and velocity might appear like this.

Assume the following data:

✔ Remaining product backlog is 500 story points.

✔ Your sprint duration (timebox) is one week, Monday–Friday.

✔ The development team velocity averages 20 story points per sprint.

✔ Today is Monday, January 5, 2015.

✔ Your annual development team cost is $100,000 per team member and you have seven members, that is, $700,000 annually or $13,462 weekly.

Within minutes, you're now able to make a solid estimation of the cost and delivery date of the project. Given this data, your project will entail 25 sprints, and therefore it will take 25 weeks to complete. Your cost will be $336,550, and your completion date will be Friday, June 26, 2015.

What happens if your development team increases their velocity to 25 story points per sprint? Just plug in the numbers. Now, you'll only need 20 sprints. Your cost will drop to $269,240 (saving you $67,310), and your final delivery date will be Friday, May 22, 2015. This is the benefit of having a dedicated scrum master who is able to remove impediments and organizational drag on the team in order to increase velocity.

Chapter 5

Release and Sprint Planning

A complex system that works is invariably found to have evolved from a simple system that worked. A complex system designed from scratch never works and cannot be patched up to make it work. You have to start over with a working simple system.

— John Gall

Release and sprint planning is really where the rubber hits the road. As I've mentioned before, with scrum, you'll do more planning than ever before, but it's focused, results oriented, and packaged such that you'll wonder how you ever managed projects without it.

In this chapter, you find out how to plan the release of project features in a logical and organized way. The purpose of release planning is to mobilize the wider project team around a specific set of functionality that the organization wants to release to the marketplace. This is when such departments or stakeholders as the marketing department, field support, and customer service get mobilized and prepared to support functionality that end customers are going to be using in reality.

I also walk you through the scrum event of sprints. Scrum at its core is the sprint cycle. I show you how to use this valuable process and get the best possible results.

A *sprint* is a fixed timebox within which development is done to produce working, potentially shippable product. A typical sprint might be one or two weeks in duration, but could be as little as a day and as much as a month.

You'll understand how prioritizing releases and sprints accelerates time to market and maximizes return on investment (ROI), and how by having feedback loops, you create the product that your clients actually want, with the features they'll actually use.

Release Plan Basics — Stage 3

I began the roadmap to value with the bird's-eye basics — your vision statement. This allowed you to establish your destination and define the end state of the project. The second stage, the product roadmap, provides a holistic view of the features that support the vision. As you narrow your focus and generate more detail, you come into release planning. This is Stage 3 in your roadmap to value; see Figure 5-1. The release planning concept is scrum. However, the release plan artifact is a common practice that many scrum aficionados use with success.

Stage 3: RELEASE PLANNING

Figure 5-1: Stage 3 of the roadmap to value is the release plan.

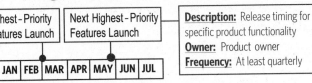

Highest-Priority Features Launch | Next Highest-Priority Features Launch

Description: Release timing for specific product functionality
Owner: Product owner
Frequency: At least quarterly

| JAN | FEB | MAR | APR | MAY | JUN | JUL |

(Stages 1 - 3 are common practices outside of scrum)

A *release plan* is a high-level timetable for releasing a set of product requirements. So you're working down, segmentally, in size from the big-picture roadmap to the mid-level release plan. (Later in this chapter, I cover the next-smaller size, which is the actual sprint.) The release plan provides a focal point around which the project team can mobilize.

Do the minimum amount possible that still creates a working product. When planning a set of features to release to the market, always ask yourself, "What is the minimum set of features that delivers value to my customer?" This is what is commonly referred to as the *minimum viable product,* or MVP.

You should release product to the market as often as you have something of value to offer your customers — the minimum viable product. Your product releases could also come on a regular schedule (for example, four times a year, at the end of each quarter). But with the advances in technology and the need to be quick to market, releases now may be monthly, weekly, or even multiple times a day in some cases.

AC + OC > V

Applying a simple formula to your project will help you know when you've achieved the best possible results. In other words, you'll know when to terminate the project as soon as the actual cost (AC) of the project added to the opportunity cost (OC) of not working on other projects is greater than the value (V) you're expecting to get from the future functionality.

As a formula, it looks like this:

$$AC + OC > V$$

This formula will help you determine when it is time to end a project. You'll see how you can achieve the 30–40 percent time savings and 30–70 percent cost savings I've realized so many times by

✔ Having stable, dedicated teams

✔ Prioritizing to avoid building features that customers won't use

✔ Iterating through consistent feedback loops with your customers

TIP

Consider the pen-pencil rule. You can use a pen to commit to the plan for the first release, but anything beyond this plan is written in pencil. It's just-in-time planning for each release.

A project may have multiple releases. For each release, you start with the goal, which is supported by the next-highest-priority features and requirements. You'll see that this is a pattern you follow at each stage of the road-map to value. Each release will have a release goal, and you only commit to one release at a time. Figure 5-2 depicts a typical release plan with an optional release sprint.

Release Goal: Enable customers to access, view, and transact against their active accounts.
Release Date: March 31, 2021

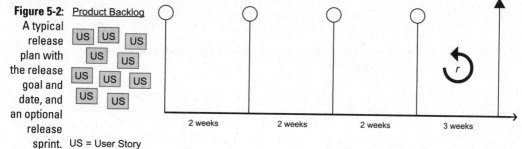

Figure 5-2: A typical release plan with the release goal and date, and an optional release sprint.

Product Backlog

US = User Story
r = optional "release" sprint

The number of sprints within each release can vary. It's dependent on the release goal and what's required to complete the requirements to achieve that goal — or, an option is to have release trains. This is where each release has a set time schedule. These could be evenly spaced or varying throughout the year. But they're set so that everyone knows when to expect the release.

At each scheduled release, the product owner decides which of the completed functionalities will be released on that date. This way, organizations and customers know to expect new features on a set schedule. Scrum teams are able to predictably organize their release plans to cadence.

Scrum is an empirical approach. Each step of the way, you inspect your results and adapt immediately to the changing needs of your customers. These fundamentals enable you to achieve significant cost and time savings while actually delivering what the client wants. You may have a bird's-eye view of four releases for your project, but you only plan in detail one release at a time. What you learn in release one may completely change what you do in release two.

Prioritize, prioritize, prioritize

You've heard this before when I talk about scrum, and you'll hear it throughout this book. Identifying the highest-priority requirements, according to business value and risk, and working with them and only them are key common practices within the agile community.

Think of each release as the next, incremental MVP (Minimum Viable Product) of your product. When planning each release, ask these questions to identify the highest-priority features:

- ✔ What makes a requirement important for this release?
- ✔ What minimum number of features providing business value to the customer do I need to bring to market?
- ✔ Which requirements present the greatest risk and should be addressed sooner than later?

In a famous Standish Group study from 2001, they showed on a representational software development project that only 20 percent of the features were used always or often by the customers. Interestingly, 64 percent of features were never or rarely used. With scrum's emphasis on prioritization, only those most important and useful features are developed first. What if your project runs out of funding and you're only 80 percent done? Based on what the Standish study found, you might not have needed the remaining 20 percent anyway. AC + OC > V means the end of the project. Redeploy that capital to a higher and better use.

The following four key reasons are why you want as small a set of features per release as possible:

- ✔ First mover advantage of speed to market and increased market share

- ✔ Accelerated end customer feedback cycle

- ✔ Maximized ROI (a dollar today is literally worth more than a dollar six months from now)

- ✔ Internal risk is reduced from such factors as organizational change and budget poaching

The product owner fully owns the release plan. They will be the ones who prioritize the requirements in the product backlog and set the release goal (as shown in the following section). While the product owner decides what the priorities are and when to release completed shippable functionality, they consult with stakeholders and the development team to make his decisions.

Release goals

Each release plan has an overall business goal associated with it, called a *release goal*. This goal is created by the product owner, and ties in directly to the product end goal, which is the product's vision statement. The release goal establishes the mid-term boundary around specific functionality that will be released to customers to use in the real world.

Having an explicit release goal expedites the prioritization process: If a requirement doesn't align with the goal, you don't have to worry about that requirement in this release. Any given requirement should earn the right of your investment. Leave it tucked away in the product backlog until it can support a priority goal.

Think of the three layers of goal setting as a prioritization filter system. The vision statement is the highest boundary. If a feature doesn't fit the overall vision, it isn't for this project. Don't even let that requirement on the product backlog. The requestor needs to go get funding for that idea separately — don't be a stowaway on my project.

Next comes the release goal. This is the mid-term boundary. If a requirement doesn't fit this goal, it stays in the product backlog. And finally, the shortest-term boundary is the sprint goal. More on those in this chapter.

Goals drive the product backlog and the release plan, not the other way around. Every feature and requirement must be thought of in terms of "does it fit the goal." This is *purpose driven development*. Goals drive what makes the product backlog. Goals drive what gets included in a release. And goals drive what gets included in each sprint.

Release sprints

Sometimes releasing product features into the marketplace requires completing certain jobs that can't fit within a normal developmental sprint. Ideally, all activities required to release a product to the market are done within a normal sprint. But if the way an organization is set up does not allow it, a release sprint may be used to accomplish such purposes as

- ✔ Verifying scaling (for example, load or performance testing)
- ✔ Broader testing activities (for example, focus groups or validating that developed functionality works with live data)

Although I prefer not to have release sprints, simply phrased, a release sprint is for "all that other stuff" that needs doing to get the product to market.

The release sprint is commonly used at the end of the normal series of sprints within a release. The length of a release sprint may be a different length than the development sprints in the release. The release sprint length depends on the types of activities and the amount of work required to release the completed product increments from each sprint. The scrum team determines all these factors during release planning.

During a release sprint, no actual development of requirements is done. All development tasks (such as testing, technical documentation, quality assurance, and peer review) are completed during each sprint to satisfy the team's definition of done, which in turn ensures potentially shippable product at the end of each sprint. But before it can actually go out to the market, other things (such as focus groups or load and performance testing) may need to be done.

Because the release sprint length and activities are often different than the development sprints, no concept of velocity exists for a release sprint. Development teams estimate to the best of their knowledge the effort and complexity of the tasks for the release sprint. They should all agree and feel comfortable with the release sprint length after it is decided.

The release sprint is a form of antipattern in organizations that cannot do scaling testing and organizational support tasks within the sprint. If you don't need it, don't do it.

Including examples already given, uses for release sprints may include the following:

✔ Conducting focus groups (keep in mind that this is not to identify new features, but to validate what you've done and identify release issues)

✔ Scaling tests

✔ Tweaking performance based on scaling test results

✔ Integrating the product within enterprise-wide systems

✔ Creating documentation such as user manuals

✔ Finalizing any regulatory requirements

Release plan in practice

So how does a release plan actually work in the real world? Follow these steps:

1. **Develop a release goal.**

   Do this first — it behaves as the target for everything else. The product owner ensures that the goal aligns with the product vision, and works with the scrum team to make sure that the entire team feels comfortable with the goal.

2. **Identify the target release date.**

   This date may also be influenced by a number of factors outside the control of the scrum team.

3. **Identify the highest-priority requirements (minimum viable product, or MVP) on the product backlog that support the release goal.**

4. **Refine the requirements estimates, as needed.**

   Sometimes issues and/or synergies are discovered when the development team looks at the smaller package of requirements that go into a release plan. The requirements themselves will also be more detailed and broken down (no larger than 34, see Chapter 4) than when the development team originally estimated at the product roadmap level.

5. **Identify the team's velocity.**

   If it's a stable team that has been working together on the same project, their established velocity from previous sprints is a great starting point. If the team has not established velocity, start modestly until you have run a few sprints and velocity can be ascertained.

6. **Plan a release sprint (if needed).**

   Determine as a scrum team whether you'll need one, and if so, how long it will be.

7. Finalize the release scope.

Based on velocity, total estimates of requirements and number of sprints within the release timebox, how much functionality can you include? Which is more flexible — the date or the amount of functionality? What adjustments need to be made to the release date or scope of requirements to release as much as you can within your timebox?

For instance, let's say that your velocity is 20, the release timebox is five sprints, and the total estimated points for the release is 110. This puts you ten points over what's available in the release. The product owner has a decision to make. Are the requirements that make up the bottom ten points in the release valuable enough to include, or can the release go on without them? Or does the release need to be extended one sprint, and will that be acceptable to the stakeholders and customers?

One option in release planning is to use the *release train* model. Rather than have releases of varying duration, in this scenario, each release is exactly the same length — six weeks, for example. At the end of each six week cycle, the completed functionality from each of the sprints is packaged and released. This way, a development rhythm is created, and everyone in the organization can anticipate their workload and schedule moving forward.

Use any of the estimation and consensus-building techniques discussed in Chapter 4 to refine the product backlog items in the release, if requirements still need to be refined and estimated (see the preceding Step 4). If your releases consist of a large number of product backlog items, use affinity estimating (the T-shirt sizing technique discussed in Chapter 4) for release planning.

As with all scrum documentation, I prefer the simplest tools possible. The entire release plan can be mapped out with your trusty white board and sticky notes. This allows for ease in change and immediate access. As well, it just plain saves time.

Sprinting to Your Goals

Finally, the heart of scrum! Sprints, and their built-in inspect and adapt model, are an integral scrum feature. It is through the sprint process that you are able to achieve the three agile pillars of improvement — transparency, inspection, and adaptation — that you read about in Chapter 1.

By breaking down your project into tangible pieces and then using the empirical model of scrum to assess your progress, you are able to constantly pivot moving forward. This allows you the nimbleness and ease of adaptation so sorely missing in waterfall.

Each scrum team member has the same purpose in the sprints — maximizing effectiveness in delivering potentially shippable product. I first look at the various components of sprints before I move on to sprint planning.

Sprints defined

Sprints are the essence of scrum, as I discuss in Chapter 1. They are a consistent timebox for product development by the development team. Each sprint includes the following:

- ✔ Sprint planning, including goal setting
- ✔ Daily scrums
- ✔ Development time, including regular review by the product owner
- ✔ Sprint review
- ✔ Sprint retrospective

The consistent timebox of sprints allows the development team to establish a development rhythm. It also enables scrum teams to extrapolate into the future based on empirical data like velocity. As soon as one sprint is finished, another begins. A flow of consistent iterative feedback loops is created and thereby is an ideal environment for production and continuous improvement.

Imagine that you're a runner. You are consistently training for the 100-yard dash and have become incredibly proficient at it, but all of a sudden your coach asks you to run a marathon. If you attempt the marathon at your 100-yard-dash pace, you won't finish the marathon. You need to modify your training to adjust for a marathon pace, which will require coaching, schedule, and diet changes over time. All the muscle memory and the type of endurance that your body has developed will need to be "relearned" to run a different length of race.

Planning sprint length

Because sprint goals do not change during a sprint, the answer to the question, "How long should your sprint be?" depends on your project and how long your organization can go without making changes. That is the outer edge. You have no reason to discuss going beyond that in duration. For example, if your organization struggles to go a week without needing changes, don't even entertain the idea of a two-week sprint. You won't be able to maintain the integrity of the stability of the sprint, and stability is a huge driver of performance in scrum. Instead, discuss how much shorter you can make the sprint.

Also, sprint lengths do not change after they begin and ideally do not change throughout a project, unless they are being made shorter. If a scrum team changes sprint length during a project, it comes at a significant cost: Their earlier velocity is no longer relevant. Performance is not a straight mathematical line that can be sliced, diced, and reassembled. Just because a scrum team doubles their sprint from one to two weeks does not mean that they will automatically accomplish double its historical two-week velocity.

So, why are shorter sprints better? Shorter sprints decrease the amount of time between feedback received from stakeholders, enabling scrum teams to inspect and adapt earlier and more often. Longer sprints have a diminishing return because less of a sense of urgency exists due to the multiple days still available to the team. Weekends and longer sprint meetings can also have a negative effect on efficiency.

The capacity of a development team during a one-week sprint may be either higher or lower than half the historical two-week velocity. You don't have any idea until you run a few sprints, and you don't know for sure until you run a lot of sprints.

Whereas the cost of changing sprint lengths throughout a project is significant, the cost of changing a sprint goal during a sprint is probably worse. If a sprint goal becomes irrelevant (for example, because of changes of company direction or changes in the market) before the end of a sprint, a product owner may decide to cancel the sprint. But be aware that canceling wastes valuable development resources and is quite traumatic to the scrum team and the organization. Also, the shorter the feedback loop (that is, length of sprint), the less likely a product owner would need to cancel a sprint.

One of the things we know from science is that you can't turn off your mind. It's always working. So, if you can give your development team a small number of problems to solve, and have them know that they'll face those problems tomorrow, they'll think about them consciously at work. Whether they want to or not, they will also think about them unconsciously when they're away from work. This is why the stability of sprints is so important. After a sprint starts, the developers must have confidence that the scope is stable. Ever have an epiphany while brushing your teeth? This is the dynamic. But you need two elements — a limited number of problems and confidence that you'll face those problems tomorrow. If every day a developer could be working on Project A or Project C or Project who-knows-what, this won't happen. They will only mentally engage when they get to the office and discover what's ahead of them in reality. One of the reasons that agile projects are so much more innovative is that we have this stability and thus so much more of the developer's mind share.

Cumulative flow diagrams

Cumulative flow diagrams (CFDs) provide scrum teams the visibility into the patterns of their output and help them identify possible bottlenecks in their processes.

A burnup chart, as shown on the left, is a type of CFD that shows the number of requirements that the team was able to complete within a set duration of time.

CFDs, as shown on the right, give a snapshot of how much work is in any given stage of the process, so indicators like lead, cycle, work, and wait times can be exposed to identify points of inefficiency.

Changing sprint lengths during a project makes performance indicators inconsistent over time. In addition to loss of relevancy of the historical velocity with changing sprint lengths, CFD indicators like lead, cycle, work, and wait times also become irrelevant.

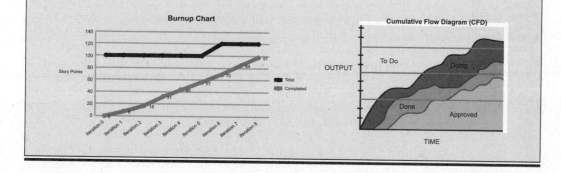

With my clients, I've found that the one-week sprint length is a nice rhythm. It gives the development team clear time off, avoids weekend "cheating" to get more work done than is within the team's capacity, yet is long enough for real progress to be made every week. This shorter feedback cycle also allows scrum teams to inspect and adapt more frequently. For these reasons, scrum teams should always be looking for ways to responsibly shorten their sprint length.

The key is to run sprints that enable your development team to realistically create tangible, tested, and approved product every single sprint. After each sprint, you will have something real that can be shown to stakeholders.

Following the sprint life cycle

Each sprint has the same process — sprint planning, daily scrums, a sprint review, and a sprint retrospective. Sprints are developmental cycles that repeat until your project is complete. Requirements (often in the form of user stories) are developed, tested, integrated, and approved within each sprint. And the process continues sprint after sprint. Figure 5-3 depicts a one-week sprint life cycle.

Figure 5-3: The one-week sprint life cycle.

		SPRINT PLANNING	SPRINT (1 Week Sprint)	Design / Test ↓ Test ↑ Develop ↘ Integrate ↘ Test ↗	SPRINT REVIEW	SPRINT RETROSPECTIVE
US		Sunday Evening	Monday Morning → Friday Morning M T W T F		Friday Morning	Friday Morning
India		Monday Morning	Monday Afternoon → Friday Evening M T W T F		Friday Evening	Friday Evening

When scrum teams are distributed offshore with team members in faraway time zones (like US and India in this example), arrangements need to be made for all team members to attend each of the sprint meetings. To account for time zone differences, the domestic team members might join the meeting Sunday night while it's Monday morning for the offshore team members. Then at the end of the sprint, the domestic team members finish the sprint Friday morning and take the rest of the day off while the offshore team is joining the sprint review and retrospective Friday night. Rotating each sprint might be appreciated on each end, so that each team member doesn't always have to work on Sunday nights or Friday nights.

The key is that after each sprint, the scrum team learns new things. Change happens; it's inevitable. Responding and adapting to it should be considered progress, not failure.

Taking a queue from mathematics

Queuing theory is the mathematical study of waiting in lines. Studies have found that when customers are waiting in a restaurant for a table, they will wait twice as long if they are given something satisfying at the start. For example, if they're asked to sit at the bar and offered the ability to order a drink or even given a tasty sample, they'll stick around longer and wait for that busy table to be cleared.

The same principle is working for you in scrum. At the end of each sprint, you will have something working and tangible to place in the hands of stakeholders. This "early and often" concept is a known technique for raising customer satisfaction.

Don't go chasing waterfalls

Scrum is different from the traditional waterfall method, in which all items are in a package and that package is matured. So if changes come in halfway through the project, the impact of those changes is nebulous and woven across multiple requirements. This unknown impact is what made change a dirty word in waterfall.

Some who are new to scrum and hold on to waterfall ways may mistakenly view a sprint as simply a smaller timebox than before for completing tasks, which are part of an overall upfront plan:

✔ They'll set multiple sprints up front at the beginning of the project, and identify the exact requirements and tasks that will be done during each sprint.

✔ They'll hold very brief sprint reviews as status reports about the product backlog, rather than product increment demonstrations.

✔ They'll hold brief sprint planning meetings to confirm the original plan.

The increased frequency of review of the original plan seems nice to a team new to agile thinking but completely misses the point and falls short. This is still waterfall.

The sprint life cycle allows for the easy incorporation and adaptation of change based on reality. This is empiricism.

Change is easy in scrum, because at the end of every cycle what was created was done so to completion. When you go into your next sprint and work on items from the product backlog, it doesn't matter whether those items have been on the product backlog for four months, four weeks, or four minutes. Old or new, each product backlog item gets prioritized not by the order in which it was received, but by the order in which it will deliver the highest value to the customer.

In my experience, the Monday – Friday workweek is a natural, biorhythmic time frame. Whether one week or two, teams need the weekend break, and it fits naturally with our life patterns. So avoid off-kilter sprint patterns of Wednesday – Tuesday or the like.

Planning Your Sprints — Stage 4

The planning of sprints is Stage 4 in the roadmap to value. See Figure 5-4. All the work to be accomplished during that specific sprint is planned here. Each sprint planning session is timeboxed to no more than two hours for each week of the sprint. If you have a one-week sprint timebox, you have a maximum of two hours to plan your sprint, for example.

Stage 4: SPRINT PLANNING

Figure 5-4:
Sprint
planning —
Stage 4 in
the roadmap
to value.

Description: Establish specific iteration goals and tasks.
Owner: Product owner and development team
Frequency: At the start of each sprint

Sprint goals

A goal is created for each sprint. The product owner initiates the goal discussion, identifying the business value objective that needs to be met. After the team is clear on the goal, the product owner chooses the requirements from the product backlog that best support the goal. As with the release goal, the sprint goal drives the requirements developed, not the other way around.

The sprint goal itself must support the release goal, which supports the vision statement. This goal decomposition and alignment are essential for ensuring that you are doing purpose-driven development.

The development team is critical in creating the sprint goal. Because they're the ones doing the actual work, while the product owner establishes the direction, or the "what," the development team establishes the "how" and "how much."

If your development team has an established average velocity, it may be used as input in determining the amount of work they will take on during the sprint.

The development team can also use velocity for stretching, testing its limits, or backing off if they're struggling to achieve the goals set. If they've been achieving 34 story points comfortably, they might push it to 38 or 40. If they've been struggling to achieve 25, they might lower it to 23 while the scrum team figures out organizational drag that can be removed.

Both phases of sprint planning occur in the single sprint planning meeting at the beginning of the sprint. Phase I is where the product owner, with input from the development team and facilitated by the scrum master, determines what needs to be accomplished (the goal). In Phase II, the development team determines how to achieve the sprint goal and develops the actual sprint backlog of supporting tasks.

The sprint planning meeting may not always go smoothly, especially at first. You may slip down rabbit holes, discover tangents, and unearth different estimations of what's possible. This is where a strong and deft facilitator is needed in the form of the scrum master. It's their job to make sure that the session stays on track and the heat stays on low.

Phase I

At the start of Phase I, the sprint goal is created, and the development team must fully understand it, because it will provide the boundaries and direction for the work they will do throughout the sprint. The product owner then selects a portion of the product backlog that supports the goal. This won't necessarily be the final sprint backlog, but is the forecasted functionality that if finished in the sprint, would satisfy the sprint goal. It's what the development team will work from to achieve the sprint goal and determine the actual sprint backlog.

Phase I gives the development team and product owner another opportunity to clarify any existing requirements or identify new ones that are needed to achieve the sprint goal. This would also be the time to give the final size estimation on any clarified requirements and size any new requirements for the sprint. Remember my yardstick: If any requirements are sized higher than an 8, they're too big for a sprint (see Chapter 4).

I like to bring between six and ten product backlog items into each sprint. This is usually the right balance of being able to deliver a product increment with substantial functionality as well as litmus that each individual item is sufficiently broken down.

The only requirements discussed in sprint planning should be those estimated between 1 and 8 on the Fibonacci scale. This isn't a scrum rule, but it aligns with our affinity estimating model (see Chapter 4) and has been an effective way for many teams to keep focused on properly refined requirements that can be completed within a sprint. For more on Fibonacci numbers, see Chapter 4.

Phase II

When the goal and the supporting requirements have been determined by the scrum team, the development team breaks down those requirements into individual tasks — how they will turn product backlog items into the product increment. The tasks for each requirement should explicitly satisfy the team's definition of done. For instance, if the definition of done includes integration with system "A," at least one task for the requirement should be "integration test with system A."

Ideally, each task should be able to be completed in one day. This gives the development team a tangible, realistic time target as they break requirements down into tasks. It also sets a benchmark from which the team can be alerted to any development problems. If a task is taking multiple days to develop, an issue might need to be addressed with the task or the developer.

Development teams may choose to estimate the tasks for each requirement in hours if the organization wants that level of visibility. But many teams simply use velocity and complete/not complete of product backlog items to adequately visualize sprint risk.

The development team is forced to be the most detailed here, which helps to sharpen the mind. They can really dig down and look at what needs to be done.

By the end of sprint planning, the development team should be clear on how the chosen sprint backlog items support the sprint goal and how the work to complete those backlog items will be done. This does not mean that all (or any) of the tasks on the sprint backlog get assigned at this time. Rather, each day the development team will self-organize by having each developer pull a task and work on it to completion. (You find more on "pull" versus "push" later in this chapter.)

Your Sprint Backlog

The sprint backlog is created in the sprint planning session and is the ordered list of requirements and tasks necessary to achieve the sprint goal.

A sprint backlog might contain the following information:

- ✔ The sprint goal and dates
- ✔ A prioritized list of the requirements (for example, user stories) to be developed in the sprint
- ✔ The estimated effort (that is, story points) required to develop each requirement
- ✔ The tasks required to develop each requirement
- ✔ The hours estimated to complete each task (if needed)
- ✔ A burndown chart to show the status of the work developed in the sprint

The burndown chart benefit

Burndown charts are a way to visually represent progress achieved within the sprint. They depict the amount of work accomplished versus the amount left to go. This figure shows an example:

✔ The vertical axis represents the work left to be done.

✔ The horizontal axis depicts the time still available in the sprint.

Your sprints will show a diagonal line from the upper-left corner to the lower right, which represents what an even and consistent burn would look like — though in reality, you won't have a perfectly even burndown.

Some burndown charts also have a line showing the outstanding story points. This allows you to quickly and easily see the status of your sprint from both time and relative estimation perspectives.

You can create your own burndown chart with Microsoft Excel. Or, you can download one that's included within my sprint backlog template at www.dummies.com/go/agilprojectmanagementfd.

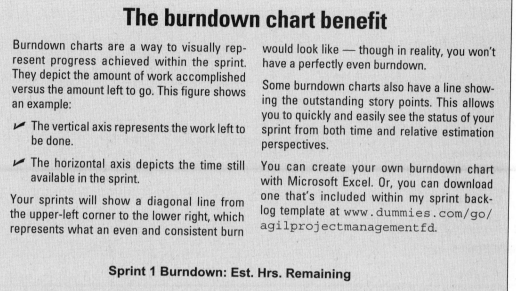

Sprint 1 Burndown: Est. Hrs. Remaining

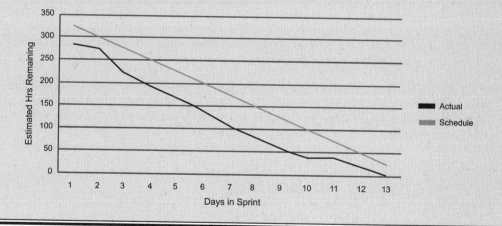

The burndown chart is generated from the sprint backlog. The sprint backlog should be updated every day, and only the development team can do this. At the end of each day, each developer updates their task (whether on a 3x5 card, on a spreadsheet, or in an electronic tool) by entering the number of *remaining* hours (*not* the number of completed hours) that are left to complete the task. That's it. One number. It takes seconds and the results are invaluable. See Figure 5-5 for a sample sprint backlog.

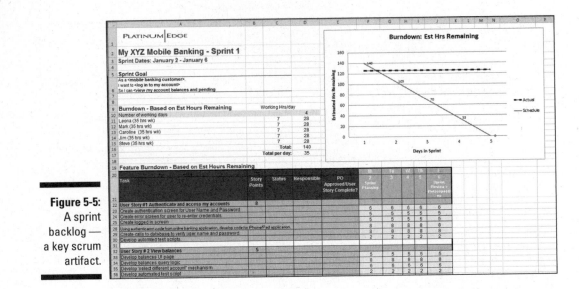

The sprint burndown chart is an information radiator that shows anyone who wants to know the status of the sprint. Burndown charts get generated automatically as development team members update the amount of time left on their one active task at the end of each day. (Go to www.dummies.com\extras\scrum for a sprint backlog and burndown chart template.)

The burndown chart shows the amount of time remaining for the sum of all the requirements on the sprint backlog. Compared with the trend line, it provides a daily level of status detail for a scrum team that you can't get with traditional project management techniques.

Capacity for backlog

How much capacity is really in a day? If you're looking at the number of hours per day that a development team member will actually be able to devote to his main job — developing! — allow for less than eight. Every organization has a certain amount of overhead. I find that for most organizations, somewhere between five and seven hours is a normal effective work day.

An average of 16 hours per week are wasted on unclear objectives, poor team communication, and ineffective meetings.

How much capacity is really in a sprint? In a one-week sprint, scrum teams will spend up to two hours in sprint planning, up to one hour in sprint review, and up to 45 minutes in a sprint retrospective. That's about four hours in sprint meetings. (Do you have to use all four hours? No. Can you go over the limit for any given meeting? No.)

That accounts for four of the five scrum events (I'll assume that a maximum 15-minute daily scrum won't impact development time), but don't forget product backlog refinement. I find that development teams will, on average, spend 10 percent of their time each sprint in product backlog refinement activities. This translates to about three to four hours in a one-week sprint.

So, for a one-week sprint, each developer will spend between seven and eight hours in sprint events, which takes care of one full workday for an efficient organization and about a day and a half for a less efficient organization.

Is there any buffer in scrum? Sure there is. Consider that a development team has 165 hours available to them for a sprint. They shouldn't take on 164 hours under the false assumption that everything is going to go exactly according to plan. Buffer will vary from team to team, but make it transparent.

So, capacity for one developer for a one-week sprint would be between 18 and 27 hours, depending on the organization's established effective workday. Take this into consideration when identifying a development team's capacity during sprint planning. This is assuming that no paid holidays, vacations, or other time off is planned that will keep developers from developing.

Who said scrum is rudderless? You can't get much more disciplined than this.

What an incredible impact having a dedicated and effective scrum master means to a development team's capacity. By removing the organizational drag (impediments) that keep effective workdays from increasing from five to seven hours, the impact can add up to an additional nine workhours in a one-week sprint per developer. For a development team of seven, that's a potential 63-hour efficiency increase. Scrum masters add value.

What happens if at the end of sprint planning, the development team finds that the number of estimated hours for their tasks from the sprint backlog is more than their capacity? Do they hunker down and work overtime? No, the product owner has a decision to make: Which sprint backlog items will be moved back to the product backlog to get the number of hours below the development team's capacity?

The value of the iterative planning process is easily visible within sprint planning. By the time the work to be done is outlined and broken down to the task level, you will have done so in a way that minimizes time waste and maximizes business value and ROI. This is because the roadmap to value, from the vision statement all the way down to the sprint level, has enabled continuous prioritization and progressive elaboration of only the most important product backlog items.

Working the sprint backlog

I see development teams get distracted and go off target by making some common mistakes. Follow these practices to counter those mistakes when working with the sprint backlog:

- Make sure that requirements are broken down into tasks that accurately and completely reflect your definition of done (see Chapter 4).

- The product owner should not accept a requirement until it completely satisfies the sprint definition of done.

- The entire development team ideally works on only one requirement at a time and completes that requirement before starting another. This is called *swarming*.

- Swarming can be accomplished by such activities as

  - Each team member working on individual tasks related to the same requirement

  - Pairing two people on one task to ensure quality

  - Team members shadowing each other to increase cross-functionality

- As development teams swarm around one requirement at a time, this ensures cross-functionality and that every sprint will have something tangible accomplished at its end.

- Each requirement must be fully developed, tested, integrated, and accepted by the product owner before moving on to the next requirement.

- Don't assign multiple tasks to individual development team members. Each day, the development team coordinates priorities and decides who will do what. A developer should only be working on one task at a time until that task is completely done. This is called a *pull mechanism*. Don't fall back into the traditional method of a manager assigning tasks out to team members.

Push versus pull

Traditional project management follows the push model of assigning tasks to individuals when they're identified. Each individual manages and focuses solely on the tasks in their personal queue. This queue builds up over time, and attempts are made to redistribute task load across team members to avoid over/underloading. The trouble with push systems is that it's difficult to know the status of things unless everything is either unstarted or all the way complete. This also has a tendency to contribute to team members operating as silos rather than cross-functional teams.

Pull models, like scrum, maintain all work in a common queue, and items are pulled from the top by individual developers (which assumes proper ordering and prioritization by the product owner). You don't need the redistribution of task load, and it provides a natural pause for developers to evaluate where they can help others on open tasks before pulling a new one. Development teams are also more likely under a pull model to work on backlog items much closer, if not exactly, to the original order of priority than a push system. Bottlenecks are less common, and overall workflow is more predictable.

Push systems encourage individual-centered (silo) goals. Pull systems support collaboration for the sake of achieving product-centered goals.

For example, at the grocery store, you can choose between a push and pull option when you go to check out:

✔ The push option is chosen by going through a checkout line with a dedicated clerk for that line. The line is "assigned" to you, because you chose it and you're standing in it. You're stuck with it unless another line empties, and you get to it before someone else does.

✔ You can choose the pull system and increase your chances of getting through as quickly as possible. Do this by selecting the self-checkout option, where four to six individual checkout stations are ready for whoever is next in line. Rather than being committed to a single checkout line for the remainder of the checkout experience, you'll be able to take advantage of the next open self-checkout station as soon as it's available.

Swarming on requirements stems from the lean concept of work in progress (WIP) limits. When a development team has a lot of work in progress, it delays taking the actions necessary to finalize that work and rear-loads issue correction. Your WIP limit should ideally be only one requirement at a time for the development team and only one task at a time per developer. The development team usually finds that their tasks get completed sooner than if they had started them all at the same time. Having only one requirement "open" at a time is also an effective way of exposing process bottlenecks, which can then be addressed and fixed for faster throughput.

Sprint prioritization

Each sprint has its own life cycle, as shown in Figure 5-5. Within each sprint, each requirement has its own prioritization and life cycle, too. Each requirement and task are developed, tested, integrated, and approved before moving on to the next-highest-priority item. See Figure 5-6 for a representation of this.

The sprint backlog items are prioritized from highest to lowest and developed in that order. Only one requirement is worked on at a time by the development team. When that requirement is finished, they move on to the next-highest-priority one rather than picking one lower on the list that might be easier or more interesting.

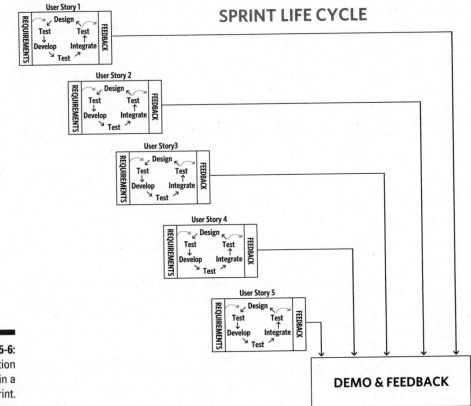

Figure 5-6:
Prioritization within a sprint.

Chapter 6

Getting the Most Out of Sprints

Sprints are the essence of scrum, so it's worth spending an entire chapter on them. You have the gist already — they're fixed timeboxes designed so that your development team can create a development rhythm. They also nurture the inspect-and-adapt premise.

But that's not all they do. In this chapter, you'll be introduced to the daily scrum, an invaluable 15 minutes spent every day that will focus and organize your short-term goals like never before. Facilitated by the scrum master, your project will stay on track as the scrum team deals with impediments and coordinates the day's priorities.

You'll also be exposed to the sprint review and sprint retrospective. Within these two meetings, you will take the concept of inspect and adapt to new levels. Stakeholders will review the product developed and provide the product owner with immediate feedback, and the scrum team itself will assess how the sprint went in reality and incorporate any improvements in their process.

I reveal all of this and more in the following pages.

The Daily Scrum — Stage 5

The daily scrum is one of the five scrum events and Stage 5 on my roadmap to value. See Figure 6-1. As you have noticed, planning is huge in scrum. You don't set a goal, forget it, and then gather together six months later to see what happened. You inspect and adapt every single day, and even throughout the day.

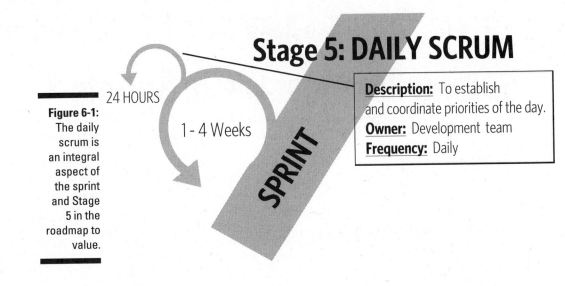

Figure 6-1:
The daily
scrum is
an integral
aspect of
the sprint
and Stage
5 in the
roadmap to
value.

Stage 5: DAILY SCRUM

24 HOURS

1 - 4 Weeks

SPRINT

Description: To establish and coordinate priorities of the day.
Owner: Development team
Frequency: Daily

Because a development team swarms each day to attack a single require-ment, coordination is key. The removal of impediments is also crucial for developers to be able to work so closely together to deliver potentially ship-pable increments within short iterations. The daily scrum is how you do that.

If you manage your projects by weeks (that is, weekly project manager status reports, delayed up to a week, that may or may not get reviewed promptly that day), you slip by weeks. In scrum, you may still slip, but only by a day, because scrum teams manage by day, through the sprint backlog, daily scrum, and daily and direct interaction.

What's a daily scrum?

As its name implies, this is a daily event that takes place during each sprint. The timebox is 15 minutes max, no matter the overall length of the sprint. Meetings in scrum, like artifacts, are barely sufficient. Anything longer than 15 minutes would eat into valuable developing time. Besides, it's plenty of time to accomplish everything necessary.

The purpose of the daily scrum is to coordinate the day's sprint activities and identify impediments keeping the development team from accomplish-ing their sprint goal. Every member of the development team participates, so everyone is dialed in to what the entire team is working on. If an impediment comes up during the daily scrum, it is dealt with following the daily scrum. It's a coordination meeting, not a problem- or complaint-solving meeting.

The scrum master either personally removes impediments or facilitates their removal. Some impediments might need to be removed by the product owner, or may require a discussion between a development team member and a nonscrum team member.

Daily scrum are an opportunity to inspect and adapt in the moment!

Because a daily scrum is only 15 minutes, everyone needs to be on time and ready. You'll find a direct correlation between how late a meeting starts and how loose the focus is after the meeting starts. Teams may have different ways of achieving punctuality, such as

- ✔ Start your daily scrum a half an hour after the normal workday begins.

  This gives your development team members time to get coffee, answer emails, discuss the previous evening's antics, and cover anything else in their morning ritual.

- ✔ Penalize members for being late in a friendly and spirited way.

  Have them pay a certain amount into a celebration fund for each minute they're late. Or have them sing their college team song at full tilt. Get creative and make it uncomfortable enough that it stops tardiness.

A scrum team in Portland implemented a "$20 or 20 push-ups with multiplier" incentive. For the first time being late, team members paid $20 or did 20 push-ups. Next time, $40 or 40 push-ups, and so on. This was invented by the team, not imposed on them. It worked for them, and it definitely prevented tardiness.

Participants in the daily scrum are the development team members and the scrum master. The scrum master ensures the meeting takes place and the development team directs it. The product owner should attend, and must attend if the development team specifically requests it. The product owner may provide clarifications on prioritization as needed, and anyone else involved and interested can listen in. They just can't say anything. This way they can enjoy the daily transparency and be involved in the daily process, but they can't hinder or derail it.

A common misconception with daily scrums is that it's a time for the development team to report to the product owner or a time for product owners to introduce new requirements or update a sprint goal. This defeats the purpose of short iterations wherein developers can focus on a set of tasks and crank them out in support of a well-defined business goal. The daily scrum is not a business status reporting meeting. It is a coordination meeting to enable high performance.

As soon as the daily scrum starts to feel like a status reporting meeting, or development team members start addressing their "report" to one individual (for example, an informal team "lead" or the scrum master), it has missed the point. It's peer to peer. It's not about each person reporting to one individual, such as the scrum master or the product owner. Keep it about coordination as a self-organizing team, identifying impediments and ensuring that they get removed as soon as possible.

Often during daily scrums, I'll look down at my shoes or even wander away. This way, if people are reporting to me and trying to get my attention, I'll respond by saying, "Why are you addressing me? This meeting is for you guys." It works well to readjust perspective of why we're having the meeting to begin with.

What's achieved in a daily scrum?

The development team meets, and three statements are made by each development team member. Each statement is made in the context of how it is helping the team achieve its sprint goal:

- ✔ Yesterday I accomplished this . . .
- ✔ Today I'm going to focus on . . .
- ✔ The things impeding me are . . .

The daily scrum is how the development team self-organizes and self-manages. Each day, they decide who will do what and who will help whom. It is not dictated to them by a project manager or some other nondeveloper.

Imagine a scrum team gathering around their sprint backlog or task board at the beginning of the day. Each individual can see at a glance the progress made the day before, and then each person proactively chooses a new task for the current day. They coordinate where help is needed to accomplish the task before the day ends, and then go straight to work.

As I discuss in Chapter 5, tasks should be broken down so that they can be accomplished in a day or less. Even then, when developers are left to themselves for days on end without coordinating and swarming as a team, they can get bogged down in unnecessary details or problems that could be easily resolved with two sets of eyes. Daily scrums synchronize a team, and everyone goes to work with complete ownership in helping each other do what it takes to get to done. Come the next day, the team members are more excited to talk about progress rather than a dry status report that goes something like, "I'm still working on that thing I talked about yesterday and the day before."

A squeaky dog toy in scrum? That's what I use to toss to a random member of the development team, as I never want a set speaking order. Set speaking orders encourage people to check out until it's their turn (and after), or worse yet, show up late just before it's their turn "to go." If anyone takes too long, I switch to a timer ball that alarms or to a ream of paper — it weighs five pounds — and have them talk for as long as they can hold it out to the side. This keeps the daily scrum fast, forward moving, and fun.

As part of the daily scrum, I like to have scrum masters participate beyond facilitation by addressing the impediments that are identified and/or in progress. For instance, the scrum master says after the team members have spoken:

- Yesterday I removed this impediment . . .

- Today I can remove this impediment . . .

- The impediments I can't remove are . . . and I'll see whether so-and-so can help me.

Studies have shown that meetings conducted standing up are 34 percent shorter than those sitting down.

The following tactics can keep your daily scrum meetings quick and effective:

- Diligently start on time.

- Conduct the meeting standing up.

  No one has a chance to slump in his chair and relax. Rather, it's as if they're on the move already.

- Focus the meeting on coordination, not solving problems.

  Impediments get removed after the daily scrum.

- The scrum master is the meeting facilitator and, as necessary, keeps the meeting on time and on track, and makes sure that only development team members participate. The scrum master's "touch" should be as light as possible.

  A title for a documentary about a day in the life of a scrum master might be *Stand Back and Deliver*.

- Cover only immediate issues and priorities in relation to that very day as they support the sprint goal.

- Gather around a representation of the team's sprint backlog (the task board, discussed in following section) to ensure context and focus.

  Don't allow vague statements or rely on team members' memories of what's on the sprint backlog.

When impediments are uncovered in the daily scrum, they can be dealt with by the scrum master hosting an *after party*. An after party takes place immediately following the daily scrum involving only those who need to be involved, and is for addressing any issues that came up during the daily scrum, such as one developer asking another developer how to resolve a specific problem with their task, or discussing ways to resolve two conflicting tasks.

Team Task Board

A *task board* is one way to display the sprint backlog. While it's common for scrum teams to manage their sprint backlog in a digital format, all you really need for a task board is some wall or whiteboard space, some 3x5 cards and sticky notes, and some tape! See Figure 6-2 for a sample task board.

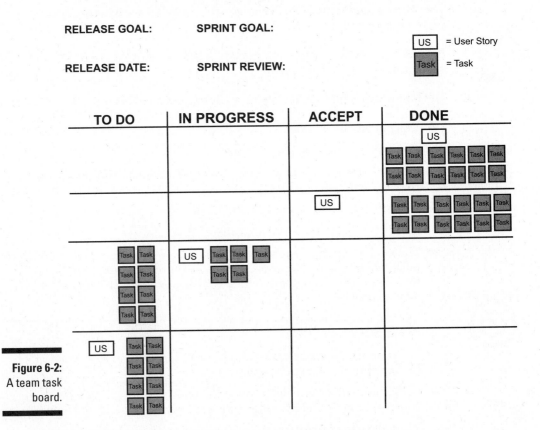

Figure 6-2: A team task board.

...excellent because they're a quick and effective way ...ntire sprint at a glance. Having the task board within ...t team and product owner ensures that they instantly ...'s not, and everything in between. Use these basic

...print goal

...lease goal

...ates can also be included.

...o right)

...requirements and tasks in the sprint that are yet to

...ll from the top of this list to start a new task. If more ...oper wants to take the same task, they can either ...can shadow the other, or they can decide as a team ...t handle it.

...e current product backlog items and tasks that the ...eam is working on.

...t have different colored dots or stickers to desig- ..., or to identify tasks that are blocked by an impedi- ...progress (WIP) limits, if used, should be displayed ...After developers complete a task, they look here ...they can help get to done. Otherwise, they pull the ...To Do and verify with the team that it's the right ...next.

...requirements that are awaiting acceptance by the

...ent is rejected, and enough time is left in the sprint, ...In Progress. Otherwise, the requirement gets moved ...duct backlog for consideration in a future sprint. ...d later in this chapter.)

...irements that the product owner has accepted as

...am can move the requirements from To Do to In ...he product owner can move them from Accept ...re the only ones who move tasks around on the task board from To Do to In Progress to Accept, and after a requirement is accepted by the product owner and moved to Done, the development team moves tasks with it. Otherwise, if a requirement gets rejected, the development team moves tasks back to In Progress to rework them, or creates new tasks to address the reason that the requirement was rejected.

The Kanban board

Kanban is Japanese for "signboard," "billboard," "signal card," or "card you can see." In the 1950s, Toyota formalized this concept to standardize the flow of inventory parts in its production lines. In essence, Kanban boards contain cards that represent single pieces of work. Each card acts as a signal of status and indicates when new work can be pulled in.

This practice helped inspire lean thinking and manufacturing practices, and many agile teams use something like a Kanban board system today. Task boards function much as a Kanban board, in that they provide a visual status (signal) of exactly where each task (piece of work) is in the overall process. This level of visibility makes it easier for development teams to be disciplined at adhering to WIP limits and swarming on requirements to get to done.

The physicalness of the task board, like the product roadmap, increases engagement and flexibility with development team members. It's real. It's tangible.

Requirements in the Accept column shouldn't be allowed to pile up. Ideally, you shouldn't have a day's break between the card being placed in Accept and either placed in Done or rejected for further development. If a delay occurs, the product owner needs to be coached in not letting stories accumulate waiting to be accepted. You have no reason for delay if the product owner is a dedicated scrum team member who is available to the development team at any time for clarification, the requirements have been detailed down to a single action or integration, and the requirements have passed the definition of done. It's critical that the development team knows that their work is done and they can "swarm" the next requirement.

Swarming

In Chapter 5, I introduced the concept of *swarming* in the context of the sprint backlog. Swarming is the act of all development team members working on only one requirement at a time during the sprint. Although not a principle specific to scrum, it is such an effective way for teams to execute their sprint backlog that it warrants some more discussion.

Again, one of the main benefits of scrum is that development teams start and finish requirements to satisfy their definition of done to produce a potentially shippable product increment within a relatively short timebox, and to repeat that cycle with lessons learned again and again. The goal is to finish, not just start, as many requirements as possible.

Swarming enables teams to enjoy the following benefits:

- Maximized chances for success with the skills and abilities of the entire team focused on a single requirement.
- Complete the entire cycle of plan, design, develop, and test to completion for each requirement.
- Resolve issues and impediments today, in the now.
- Dramatically decrease the introduction of defects into a product up front through pairing and single-tasking (versus multitasking).
- Eliminate single points of failure in knowledge, process, and skillsets.
- The most important requirements get done, done completely, and get done first.

When team members see all their fellow developers working on a task, and none are left for them to work on the same requirement (the user story), it's perfectly natural for them to consider it more productive to go start on a new requirement rather than help the others out on the current requirement in progress. However, this tendency can get out of hand to the point where teams find themselves with multiple requirements started, but none of them finished. By shadowing, pairing, researching, or helping in whatever way gets the task to done, development teams will avoid this risk.

Stay focused. Stop starting and start finishing.

This process ensures that in every sprint, *something* will get completely developed and be available to show stakeholders. Every sprint will produce "shippable" results. The development team's efforts are focused, their teamwork is enhanced in that they're encouraged to help each other, and the iterative process of scrum is put into play.

Recently, Microsoft conducted a study on the effects of multitasking. The results were that multitasking just doesn't work. On average, it takes 15 minutes to get your brain back to the level it was at before you answered that phone call or email. Studies have also shown that an interruption as short as 4.4 seconds will triple the number or errors made on subsequent tasks requiring sequencing. Reducing multitasking in your development team will get you a sound head start on achieving the 30–40 percent increased product-to-market time I've seen so often.

Thrashing is when developers jump back and forth between projects, requirements, and tasks — context switching. Thrashing increases the time required to complete tasks by 30 percent. If you don't have enough people to take on the workload as dedicated, swarming developers, you definitely don't have time to thrash them.

If a requirement placed in the Accept column is rejected by the product owner, the developers have several options:

- Finish their current tasks, and when those are finished, they swarm the rejected requirement.

   This might be the best option if plenty of time is left in the sprint to complete the current tasks and the rejected requirement.

- Abandon their current tasks to swarm the rejected requirement.

   This might be the best option if not much time remains in the sprint to finish both.

Unfinished requirements

Even high-functioning development teams that estimate well, swarm, and stick to a WIP limit of one throughout each sprint may end up with incomplete or unstarted requirements left on the sprint backlog at the end of a sprint.

This might be okay, as long as they have swarmed on the higher-priority requirements to completion, and they have working product increments that can be shipped.

But what do you do with those remaining requirements? Work over the weekend to finish them? Work on them "under the table"? Show their in-progress status to the stakeholders at the sprint review, even though they're not done?

None of those. If a requirement is not started, or was started and not completed, the product owner puts it back in the product backlog in its entirety (keeping all notes, tasks, and documentation intact, of course) and then reprioritizes it against the rest of the product backlog. The product owner may potentially pull it into a future sprint according to its new priority.

Based on what was completed during the sprint, the unstarted or unfinished requirement may no longer be necessary, or at least may not be as high a value as it was before. What's done may be enough, and it may be time to move on to a different feature.

Whatever effort was made on it, because it was not finished, is not included in the team's velocity for that sprint. If the requirement does make it into a future sprint, it will need to be refined, clarified, and reestimated based on the remaining work to be done. You can't bank or cache story points.

An exception to this may be that you find, after working on an unfinished requirement, that you can split it so that you finish one during the sprint and the other goes back into the product backlog to be reestimated and reprioritized.

In any case, every requirement, at any time, needs to earn the right of your investment.

Lesson learned from all of this? Swarm and get to done.

The product owner decides the priority when faced with this decision. Other variables than time left in the sprint may influence the product owner's decision. As the team inspects their learning and adapts throughout a sprint, the rejected story may become less valuable to achieving the sprint goal than the next requirement in progress, and so even though time is left in the sprint to do both, the risk of not finishing the in-progress requirement might be higher than not finishing the rejected requirement.

In any case, attention to priority and close daily coordination with the product owner throughout the sprint keep the entire scrum team (including the product owner) on focus and on task, literally.

Scrum teams should always be pushing themselves. If development teams accomplish 100 percent of their sprint backlog every time, they may not be pushing themselves to their limit. A high percentage of sprint backlog completion should be the goal, but it should not be expected that scrum teams will hit 100 percent every time. As development teams push themselves, scrum masters, like aeronautical engineers, help the scrum team find ways to reduce drag to become more effective and accomplish more in each sprint. As long as teams are finishing what they start each sprint and increasing velocity, they are realizing the continuous-improvement benefit of scrum.

The Sprint Review — Stage 6

The next stop on my roadmap to value is Stage 6, the *sprint review*. See Figure 6-3. This scrum event is integral to the inspect-and-adapt process of scrum, and takes place at the end of each sprint.

The purpose of the sprint review is for the product owner to get organizational feedback on whether they are moving the product in the right direction. It is also a great opportunity for the "talent" (development team) to stand up and show off what they've accomplished. They get full credit for what they've achieved, and what they haven't.

Figure 6-3: The sprint review is a scrum event and Stage 6 of the roadmap to value.

Stage 6: SPRINT REVIEW

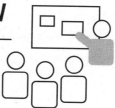

Description: Demonstration of working product
Owner: Product owner and development team
Frequency: At the end of each sprint

Empirical exposure modeling goes back to the beginning of time, as you read in Chapter 1. However, somewhere along the way, it got lost in project management frameworks. Agile practices and scrum have brought it back with a roar. The entire sprint process — from sprint planning to the daily scrum and now the sprint review and sprint retrospective — reaps the full benefits of the empirical model and its premise of inspect and adapt.

This meeting at the end of each and every sprint ensures that the stakeholders are completely up to date on what was accomplished in the sprint and have a fantastic forum for delivering feedback directly to the product owner, with the development team listening in. As well, stakeholders now have working, "shippable" product in their hands. I look at this in more detail.

The sprint review process

The sprint review is timeboxed to one hour per week of sprint, and it takes place at the end of the last day of the sprint, usually a Friday. So if your sprints are one week in duration, you would allocate one hour each Friday afternoon. Remember to allow for this time expenditure during the sprint planning session.

The participants in the sprint review are the entire scrum team and the stakeholders, in these roles:

- ✔ **Scrum master:** Facilitates the meeting and ensures that it stays in focus and on time.

- ✔ **Product owner:** Briefly reviews the sprint goal and how well the scrum team met the goal, fills in the stakeholders on what items from the backlog have been completed, and summarizes what's left to go in the release.

The sprint review is not the place for the product owner to provide feedback on the completed functionality. It is for the product owner to receive feedback from the stakeholders on the direction that they are taking the product. The product owner accepts or rejects each requirement, as it is completed, not at the end of the sprint. The product owner approves the requirements before they're demonstrated to the stakeholders.

- ✔ **Development team:** Displays and explains the completed requirements.

- ✔ **Stakeholders:** Ask questions and provide feedback.

The process begins with the development team preparing for the review. Consider the following guidelines for sprint review preparation:

- The development team prepares for the sprint review in the minimal amount of time (20 minutes max) and without presentation material to showcase the requirements that they've completed.

- No formal slides should be used in a sprint review.

  The development team should spend as much of their time developing the product as possible rather than preparing theatrics.

- Only the requirements that have been deemed "done" (according to the definition of done) and approved by the product owner are demonstrated.

- The development team showcases the "shippable" functionality of the requirement, that is, how it works in the real world.

If you spend time showing stakeholders what could or should have been done, that means you're giving a rigged demo, and you haven't done anyone any favors. Stakeholders never expect less; they always expect more. By making it look like your product increment works when it really doesn't, you'll have increased your workload for the coming sprint, because you'll have to make work what you showed should work, plus all the new work you'll plan for. Demonstrate working product increments only. No rigged demos! They take time to create and that is valuable time away from development.

Stakeholder feedback

Critical to the success of the sprint review is stakeholder feedback. It's this constant cycle of communication that keeps the project on track and producing what the stakeholders want. While stakeholders can't tell development team members how to develop requirements, they can provide insight on which requirements and features they want developed to the product owner, and how well the implementations serve the customer's needs.

This feedback loop serves another purpose as well: It keeps the development team involved and therefore emotionally engaged in the project.

When Daniel Pink studied motivation, he found that one of the three key elements was having a sense of *purpose* in what people were doing. Showcasing the developers' hard work and being directly involved in feedback and planning help do just this. It's called *ownership*.

Feedback is a common theme throughout scrum. Figure 6-4 illustrates just how many different layers of feedback are involved in the scrum framework. Each time feedback is received, it gets cycled back into the product backlog and sprint planning sessions. This is truly inspect and adapt.

Figure 6-4:
Multiple layers of feedback exist in a typical scrum project.

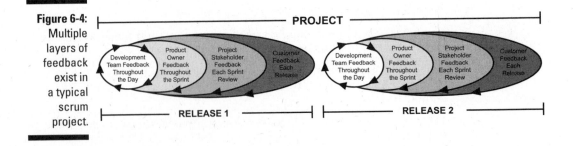

Product increments

The *product increment* is the final of the three scrum artifacts. (I discuss the product backlog in Chapter 3 and the sprint backlog in Chapter 5.)

Within a single sprint, the product increment is working product deemed done by the product owner and is now potentially "shippable." It's *potentially* shippable because the product owner may not decide that it's ready to ship until a later date. But the good news is that it's ready to ship as soon as the product owner is ready.

A product increment has been

✔ Developed

✔ Tested

✔ Integrated

✔ Documented

During the sprint review meeting, this product increment is what is demonstrated to stakeholders. The inspect-and-adapt sprint life cycle continues as feedback is taken and translated into requirements. These requirements may then get elaborated during product backlog refinement activities, as they rise in priority for consideration in future sprints and eventually become new product increments.

The sprint review is about improving the product. Here's how scrum teams can make this continuous improvement happen for their team and process.

The Sprint Retrospective — Stage 7

The seventh and final stage in the roadmap to value is the sprint retrospective. See Figure 6-5. This is yet another scrum event that takes place after every single sprint.

Figure 6-5: The sprint retrospective, the seventh and final stage in the roadmap to value.

Stage 7: SPRINT RETROSPECTIVE

Description: Team refinement of environment and processes to optimize efficiency.
Owner: Scrum team
Frequency: At the end of each sprint

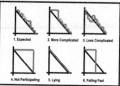

The purpose of the sprint retrospective is to provide an opportunity for the scrum team — scrum master, product owner, and development team — to assess what went well in the sprint that just finished, and what can be improved. It's inspect and adapt one more time, with a focus on the people, processes, and tools that the scrum team is using.

The outcome of the retrospective should be plans of action to continuously improve at scrum, people, processes, and tools every sprint. While the scrum framework is simple (three roles, three artifacts, and five events, as shown in Chapter 1) and doesn't require tweaking, each individual scrum team will have its quirks and nuances because of the nature of such aspects as their product, organization, and development methods. Through the process of inspect and adapt, you're able to hone those individualities so that they're aimed toward the project goals.

Because the sprint retrospective asks for input and feedback from all scrum team members, it also increases ownership through engagement and a sense of purpose. The team spirit is enhanced. This in turn leads to an increase in productivity and velocity. This is self-management.

It's critical in sprint retrospectives to create a trusting environment. Each person's view is listened to and respected, and nothing is taken personally. Trust is the key to the retrospective not being a labyrinth of euphemism or politics. The scrum master has a pivotal role in creating the environment of trust.

The sprint retrospective may unveil problems within the team. This is where an adept scrum master can facilitate the event such that these issues are dealt with in an equitable and low-intensity environment. This is not a time for venting. It's a time for actionable plans for improvement.

The sprint retrospective process

The sprint retrospective takes place at the end of every sprint, after the sprint review and before the next sprint's planning session. It's often done as last thing on the last Friday of the sprint. For each week of sprint, 45 minutes is timeboxed for this event.

The entire scrum team participates, and at the team's discretion, other people may be invited (like customers and stakeholders) if the team believes that they may have valuable insights to needed improvements for the scrum team.

In preparation for the retrospective, everyone should consider how the sprint went and jot down any ideas or concerns. As always, use simple tools like sticky notes — avoid formalities and presentations. The idea is to recognize internal, team inefficiencies and rectify them.

While the scrum master facilitates the meeting, everyone participates at a peer-to-peer level. The purpose of the sprint retrospective is to inspect the sprint that just ended to

- Identify what went well in the sprint, with regard to such interactions as processes, tools, and team dynamics
- Discuss and discover opportunities for improvement
- Define an action plan for implementing the improvement(s)

In the retrospective, remember to emphasize and give equal airtime to what went well. Don't gloss over it quickly. It's important to focus on the positive and to identify what's working well so that *you keep doing it!* Rejoice as a team in your successes! Especially during initial scrum implementation, it's important to recognize the wins, big and small. An effective way of keeping things positive and avoid isolating people during a retrospective is the sandwich technique. Start with positive, work through the negative, and then end with more positive.

Key to the retrospective discussion is that it's action oriented and not focused on justifying. When discussing what went wrong and you hear the word *because,* it's a good indication that the discussion is heading down the path of justifying why someone did something a certain way, and then begins the finger-pointing and defensiveness. You want to keep moving forward with issues and actions like, "This is what I experienced, and this is what might work better going forward." Don't get bogged down in, "I did it this way because . . ."

Esther Derby and Diana Larsen have written an excellent book called *Agile Team Retrospectives: Making Good Teams Great* (published by Pragmatic Bookshelf). Check it out for more tips and techniques on sprint retrospectives and other agile practices.

In *Agile Team Retrospectives,* Derby and Larsen point out that there is more to finding out what went well and what improvements need to be made than simply asking the same three questions at the end of every sprint. Retrospective facilitation takes preparation and strategy to get maximum participation, candor, and useful data from team members. If you're a scrum master, this is a great resource for generating ideas for activities and developing your facilitation skills.

Although it's an acceptable place to start if you've never done a retrospective before, their model for structuring a retrospective consists of more than just showing up and going around the room answering these questions:

- What do you think went well?
- What would you like to change?
- How should we implement that change?

To maximize retrospective effectiveness, I recommend their process:

1. **Set the stage.**

   This is a different meeting than most meetings that team members will attend. The thought of open discussion about team issues tends to immediately put people on edge, so you want to establish ground rules for productive communication and clarify expectations and purpose from the very beginning.

2. **Gather data.**

   Making decisions based on superficial, bad, or incomplete data can do more harm than good. You want to uncover important topics, jog memories, and correlate experiences that need to be addressed. You want to know not only what people think but also how they feel about it.

3. **Generate insights.**

   With the deeper ideas on the table, now what? Many teams stop short of the true benefits of the retrospective simply by gathering the data but doing nothing with it. Just as the best designs come from self-organizing teams, so do the best insights about what happened come from teams that take the time to explore what the data means.

4. **Decide what to do.**

Only through action can change and adaptation take place. Action requires a plan. Deciding what to do shifts the team's focus to moving forward — to the next sprint.

5. **Close the retrospective.**

Closing provides the opportunity to "scrum the retrospective" through activities that evaluate the effectiveness of the retrospective experience and identify ways to improve it. It also encourages expressing appreciation. Ending on a positive note through appreciation goes a long way.

Each aspect of the retrospective can be facilitated by a number of activities that are engaging and provoke individual thought and group discussion. Examples include Triple Nickels, Five Whys, SMART Goals, Temperature Reading, Team Radar, and Mad Sad Glad.

To stimulate discussion in retrospectives, frame any of these activities around specific contexts, such as

- What is keeping us from increasing our velocity from 36 to 38?
- Does everyone have the tools that they need to do the job?
- Do any impediments keep repeating?
- Is our daily scrum effective at identifying impediments and coordinating daily priorities?
- Is our team lacking certain skills, and how can we resolve them?

Some scrum teams will need to be coaxed and prodded to get engaged. They may be hesitant at first to say what they truly feel. Others will be the opposite. They may all want to talk at once and be bursting with ideas and input. This is where a perceptive and proactive scrum master (facilitator) adapts to work with either type of group, or anything in between, to achieve the best results.

The results from the retrospective should be put into the product backlog as "improvement" items. It should be a scrum team agreement that at least one goes into every sprint. Bring at least one priority retrospective item into the next sprint — it might be from the latest retrospective or a previous one. After all, why wait? The purpose is to inspect and adapt, so don't delay the adapt part!

The inspecting and adapting perspective given in the official Scrum Guide (`http://scrumguides.org`) is a good place to wrap up this scrum framework overview section before looking at scrum in the real world:

> "Inspections are most beneficial when diligently performed by skilled inspectors *at the point of work*." (Italics added for emphasis.)

> The scrum guide (`http://scrumguides.org`) goes on to elaborate that adjustments are made as soon as possible. Adjustments occur as soon as an inspector realizes that the work has moved outside the limits and will cause unacceptable product.

> Scrum is about planning the right things at the right time. It's about responding to changing markets and lessons learned. It's about continually learning and assessing, minimizing risk, and maximizing value at every step — each point of work.

Part III
Scrum for Industry

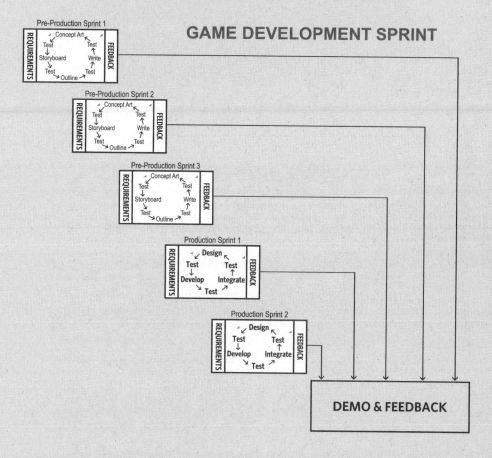

GAME DEVELOPMENT SPRINT

Pre-Production Sprint 1

REQUIREMENTS — Concept Art, Test, Storyboard, Test, Outline, Test, Write, Test — FEEDBACK

Pre-Production Sprint 2

REQUIREMENTS — Concept Art, Test, Storyboard, Test, Outline, Test, Write, Test — FEEDBACK

Pre-Production Sprint 3

REQUIREMENTS — Concept Art, Test, Storyboard, Test, Outline, Test, Write, Test — FEEDBACK

Production Sprint 1

REQUIREMENTS — Design, Test, Develop, Test, Integrate, Test — FEEDBACK

Production Sprint 2

REQUIREMENTS — Design, Test, Develop, Test, Integrate, Test — FEEDBACK

DEMO & FEEDBACK

In this part . . .

- Applying scrum beyond software.
- Avoiding excessive upfront design in hardware and tangible goods production.
- Improving education, saving and protecting lives using scrum.
- Adapting to disruption in publishing and digital media.
- Visit www.dummies.com/extras/scrum for great Dummies content online.

Chapter 7

Software Development

"You don't actually do a project; you can only do action steps related to it. When enough of the right action steps have been taken, some situation will have been created that matches your initial picture of the outcome closely enough that you can call it 'done.'"

— David Allen

Chapter 1 explains the origins of scrum having been the application of concepts outlined in a 1986 Harvard Business Review article entitled "The New New Product Development Game." Software development is the context within which scrum creators formalized agile values and principles and within which the scrum framework was born and raised. Therefore, it's no surprise that scrum is easily applied to this industry.

The "New New Product Development Game" applied the game of rugby to new product development in the context of the need for increased speed and flexibility. In contrast to a relay race, the article states, "Instead, a holistic or "rugby" approach — where a team tries to go the distance as a unit, passing the ball back and forth — may better serve today's competitive requirements."

As technology advances, so does its complexities. New challenges arise, and project management frameworks that endure will be those that allow for and enhance change.

In this chapter, I show you some of the challenges that the software industry faces and describe how scrum helps address them. You'll see scrum applied in contemporary examples, and understand how the framework allows you to be as nimble and fast as this exponentially growing world of technology.

It's a Natural Fit

Software development is creative in nature. The sky isn't even the limit as ideas, concepts, and reality go way beyond that now. Necessarily, the design solutions employed often are as creative as the products they serve.

Given the empirical nature of scrum, it fits this environment perfectly. Scrum doesn't tell you how to do anything. It simply lets you see clearly (that is, it exposes) what you are doing and assess from there.

A huge variety of languages, tools, methods, and platforms exist to solve these complex problems. Scrum doesn't tell you which ones to use. Rather, this framework lets teams self-manage to optimally decide which ways are best for their specific circumstances. As you've read, it does this through unfettered *transparency,* frequent *inspection,* and immediate *adaptation.*

The very nature of scrum allows for solution finding. It allows you to do this every day, every sprint, and with every release. Both the product and the process are nurtured for creativity and excellence.

Traditional project management methods and frameworks are predicated on being able to accurately predict the future. They are linear and sequential. They act as a *waterfall.* (You can read all about waterfall approaches in *Agile Project Management For Dummies,* by Mark C. Layton [published by John Wiley & Sons, Inc.].) What's important here is to understand how technology and design needs have far outgrown this change-averse framework.

Waterfall project management entails progressively maturing a set package of requirements in different stages; completing one stage before moving on to the next, such as designing all requirements for the entire project before doing any development; and then completing all development work before doing comprehensive testing, which is left to the end. With scrum, these phases are cycled repeatedly throughout a project, such that a continuous circle of design, development, testing, integration, and feedback are achieved each day, sprint, and release.

As projects became more complex, the natural boundaries of waterfall became abundantly clear. Multiple phases and long delays existed before coding even began, early performance was no indicator of later performance because each phase's tasks were fundamentally different, code testing was rear-loaded toward the end of the project when the team had the least amount of time or money, and end customers did not interact with the product until it was too late to incorporate their feedback. Projects were delayed or never completed, and more often than not, the end product came up short.

Winston Royce had it right

In a strange quirk of history, the man mistakenly attributed with introducing the waterfall framework to large software projects had actually emphasized the basic agile and scrum principles of inspect and adapt.

Winston Royce was a computer scientist and for many years a director at the Lockheed Software Technology Center. He published a paper entitled "Managing the development of large software systems." In it he described several different methodologies, among which waterfall and an early iteration of agile were discussed, as shown in this figure.

A quote from the man himself clearly warns of the pitfalls later to be endured with waterfall. How strange that the very system he's mistakenly credited with inventing is the same system he was warning us about.

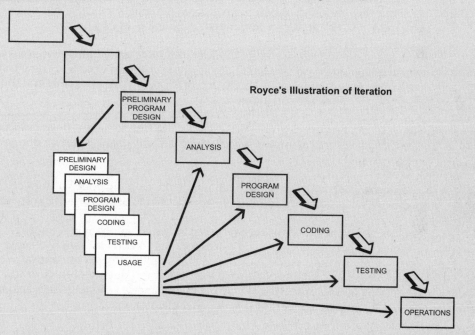

Royce's Illustration of Iteration

The testing phase which occurs at the end of the development cycle is the first event for which timing, storage, input/output transfers, etc., are experienced as distinguished from analyzed. . . . Yet if these phenomena fail to satisfy the various external constraints, then invariably a major redesign is required. A simple octal patch or redo of some isolated code will not fix these kinds of difficulties. The required design changes are likely to be so disruptive that the software requirements upon which the design is based and which provides the rationale for everything are violated.

Royce clearly warned of the pitfalls inherent in leaving testing as a separate phase at the end. He said it was "risky and invited failure." In turn, he suggested an iterative approach that tested frequently and made adaptations based on the results. Every step linked back to the previous one.

Scrum emerged from the need to find better ways to build software. In this chapter, I show you how scrum works with software development, its roots. However, keep in mind that the scrum framework can be applied to any project where you can encapsulate the work and prioritize that item against other items.

Software Flexibility and Refactoring

Scrum works well with software for a variety of reasons. Here I look at a few.

As you read in Chapter 4, the cost of fixing defects increases exponentially the later they're found. Catch them early and fixing is a hassle, but doable. Catch them later and the accumulated technical debt can be costly.

Building in quality every step of the way to reduce and eliminate defects is a scrum advantage. You've seen in the sprint sections in Chapter 5 how testing each and every requirement and its integration with others is integral to the process. Yet mistakes still happen.

Software can be very flexible. Although it's not free to have a developer refactor code, the physical impact is virtual, so in many cases it can be done with relative ease.

Refactoring code is the process of changing the existing code without changing its outward behavior to improve nonfunctional aspects of the system.

Refactoring is inevitable in scrum (in a good way), and you'll do more of it than ever before, because you're responding to and embracing change. Fortunately, scrum's empirical approach disciplines teams to continuously inspect and adapt to improve the health and quality of their product. Identifying needs for technical improvements and prioritizing them against new development are part of this ongoing maintenance.

Refactoring code is like maintaining your car. You hear the rattle, notice the little red light come on, or smell something electrical. You know if you don't do something, those problems are going to get bigger. You can pretend you have a choice, but you really don't. So, like with refactoring code, you take the little steps necessary to make sure that your vehicle is running smoothly. Maybe you just need more oil or a bolt tightened. But if you wait, your engine could seize or a part could break, leading to much higher expense and time wasted.

With scrum and software, refactoring allows you to make a working module that is scalable, extensible, and stable. In today's world of The One Who's First Wins, this type of efficiency in quality control is priceless. Refactor early. Refactor often.

Release often and on demand

Deploying new products to the market no longer requires packaging and shipping. Thanks to the Internet, the cloud, automated testing, and continuous integration, you have the flexibility to plan your releases on demand and as often as needed to suit other factors, like market readiness, customer expectations, and marketing campaigns.

You now have a much higher degree of flexibility in the product that you create and the timing in which you release it to your customer. Money previously allocated to hard-copy product is now diverted to more pressing and profiting needs. The Download Here button makes life easier in so many ways, and in many cases such as SaaS (Software as a Service, covered in this chapter), updates are pushed out automatically, even eliminating this step.

Behemoth tech companies like Facebook, Amazon, and Google deploy code to production multiple times a day. In the case of Amazon, it's 3,000 times a day. Now that's fast!

With scrum's emphasis on producing "shippable" product after every sprint — or even within sprints — you now have even more flexibility in planning product releases. You don't have to wait until the end of a project to release. You can do it incrementally in stages and continuously, with tested, integrated, and approved functionality.

Customize your release sizes

No matter how often you release, smaller is generally better. Similar to the flexibility of releasing often and on demand, the size of product that you release is now incredibly flexible with scrum, based on functionality, target dates, and market conditions. Is it one tiny requirement that rounds out a larger previously released one? Or is it a granddaddy new generation that's about to be birthed?

From a single line of code to a full bundle of functionality, it's all been through the same thorough process. Quality is the essence of flexibility — and it's the essence of scrum.

Inspect and adapt as you release

With the ability to customize both the timing and size of your releases, you're also able to receive immediate customer feedback. Each time that you release product, you're able to assess the results and make any necessary changes. Both analytics and customer service are able to collect data quickly, and from this input, you fine-tune future development and enhancements.

With scrum, you inspect and adapt daily, after each sprint and after every release. And as you've discovered, these can happen as often as you like and will suit your project. In fact, the more you release, the more you can inspect and adapt.

You can even tailor the quantity and focus of feedback. Smaller releases might have more targeted feedback. Larger releases might receive broader evaluation, and from this, smaller targeted future releases can be set.

The *sprint retrospective* (see Chapter 6) idea of inspecting and adapting your process works here too. You adapt your process at every iteration rather than only once in one sweltering meeting at the end of the project when everyone's just relieved that it's over and ready to start on different projects.

The point is, in this world, the customer has a lot to choose from, and new products hit the market every day. To survive and excel, you must be at least as nimble as and certainly faster than the next guy. Scrum provides the framework for just this.

Embracing Change

While scrum's effectiveness and speed make it a natural in so many situations, it's still different for many companies that continue to work in hierarchically structured organizations. This very fact alone can cause problems. Incorporating new ideas and breaking away from old habits can be challenging. Some corporate cultures are open to change; others have more difficulty. I briefly mentioned this in Chapters 2 and 3; it's human nature to find comfort in habits. And it takes effort and energy to break them.

It all boils down to the revealing of value. When the parties involved clearly understand WIIFM (what's in it for me), they'll accept the changes more readily. As they begin to experience the benefits of early release and adaptation, the conversion will go more quickly. I look at some specific issues.

Development team challenges

In traditional, top-down management cultures, implementing scrum while still maintaining status quo won't work. The development team can be frustrated with double work if they aren't solely implementing scrum. And managers get off kilter with moving forward on projects that aren't all planned out up front, and that don't provide the reams of reports and analysis that they're used to. Similarly, things like "My boss is on my team" is an antipattern to self-organization and self-management.

With scrum, they can ease into inspect and adapt one sprint at a time. The first sprint reviews may be difficult to get managers to participate in appropriately as stakeholders. Equally challenging, it takes a fresh mind-set to see "working software" as the new benchmark of success (see the sidebar "Spotify versus Healthcare.gov," later in this chapter).

However, if they stick to it, and give the benefits of scrum time to manifest, they will see immediate practical, quality results. They'll discover that they have something real to work with after each sprint, and that it accumulates at a logical and rapid pace. The wasted time spent on writing reports and managing status has been replaced by creating real, usable product, where status is clear because it's real.

Aligning business with technology

Traditionally, the business side of an organization and software engineering are separate, and many times, at odds. For decades, they've operated as silos within the same organization:

- The business serves the market and the shareholders, and is under extreme pressure to deliver value quickly and adapt to a constantly changing marketplace.

- The technologists want sustainable architecture and foundations with as little technical debt accumulation as possible.

Scrum brings these two parties together. With a representative from the business (product owner) a full-fledged member of a scrum team (a peer to each of the others), and with stakeholders involved throughout the sprint and directly providing feedback at the end of every iteration of work (sprint review), you'll never find a more beautiful alignment and facilitation of collaboration and joint ownership. Thanks to scrum, the right people are making the right decisions about the right things at the right times. Finger pointing is no longer relevant. Progress is exposed at all times to all parties. Inspection and adaptation points exist all along the way. Self-organization and self-management mean that we're all in this together.

A stakeholder's aha moment

Samir Bellouti, a scrum master in Canada, shared his experience integrating scrum with a new client in a blog post at Scrum Alliance:

"During the Sprint 5 planning meeting we had a breakthrough. After hearing that we could not complete a feature by a certain date, our business sponsor reacted in a surprising way. Rather than bemoaning the loss she thanked us for the advance notice. 'Usually I only find out a month before we're going live that I'm not going to have a certain feature. This time, I know five months in advance. That gives me some options.'

"This was a very big step forward in terms of the relationship between the IT department and the business. They can finally see the impact of a change on the overall schedule. Moreover, they understand that they have to cut some other backlogged items in order to have their change done. This helps them to deal with the reality: a change has a cost and the development team has a limited capacity . . ."

— *How Scrum Helped Our Team*, Scrum Alliance, Samir Bellouti, June 1, 2009

Real-world change

Not long ago, I provided scrum training for one of our software clients. Before the training, the client had been working on a research and development project, involving new technology, and had been given an arbitrary deadline for completion of a comprehensive scope of features set by senior management.

The client hadn't yet implemented scrum, so the team initially came up with a proof of concept of features and requirements fairly quickly, which won buy-in from management to proceed with the full-scale project. However, the product backlog was vague, and the team spent unbudgeted months developing a demo version for management.

The development process was slow and fraught with technical surprises. The team not only missed the first release date but also the next several rescheduled release dates. It was here that we trained them and the scrum framework was implemented.

For many of the same challenges I pointed out in the preceding section, at first the entire project team held on to traditional practices (up-front design, fixed scope and schedules, and renaming waterfall artifacts and events as scrum). But they pushed ahead, held consistent sprint reviews with stakeholders, and survived a series of tough and uncomfortable conversations about missed deadlines and how the aspects of scrum could help resolve these challenges.

After just a few sprint reviews, and the clarification of roles (especially getting a dedicated and fully trained product owner) and removal of some impediments, the crystalline transparency so inherent in scrum began to shine through. Walls were broken down between the scrum team and stakeholders and customers (actual end users were involved in every sprint review), communication improved, and the project was replanned with a proper vision, roadmap, and product backlog. From this retooling, a release schedule was re-created based on the team's newly established velocity and product backlog estimates. Long story short, from this point on, it was months, not years, until the minimum viable product (MVP) was released. The project plan was now based on priority, customer feedback, and empirical data (for example, velocity).

In the process of these initial attempts at sprint reviews, they were able to identify a key stakeholder (in this case, an actual customer who would be using the product) who hadn't been attending the sprint reviews. She was invited, and her involvement provided crucial feedback on the product. As the other stakeholders observed the scrum team's willingness

and speed at inspecting and adapting, trust skyrocketed and ownership and collaboration by all (including stakeholders) improved amazingly.

In the end, the product released reflected much more accurately what the customer wanted than in the original plans; extra features were prioritized and left out, something a stakeholder and the product owner decided, not the development team; a minimum viable product was released in full working order; and the stakeholders were fully engaged and involved in training the end users in the software. In fact, they ended up collaborating with the product owner on every aspect of the rollout.

Up-front engineering

The propensity for development managers, project managers, and developers themselves to plan out everything in advance has deep roots:

- ✔ Most schools still teach up-front engineering (see The Marshmallow Challenge in Chapter 1). Fresh out of class, they know to plan first and develop second.

- ✔ Waterfall enforces the "plan all and then develop all" mind-set. It is built around completing one phase entirely, like designing, before moving on to the next, like developing. In waterfall, up-front engineering is part of the foundation upon which everything else rests.

Given this background, you'll actually find a stigma to changing something after a project starts. But as you know, in my mind-set, and within the framework of scrum, change is ideal. All changes are learning. You will incorporate change every day, after every sprint, and in each release. You will find out how to seek out change. In scrum, change is progress.

On top of this, when management and developers have invested time and energy in planning something, it's hard to just drop those plans and potentially suffer sunk costs.

Sunk costs are those funds that have been spent on a project and cannot be recovered. In waterfall, sunk costs were more common as projects were planned and funded up front. If they failed along the way, you had nothing to show for their effort. With scrum, you have the concepts of failing fast or incrementally accumulating fully built functionality. Instead of sinking a lot of money into projects up front, you can allocate funds along the way. If the project ends earlier than intended, you either lose less money in the form of sunk costs, or you make a great business decision that maximizes the return on investment (ROI) of your limited investment. With scrum, your days of "catastrophic failure" are gone.

If 64 percent of some software project features are never or rarely used, think of the wasted time, energy, and resources involved in planning, designing, developing, testing, and documenting what is not used. With scrum, the dominant paradigm of planning everything in advance is dispelled.

I've seen development teams, working waterfall, take weeks and months in planning. And I've seen scrum teams plan features and systems with the same magnitude in a matter of hours.

Because scrum teams understand that they don't know everything up front, they don't rigorously plan what they don't know. They assess and adapt along the way as new information is garnered and as priorities are continually reassessed.

A scrum lesson learned

7Shifts is a restaurant scheduling company founded by Jordan Boesch and his wife, Andrée Carpentier. As they were building their business, they ran into a client who, unintentionally and without spending a cent on their products, helped them convert a waterfall habit into a scrum solution.

This prospective client, a restaurant owner, asked for some features on his app, one of which was a budget tool. No problem. Jordan went off, designed all the features to completion, including the budget app, and presented them to the client. Unimpressed for some unknown reason, the client said no thanks and was never heard from again. Result: lots of up-front planning and development without any feedback from actual users.

Mystified, Jordan plugged along with his business, leaving the budget tool app included but never really inspecting it further. One day, he ran some analytics on the tool to see how much it was being used by his clients. The data showed that only 2 percent of his clients actually used it.

Jordan set out to fix the app. He started by asking existing clients why they weren't using it. They explained that his program required them to manually enter an estimated dollar amount, when it could have easily been automatically calculated with some tweaks.

Jordan released an update to the app with amazing success. What he learned was to plan only what you know, talk to your customers early, inspect, and then adapt until they're happy.

Emergent architecture

In line with the restaurant app and budget feature story in the nearby side-bar, emergent architecture is seen by many programmers as a sign of failure. They want the entire product to be planned up front, leaving no code-stone unturned. However, this isn't realistic or practical.

Emergent architecture is the progressive elaboration of the architecture for your application or enterprise based on the requirements that are currently in development to achieve and maintain stability and scalability. The goal is to refactor the architecture based on the reality of working software, rather than architect the entire system based on hypothetical guesses.

If your sprints are one week long, you'll be refactoring small batches of architecture. If you wait until the very end of the project, as in traditional frameworks, you're refactoring for months or years of architecture. Refactor often. Refactor early.

You begin with macro-level architecture decisions based on the holistic view of the requirements that you have from the product roadmap. Then in your first sprint, ask what the requirements and architecture are for this sprint. Let the sprint goal drive the sprint, and if that goal requires code refactoring, don't wait. Your product should work in reality every single sprint. With scrum, you will refactor more often, but that's what you want. Just like requirement change isn't the enemy, neither is code refactoring.

At the beginning of the project is when you know the least. Why do detailed planning or build parts of the system that won't be used at this point? A lean principle is aptly applied here: Decide at the last responsible moment. The earlier you make a decision in the project, the higher the risk of that decision being wrong and the likelihood of "throwaway" work. The later you decide, the more information you have to make that decision. Therefore, you have a lower risk of making a mistake.

Refactoring should be built into every requirement estimation. As new requirements come to the top of the list and get refined, architecture will emerge in the minds of the development team. As they estimate and plan, they plan the refactor into it.

Applications in Software

It's one thing to understand the theory behind scrum's success; it's quite another to see it in action. While I can't take you into the field with me, I can bring the field to you in the following sections. I show you some of the challenges being faced, and describe how scrum's unique adaptability comes into play.

Many technology companies are already using scrum to great success. It allows them to be faster and more flexible to stay competitive.

Video game development

This hugely popular and complex area of software development can utilize scrum to great success. You find four basic reasons:

- ✔ **Flexibility:** With scrum, you start with the basic features and grow the game into more complexity. This happens organically and therefore you're always developing what's most important next.

- ✔ **Finding the fun:** Developers can add the fun in small, iterative doses. Those features that add the most value in terms of fun (a critical element of any game) get added first.

- ✔ **Cost savings:** Most games fail to break even financially. Scrum's cost-saving nature is a company saver. Even if funding is cut halfway through (assuming that the minimum playtime is met), you still have the most important 50 percent of the features fully functioning and, if not yet marketable, at the very least reusable.

- ✔ **Regular and frequent feedback in at least two forms:**

    - Daily from the product owner

    - At each sprint review from the stakeholders (such as publisher and marketing)

    Gaming is all about keeping the customer happy and engaged. Feedback within scrum is incorporated quickly, so the end result is actually what the user wants.

Development stages

For games, the technical development generally follows three stages, as shown in Figure 7-1 for the general flow of game development.

Development follows three stages:

1. **Pre-production:** This is where artists, directors, and engineers come together to "find the fun." It's a prototyping and proof of concept phase to determine whether the game is a good, fun idea before they enter it into production and more money is spent.

    Especially with mobile games, engineers can prototype without any art very quickly. But with any games, teams can validate the idea of the game, define it, develop concept art, ensure funding, and assemble a development team.

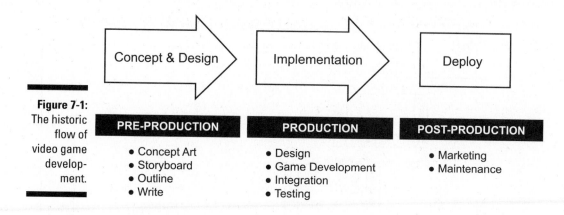

Figure 7-1:
The historic flow of video game development.

PRE-PRODUCTION	PRODUCTION	POST-PRODUCTION
• Concept Art • Storyboard • Outline • Write	• Design • Game Development • Integration • Testing	• Marketing • Maintenance

2. **Production:** The proof of concept gets developed by directors, artists, and engineers.

3. **Post-production:** Professional testers hit the "finished" product, beta testers follow, and sales, marketing, and support begin.

As this process implies, publishers typically engage with studios under traditional waterfall contracts and structures, paying the studio only at certain long-term milestones. This often implies that the publisher goes for long periods of time without seeing progress.

Under a scrum model, the game development process looks more like what is shown in Figure 7-2. Here you can clearly see the ongoing testing necessary for QA. After each task, whether it be concept art, storyboarding, writing, or prototyping, the task is tested and either moved on or further developed.

With scrum, publishers identify and kill the nonfun stuff more quickly and have greater control over quality, because they participate regularly in sprint reviews and pay studios incrementally, in line with the delivery of working game increments.

Short sprints keep a flow of outbound content that attracts and retains consumers. Scrum gets something playable more quickly to such stakeholders as publishers and focus groups. This allows developers to quickly emphasize the fun factor and eliminate sooner the gameplay elements that aren't entertaining. This can also save wasted art creation costs.

Marketing

Games have traditionally been sold as retail products. However, as they become increasingly popular, online and digital distribution is shifting the emphasis from retail to digital delivery. A huge need exists to constantly and quickly update and add, and then push out content to a game. It is the difference between surviving or not. The barrier to entry continues to lower

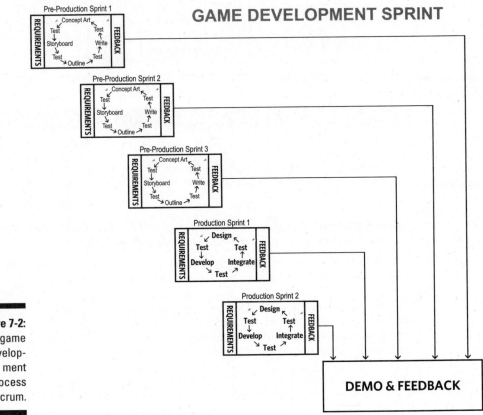

GAME DEVELOPMENT SPRINT

Figure 7-2:
The game development process with scrum.

as basic game-making tools become easier to use and less expensive than ever, and Apple and Google are convenient and inexpensive platforms to sell through (it only costs about $100 to set up a developer account through which you can release game apps). Speed to market is critical.

Game sales are overwhelmingly seasonal, with over 50 percent of the industry's revenue coming from the Christmas season alone. This is a major contributing factor to the crunch time that many teams regularly face, because the holiday season imposes a hard deadline.

Scrum's priority-driven product backlog ensures that the highest-priority "fun" will be delivered with minimized crunch time. This not only makes management happy but also helps reduce employee burnout.

Art

Art is a significant portion of the development work required. Console and PC games require a lot of art and animation assets, adding up to 40 percent or more of the overall cost of a game title. Technical or gameplay issues late in production are costly.

Art, being the most costly, is tempting to outsource overseas more and more. However, trouble with time zones and communications almost always leads to delays, rework, and dissatisfaction in finished product quality.

Scrum allows artists and developers to work on the same team, rather than as silos, with the same goals in sight and real-time communication on what will work and what will not.

Timeboxed delivery (sprints) of art assets keeps everyone on schedule with deadlines that they set as a team and a steady flow of deliverables to market, keeping waste to a minimum.

To optimize collaboration, teams should be onshore and in-house (colocated). Onshore and colocated teams actually keep delay and rework costs down.

Many times, larger game titles require larger development teams than nine people: for instance, 15 or more developers, 10 or more artists, and 30 or more on the QA team. For a thorough discussion of how scrum scales across larger projects, see Chapter 12.

Wooga, a social game developer, releases a new version of its game on Facebook on the same day of each week, every week. The developers take the weekend to refresh their minds before hitting the next sprint again on Monday. The one-week sprint, although rigorous, forces them to be disciplined in their work and avoid delays due to dependencies with other teams. Although they release on the same day each week, they'll still release earlier if a feature is ready. Development team members regularly submit new ideas, and those ideas often get prioritized and developed in the next sprint, which adds to team morale and ownership in the product.

Because gaming technology is changing so rapidly, to perform well and succeed in the gaming sphere, nimbleness and speed are paramount.

Ideally, games can't "ship" with fewer than 10–12 hours of playtime for a single-player game. So while this may be the release goal, after every sprint, publishers can review the working software and provide invaluable feedback.

The definition of "done" may differ between pre-production and production. Be sure to clarify both up front. For instance, a pre-production sprint's definition of done may include different types and levels of documentation and artwork standards than a production sprint.

Clouds and services

Cloud and "as-a-service" development companies use scrum to get their products out the door quickly and effectively. They leverage the power of the Internet.

Cloud

Clouds in software and IT do not refer to droplets of water. (After all, water and electronics don't mix well.) Cloud computing is actually the networking of large groups of remote servers that enable centralized storage of data and other software functionality. Software services in "the cloud" provide online access for customers to access their data and use the software, usually through a web browser. Clouds may offer public access, private access, or a mix of both.

SaaS

Software as a Service (SaaS) is a model of distributing software applications that are hosted by a service provider and made available to users over the Internet. No installation on personal computers or devices is needed. Customers usually pay a monthly fee or subscription.

Even mobile apps, which require a download, have quick downloads that can be done on the go, over Wi-Fi, or over a mobile network while roaming. Installation discs, manually entered license keys, and hours of installation steps with your device plugged in are a thing of the past. The cloud enables scrum teams to inspect and adapt to real, live data, and redeploy quickly to address that feedback.

SaaS adoption by companies rose from 13 percent in 2011 to a whopping 74 percent in 2014, according to a Gigaom Research and North Bridge Venture Partners survey.

IaaS

Infrastructure as a Service (IaaS) is a cloud-computing model of providing organizations with the outsourced equipment necessary to support IT operations, including hardware, servers, storage, and other networking components. IaaS providers own the equipment and are responsible for sourcing, running, and maintaining it. Clients typically pay per use, based on volume of data or size of equipment. These same products also enable other companies to manage their IT and operate their infrastructure in a more scrum-like way. For example, installing a new database server used to take weeks or even months. The in-house engineer had to procure the equipment and then build, configure, and install it before the database engineers could get started installing the database and migrating data. IaaS solutions now allow for this to be done virtually in a matter of minutes.

PaaS

Platform as a Service (PaaS) is a cloud-computing model that provides computing platform and "stack" (set of software subsystems) solutions. Clients typically pay license fees and/or per-use fees.

With IaaS and PaaS services like Amazon and others, IT organizations can spin up a new server in minutes! It's immediately ready for data and installation.

For instance, Oracle reports that IaaS administrative and maintenance automation reduces time and labor up to 68 percent, automated testing and provisioning speeds raise implementation by up to 50 percent, and unplanned downtime is reduced by 30–90 percent due to policy-based monitoring and management.

Customization projects

Some software is off the shelf. Some is customized to meet individual customer needs. How do you handle that with scrum? Do you need individual teams for each client?

I recently worked with a client providing logistics software, which comes with its fair share of customization to work with each unique equipment configuration and specific third-party and legacy software integrations. Before scrum, the project teams that provided the customization service to the clients were so far behind the curve that the lead time to get a new client up was costing them business.

The solution came by inviting the customization project teams (not yet adopting scrum) as stakeholders to attend the core product scrum team's sprint reviews. This allowed these stakeholders to anticipate the end product well in advance. They then provided feedback based on key customer usage that allowed the scrum team to engineer the core product in a way that required less customization for each client, as they saw ways to leverage certain features and collaborate with other client representatives.

According to Jeff Sutherland in a recently published article entitled "Agile Done Right, Agile Done Wrong" (January 16, 2014, Openview Lab), big technology companies are embracing scrum and agile frameworks. Microsoft has a 3,000-person scrum structure (multiple teams that integrate together — see more on vertical slicing in Chapter 12) for all of its developing and tooling, and it releases product after every single sprint. Google has 15,000 developers working on one branch of code. The company goes live multiple times a day, and it runs 75 million automated tests every day.

...ersus Healthcare.gov

...r the effect that ...neworks can have ...nd SaaS, I'll compare ...y and Healthcare.gov.

...olitical views of the Affordable ...althcare.gov was a massive roll- ...d computing that had myriad prob- ...quiring extensive layers of fixing. Jeff S...herland, one of the founders of scrum, called the rollout "waterfall gone bad."

Healthcare.gov was actually an agile project on the front end, but developers missed the second agile principle: working software. So the people on the front end did their part, but the lack of load and performance testing on the actual hardware rendered the software useless.

Although the plan had dozens of reputable consultancies working on the project, minimal coordination existed between them. The program was rolled out nationwide, when, true to scrum and agile, if it had been tested state by state — if inspect and adapt had been applied — many of the issues could have been dealt with early and quickly.

Spotify, the online music source, does things differently and is seeing remarkable success. It has embraced scrum and agile so much that all its scrum masters must be agile coaches. Spotify competitors are big: Google, Amazon, and Apple. You can stream live tunes through any of these.

Spotify had to be nimbler, faster, and cheaper to even think of competing. It has locations and scrum teams all over the world, and each team is responsible for a single piece of product. But even this isn't fast enough, so the company has developed *continuous deployment,* where it deploys product several times during a sprint.

So to compare two huge cloud-computing services, one done through waterfall and the other through fast and nimble scrum teams, and you can easily see in today's world the need for delivering, inspecting, and adapting working software frequently.

Continuous delivery

Continuous delivery is the practice of deploying code throughout a sprint, rather than just at the end. Who's doing this?

- ✔ **Google:** The company has 15,000 engineers working on a branch of code. That code is refactored by 50 percent every single month.

- ✔ **Amazon:** This company deploys new code every 11.6 *seconds!* This means 3,000 deployments every single day.

- ✔ **Facebook:** A team of 5,000 engineers commit to the same branch of code at least once a day. This code is deployed every day. Rather than having a dedicated QA team, all QA is the responsibility of the engineers themselves.

Chapter 8

Tangible Goods Production

Even a mistake may turn out to be the one thing necessary to a worthwhile achievement.

— Henry Ford

Given the origin of agile and scrum, it's not a far stretch of the imagination to think that it should only be used with developing software. The fact is, nothing could be further from the truth. The 1986 Harvard Business Review article "New New Product Development Game," mentioned in Chapters 1 and 7, was actually written in response to experiences in the manufacturing industries. The article used as case studies hardware, electronics, and automotive products engineered and built by companies like Fuji-Xerox in 1978, Canon in 1982, Honda in 1981, and others.

The development and production of tangible goods work beautifully with scrum, and I'll show you how.

The situation and product may vary enormously, but the tools and techniques remain the same. By following the same framework procedures I've been writing about, you'll begin to easily see how scrum can fit most any project. All you need is a list of requirements that can be prioritized.

The Fall of Waterfall

As you saw in Chapter 7, product development is occurring at accelerating speeds. It's not just software that's seeing fundamental shifts in what's developed and how long it takes. Long-term, manual activities like hauling and stacking stones for pyramids, laying steel railroad tracks across prairies, and even mapping and developing new highways are fewer and fewer.

Development cycles in most industries are shorter and faster due to the time and cost savings accrued through technology. Companies like Apple — whose products are certainly tangible — release next-generation, cutting-edge products multiple times a year.

Some argue that the scrum framework can't be applied to physical products. "We can't be building the tenth floor when we realize we need to make a change on the fifth floor!" And sometimes they're right.

Questions like that arise all the time in software development as well. A change in design might be so costly that it can't be realistically implemented, and other options have to be considered — including moving forward with no change. Maybe a different database would be preferred, but it's too costly, so the product owner decides to nix the idea and keep going as is.

Scrum is about exposure and good decisions based on empirical evidence, not about swapping out requirements at a customer's every whim. Whether with software, or whether with planes, trains, and automobiles, the scrum foundation applies: organizing a scrum team with appropriate roles, holding frequent inspection and adaptation points, and forcing decisions to happen at the last responsible moment (that is, planning at different levels of detail for the right things at the right time).

Because of the feedback loop, the customer has input over some business decisions via the product owner. This way the development team doesn't have to know all the market and customer nuances needed to make the business decisions. The product owner filters out the "noise" from all the stakeholders so that the developers only spend their time on those requirements that become highest priority. As a team, product owners and developers work together to implement the solutions to problems presented by the product owner. When everyone is working together toward the same goals, finger pointing is reduced and accountability is shared.

Engaged customers are more satisfied customers who end up getting what they want. With scrum, feedback loops are regular, consistent, and as frequent as possible, so customers get what they want at the cost they're willing to pay for it. This keeps customers involved and development teams on track. Impediments can be identified and resolved early on, and accountability is taken on by both those who do the work and those who make decisions, including customers.

Construction

The uses for scrum within the vast world of tangible goods are enormous. The speed-to-market increase and cost savings can be achieved here as in software and other areas. Construction and scrum are an excellent example.

Remember, scrum works with any project, provided that you can list and prioritize the work to be done. Obviously, construction projects have these qualities. However, they also have challenges specific to the industry. Every segment of an industry will. So it's not a matter of "Oh, scrum won't work with this because of X and Y and Z." Rather, think of it as "These are the challenges we face, and let's look at how scrum will solve them and get us faster and cheaper to market."

In the following sections, I outline specific issues within the construction industry and describe how scrum fits. You'll see how traditional problems — those that you've been dealing with your entire construction careers and thought would never leave — are dealt with by scrum.

Getting the best in bids

Competition in the bidding process for construction projects is fierce, and it shows no signs of trending toward easy. Combine this with a steady increase in the cost of construction, and you have a formula for cutting corners and potential for skipping essential steps.

None of this is news to anyone in this industry. Your bid may be pristine and provide everything that the client needs at a reasonable price, but you know it's possible that your competitors' bids will undercut you by leaving things out that you know the client needs. Scrum can help you and the client. After all, in the end, the better the client is served, the better the end result, the better your business stands, and the more potential for referrals.

Scrum provides the following:

✔ **Transparency:** Let the customer decide where they wants their money to go. They can make changes, inspect, and adapt as the project progresses. But they'll be fully informed each step of the way, as they participate in regular sessions of progress review in the sprint review and provide feedback and ask questions.

✔ **Adaptability:** Scrum allows the team to identify course-correcting issues earlier. Even when building to completion, it's better to resolve problems identified by completing a single house than it is to find out about them when ten houses simultaneously reach the same point of completion. But taking it a step further, adapting to customer feedback about a nonload-bearing wall that's misplaced is much easier to fix before electrical, plumbing, and drywall are installed.

✔ **Daily scrum team coordination:** Having an established forum for raising issues limits bottlenecks and prevents small issues from turning into big problems. ACME Pipe company failed to deliver the materials needed? The scrum master is addressing the issue now — and ensuring that it doesn't happen again — not at the end of the week when it comes up in a weekly status reporting meeting.

In Chapter 1, I talk about the three pillars of improvement with agile: transparency, inspection, and adaptation. While all three serve you well throughout scrum, the transparency issue is clearly (pun intended) key in the bidding and building process.

Scrum roles in construction

In traditional project management, the project manager role carries huge responsibilities. They're broad and all inclusive, and all too often, too much for one person to effectively bear alone. The project manager wears so many hats — coordinating between everyone involved — that efficiency and quality can bear the consequences.

Scrum provides different, clearly designated roles, to shoulder the burden. Balance is restored as scrum team members take on different responsibilities:

✔ The project manager role disappears.

✔ The product owner represents the funding customer and the stakeholders. This could be the person who was traditionally the project manager, or could be the project architect or engineer, depending on how those roles are implemented in each organization. The role is the same: the "what" and the "when" of the product being built.

✔ The scrum master role facilitates communication and interactions, removes impediments for the development team, makes sure that each person involved understands the process, and makes sure that the team environment is set up for them to succeed at their jobs. This sounds a lot like a foreman or superintendent, doesn't it?

✔ The development team consists of the subcontractors, engineers, architects, and individual tradesmen.

While these sections of the book serve as a field guide for scrum within specific industries, you can see that the scrum roles that make this framework so effective easily morph into new project types.

Customer involvement

Remember the traditional view that change in projects is bad? As you know, in scrum, change is embraced; it's a sign of progress. I seek change as clear evidence that I'm building a better product, more directly in line with what my client wants.

In traditional construction projects, you find a tendency (as in so many other fields) to involve customers as little as possible to keep changes to a minimum. They're still in the change-is-bad mind-set. However, as you've seen, the earlier and more frequently the customer is involved, the cheaper changes are and the more likely you are to actually build something the customer loves.

At the other extreme, what we don't want is *scope creep.* As customers see things take shape, they want to add more and more features, which builds additional scope into the project. This adds cost that may not have been budgeted for. In scrum, we want to reduce cost, not raise it.

How does scrum prevent this? By having scope restricted by cost, and thus time, rather than by arguments of what was "meant" by a written requirement. The customer can have any new requirement that aligns with the vision statement, but each of those new requirements is offset by not getting a corresponding lower-priority requirement, unless those lowest-priority requirements are funded by additional budget.

Scrum facilitates the customer involvement process by

- ✔ Structuring customer feedback within sprint cycles at natural breaks and milestones in the project, such as inspecting rough electrical or plumbing before hanging drywall to ensure that fixtures are lined up where the customer intended. This allows for any necessary adjustments to be made before it's too late. The customer inspects completed work at the end of each sprint and can provide valuable feedback then.

- ✔ Gaining ownership of the project, by making decisions driven by cost and return on investment within these feedback loops.

- ✔ Giving customer change requests visibility throughout the project, by showing how they will impact the remaining schedule and cost to the customer.

In the end, the transparency, inspection, and adaption process allows better communication. When everyone involved has the information that they need, the environment for excellent decision making is created.

The subcontractor dilemma

Since the building of the pyramids in Egypt, project managers and subcontractors have struggled to stay coordinated and on track. Issues still arise far too frequently, and it has to do with the structure within which these two valuable parties operate.

"Contractors and subcontractors in traditional construction procurement projects pursue their self-interests to such an extent that collaborative working has been impossible to achieve." — Journal of Construction Engineering, Volume 2013 (2013), Article ID 281236.

The challenges are several-fold. Traditionally, the project process has been difficult to coordinate because the subcontractors are numerous, while the contractors are few. Through a lack of coordination, communication, and therefore ownership in the outcome, the parties involved focus on their own benefits and outcome, rather than the project as a whole. It's human nature.

Each subcontractor is hugely specialized, and therefore a high degree of coordination is needed between them and the responsible party, stakeholders, and potential end users. But the waterfall method simply doesn't provide this environment. Fortunately, scrum does.

Here are some of the ways that scrum helps facilitate the contractor-subcontractor relationship:

- ✔ Through regular, structured scrum events (daily scrums, sprint reviews, and sprint retrospectives), communication is enhanced and vital feedback from all parties is encouraged.

- ✔ Sprints and releases are timeboxed and frequent, and each party knows exactly what is expected and when at each increment.

- ✔ The subcontractors now have input as to how much work they can accomplish in a given sprint (that is, empirical data from what has been accomplished in previous timeboxed sprints). The contractors can give their input on priorities, but the final decisions rest with the people who are doing the work.

- ✔ Subcontractors are not only given a big-picture perspective of their role, but they also are encouraged to share their knowledge and experience in making it a more efficient process (that is, self-organized teams that come up with the best designs).

✔ The contractors receive knowledge and experience from the people actually doing the work — the subcontractors.

✔ Subcontractors can bring up inefficiencies and problems early on (that is, sprint retrospectives). This feedback is critical for removing impediments.

✔ Supply and procurement issues are more easily coordinated because everyone is looking down the road together, through active, in-person discussions (that is, product backlog refinement and daily scrums and real-time daily feedback from the product owner).

✔ Quality is improved through increased coordination.

✔ Material flow and staging are more easily coordinated (that is, product backlog refinement and sprint planning, including task planning of requirements).

The key here is that a disconnected set of roles and jobs are now combined into one communicating and coordinated scrum team. With scrum, you have a living organism. Each part is reliant upon and enhances the other.

Individual subcontractor teams do well using scrum to organize themselves and their work, but what about the overall project team, which is made up of multiple subcontractors? How do you get all of these teams to work as one? Well, it may not be realistic to get all teams in the same room every day, but it would be possible to get each foreman in the same room every day to coordinate the day's priorities, identify impediments, and then go to work removing them for each other to ensure that the job moves forward unhindered.

Worker safety

Safety concerns for workers are always important, but even more so now with an increased number of projects in high-traffic and -populated areas. Clear communication of risks and solutions, therefore, is more important than ever. Lives depend on it.

Scrum helps facilitate an increase in worker safety through the following means:

✔ Safety compliance regulations are more relevant and thorough than ever. Adding these to the definition of done means that documented and validated safety measures can be in place and ready for perusal during audits.

✔ Frequent and regular sprint retrospectives allow workers themselves to come forward with safety concerns and solutions. Good scrum masters can facilitate this process and make sure that the appropriate safety subjects come up.

✔ Experienced workers can share their expertise in providing solutions for all.

✔ Daily scrums can provide a forum for urgent issues.

It's likely that these things are being done already in various ways, just not using scrum terms. Transparency of safety concerns is the key, as well as providing a mechanism to inspect based on that transparency and implement actions to adapt.

Flyover Construction in Bangalore

This is a real-life example of the scrum process in action with construction. The project was building a flyover road at a hugely busy intersection in Bangalore, India. This was a crossroads where many high-tech companies had major facilities. The story is based on a Scrum Alliance article entitled "A Real-Life Example of Agile, Incremental Delivery of an Infrastructure Project in Bangalore, India" (July 2014).

Normally, a flyover project of this magnitude would take 18 months to complete. In the process, temporary roads would be created on either side of the main thoroughfare, while both flyovers were built simultaneously. Naturally, traffic is delayed during construction as temporary roads are used. And no flyovers are available until the end, when both are opened.

However, in this case, the project was conducted using scrum and incremental steps. I'll walk you through them:

✔ The highest-priority requirement (MVP) was identified as one side of the flyover for first release. Therefore, a temporary road was constructed and used on one side of the main road. Simultaneously, construction of the flyover on the opposite side of the road began.

✔ Upon completion of the first flyover, it was opened for traffic in both directions, and the opposite flyover began to be constructed. So while traffic was still delayed, the delay was reduced because at least one flyover was functional. The completion of the first flyover also created a "shippable" product increment. Swarming was done on that side of the flyover only.

✔ The same temporary road was used during the second flyover construction as the first. Time and money were saved as no new road was required. Perhaps a second temporary road would have been planned up front, but after using the first temporary road, it was found to be useful during the second phase. Inspect and adapt eliminated waste.

✔ The second flyover was completed and now both were open, while traffic was returned to the main thoroughfare. The temporary road was closed. The second MVP was complete, and therefore the end of roadmap was reached.

Seems simple, doesn't it? That's scrum. Here are some of the results:

✔ Using this incremental delivery of one flyover at a time actually reduced the overall construction time from 18 to 9 months (a 50 percent time-to-market decrease).

✔ Traffic congestion, while still there, was reduced as first one and then the other flyovers were opened.

✔ Only one temporary road needed to be constructed.

✔ As soon as one flyover was operational, risk of failure was reduced. For example, what if funding had been cut halfway through? Because one side was fully functional (that is, a shippable increment had been created), it wouldn't have been as big a disaster as if both sides of the flyover were halfway done and therefore both unusable. The highest-risk issues had been dealt with up front.

✔ The overall efficiency was improved as there were fewer moving parts at any one time.

Scrum Home Building

A home can be defined, planned, estimated, and built using scrum. The first meeting with the builder is to learn about the type of home that you're looking for (such features as the number of bedrooms, type of property, and number of garages), the quality of finishes and flooring, the landscaping, the approximate amount you want to spend, and your time frame. This gives the builder a high-level understanding of what you're looking for (the vision and roadmap). It takes about an hour.

Over the next several weeks following the initial planning meeting, buyers meet with an architect to get more specific about plans such as the desired room layouts, floors, basement, lot placement, flooring, and cabinetry. Design elements such as colors, appliances, and fixtures are not yet selected. What does get decided is what's needed to estimate the cost of the house and provide a blueprint and elevation. These are the higher-risk items that are difficult and most expensive to change later (the product backlog).

From that point, it's expected that the less risky things will change later, so those decisions are deferred until the last responsible moment. Potential risks are discussed, however, like surprises that might be found at ground-breaking.

With the blueprint comes a budget, which breaks out the details sufficiently for the builder to factor in profit and for the buyer to see each feature of the house factored in that they care about when the house is finished (that is, user stories).

The budget for each feature, like cabinets, is based on the description given by the buyer of what they want from the builder at the beginning. Within that budget, when it comes time to install the cabinets, the buyer gets to choose at that time exactly what they want. This is where trade-offs can be made, or color coordination can take place when looking at the actual home rather than pictures in a brochure in an office. Although a certain quality of wood may have sounded great during planning, the buyer may change their mind and desire a less expensive option and use the savings to put toward something else, or simply finance less at closing because of the savings.

Last Planner®

Last Planner® is a planning system used in the construction industry that takes advantage of scrum practices as well, and was partially inspired by experiments "on well managed sites run by respected engineering and building companies" that found "only 54%, one in two, of tasks planned for delivery the following week were delivered in that week."

Decentralized decision making, reduced specialty constructor costs, and early delivery of bad news are several aspects of many that make it so successful in delivering higher quality at lower costs and on tighter schedules.

Last Planner also challenges the traditional *push* systems, which typically result in dysfunctions like ceiling contractors installing ceilings before mechanical and electrical items get finished, eliminating rework (waste).

Five key conversations are at the heart of Last Planner:

- Master Scheduling, which is roadmap planning

- Phase "Pull" Planning, which is identifying dependencies and impediments, such as in daily scrums

- Make Work Ready Planning, which is product backlog refinement

- Weekly Work Planning, which is sprint planning

- Learning, which encompasses sprint reviews and sprint retrospectives

Scrum in construction is real, it's becoming common, and its benefits are just as strong as in other industries, such as software. While this is one example, many more exist. Give it a try, and perhaps yours will be the next success story.

Manufacturing

Interestingly, the lines between software and hardware are blurring. Sure, they're still different, but tangible products nowadays have a surprising amount of software within them. The car you drive, the refrigerator you cool your Mocha Frappuccino in, the reader you're reading this book on — all are full of code.

According to a 2012 IBM white paper on innovation, the amount of code in the average automobile increased by over 400 percent between 2004 and 2010. Ten million lines of code now help operate that tangible product called a car. And IBM estimates that software drives 90 percent of innovation in automobiles.

This means that new demands are placed on the manufacturing process in that it's not just connecting one widget to another. It's interlacing and integrating with complex systems, many of which are software based. In fact, software is critical to the success of many manufactured products.

All this means larger and more complex development projects and incorporating teams with a diverse array of talents. It means increased complexity in incorporating product families (not just individual products), increased risk of defects as complexity rises, and a new and full array of compliance and required standards.

It means scrum.

Lean and mean with Toyota

In the 1940s, a relatively unknown car company called Toyota devised a plan for producing cars, while still controlling its costs. Rather than partaking in the standard assembly line procedure, which required huge overhead costs, the company created a just-in-time process.

Rather than producing everything all at once, it instead built only what it needed then, for that project. Like a supermarket only replaces the items that have sold out, Toyota only built or procured the parts that it needed at that time. No huge inventory. Reduced cost.

This means that one of the several roots of scrum actually began in manufacturing.

Survival of the fastest to market

One key to winning the race to market share is being the fastest to market. This is not a new, twenty-first century paradigm. However, an equally important concept is keeping up and even leading in innovation — specifically, innovation led by customer needs and desires.

The new technologies that we're witnessing are astounding: robotics, artificial intelligence, 3D printing, and nanotechnology to name but a few. In each of these areas, new complexities in production are realized. Scrum and agile-based frameworks are ideal for problem-solving complexity.

 New technologies facilitate getting that early feedback. For example, rather than creating a new, expensive mold for a part to understand what it's like to hold it, a 3D "print" will go a long way at a fraction of the cost and time.

You can only be fastest to market if you're iterating and getting customer feedback up front, while addressing the highest-priority features and highest risk up front. Higher quality is built in through earlier testing. Scrum enables this earlier and higher quality release to market.

Maximizing shareholder value

The hierarchical bureaucracies that are traditionally part of the manufacturing industry place emphasis on efficiency, cost-cutting, and maximizing shareholder value — as opposed to adding value for customers. This is their Achilles' heel. Those companies that are excelling going forward emphasize *value to the customer*.

Scrum and its organic feedback cycle emphasize regular and frequent customer value and feedback. You've read about it for several chapters now. After each sprint, you have working, "shippable" product that you can show to stakeholders and customers. If the sprint cycle is too soon for customer input, then after each release works great too.

As stated in the principles of the agile manifesto, the primary measure of success is a working product in the hands of a customer. The earlier the better, and the more frequently the better. Scrum does both.

Strategic capacity management

In the building of tangible products, you may not have a final piece of product to place in someone's hands at the end of a one-week sprint. This is fine. Just remember to keep the progression demonstrable and the feedback cycle as short as possible.

The idea is to have regular and frequent feedback from end users. The specifics will vary with each product. So work to keep the feedback cycle as short as possible, and try to decrease the cycle when possible.

Intel

Intel has a long history of waterfall project management given its manufacturing history. And for many years and iterations, it's worked for the company. However, it too is seeing the writing on the wall.

The company decided to test scrum first on "developing presilicon infrastructure and readiness work." The idea was that if scrum worked here, Intel could implement it in other areas of the company and manufacturing processes.

In testing scrum, and deciding whether it worked within its culture and products, Intel hired a scrum coach. As you know, I'm a fan of using scrum coaches while making the transition out of waterfall. They help you identify and break old habits, integrate new ones, and generally understand the scrum framework properly.

However, even despite the coaching, transition issues arose. Not every senior manager made it to initial scrum meetings, buy-in with important people was slow, and real-world examples of why scrum works weren't being identified.

Eventually a light began to shine. What did the company find? The best way to get its teams implementing and benefiting from scrum was to use scrum by the book.

Pat Elwer, the author of this case study entitled "Agile Project Development at Intel: A Scrum Odyssey," called scrum cross-functional teams "a Task Force without the crisis!"

In summary, the case study found that the teams discovered that scrum helped the project in four distinct ways:

- ✔ A reduced cycle time of 66 percent.
- ✔ Their performance remained on schedule with virtually no missed commitments.

✔ Increased employee morale. Ironically, their lowest-morale team turned into the best-performing team.

✔ Increased transparency, which has led to identifying impediments and unproductive habits.

After the teams and management bought into the process, the power of scrum soon became apparent.

Hardware Development

As with manufacturing, many similarities exist between implementing scrum in software and hardware projects. You might hear pushback that the differences between the two products are too great; scrum can't work with both. Not true. I repeat, the basis of scrum is that if you can encapsulate the work to be done and prioritize it against other work, you can use scrum to your immense benefit.

A key element with hardware projects and scrum is to focus on feedback, early and often, just like with manufacturing. You may not have as much to work with at the beginning, but keep moving in that direction. Keep producing workable increments at the end of each sprint, and what you have to show customers and stakeholders will grow. And it'll do so with their feedback incorporated.

Which brings me to my next point: change. In hardware projects, it's inevitable too. You'll be better served to accept the fact and turn it into an advantage. Denial will get you nowhere. Fortunately, change in hardware project design and development is totally workable and practical.

Early identification of high-risk requirements

If you can find a way to discover defects and problems early on, it will save you time, money, and hassle. With waterfall, testing was left until the end. After having read so much about scrum by now, I'm sure that you can see how incredible that seems. Why test only at the end when you can test all along the way and find and resolve defects early?

Scrum forces more timely integration between firmware and software. Scrum helps break down functional silos and gets engineers working together to solve problems, rather than crashing together later as they discover problems.

In the daily scrum, which is no more than 15 minutes a day, coordination of what's been done, what's going to be done, and what impediments are in the way can be achieved. This should happen within teams and between them wherever dependencies exist.

In projects where the number of members exceeds a dozen or so, when adopting scrum, it is common practice to split into smaller teams so that each team is within the 7 +/– 2 range. Each scrum team has their daily scrum, and one member from each of the roles on each of the teams then meets for a coordinating daily scrum called a *scrum of scrums.* The format is the same as individual scrum team daily scrums. The value is that direction, dependencies, and impediments get identified and coordinated and resolved daily. See Chapter 12 for more on scrum of scrums.

Open source hardware is a gift to scrum and engineering as a whole. As open source submissions increase, organizations will be able to more quickly and creatively implement existing designs, frameworks, and architectures that will get their product to market more quickly.

Live hardware development

In the following sections, I discuss three examples of the scrum framework being used successfully in different projects. Each situation is unique, but you'll notice that the scrum principles and practices remain the same. For the most part, whatever the project, scrum can be used to develop it faster and with higher quality and ease.

Johns Hopkins CubeSat

The Johns Hopkins University Applied Physics Lab used scrum in the Multi-Mission Bus Demonstrator (MMBD) project in building two CubeSat satellites. The program itself was sponsored by NASA.

Three key elements were identified as critical to the success of the project:

- ✔ **Scrum teams:** These were made up of subsystem leads. All team members were colocated and given direct access to the NASA representative, the product owner (who was on site), for quick decision making.

- ✔ **Emphasis on a working system:** Only one design review was funded, and here CAD models were used to simulate and manipulate designs. Informal peer reviews were also conducted throughout the project. Documentation was minimal.

- ✔ **Change was welcomed and incorporated.** Daily scrums were held for coordination and identifying the best ways of addressing the highest-priority requirements. Long-term planning was eschewed in favor of responding to reality.

Wikispeed modular car

Wikispeed is an all-volunteer, green, prototype car designer. By forming self-organizing teams and using the scrum framework, the company built a functional prototype car that gets 100 miles per gallon. The teams also consistently win races because their car is completely modular. They can swap out components based on the reality of how they're running that day, on that track, in the specific weather of that day. Their competition doesn't have the same ability. Wikispeed founder Joe Justice, in partnership with Scrum Inc., garnered five key takeaways from the company's scrum experience, which it now coaches and trains organizations on globally:

- ✔ **Customers, customers, customers:** Teams went for regular and constant feedback to end users. They tested what they could every week.

- ✔ **Sprints and reviews:** Regular sprint cycles were conducted, with meetings at the end of each stating what went right and what went wrong.

- ✔ **Transparency:** Everyone knew the goals, and anyone could make a suggestion.

- ✔ **Peer-to-peer communication:** Self-organization: No one person was the boss, and everyone was equal and contributed to achieving the sprint goal each day.

Telefonica Digital

Telefonica Digital began as a hardware manufacturing firm and utilized waterfall project management. As technology changed, it began to develop more software, and by the mid-'90s, this was its main focus. At first, the company's approach to software was waterfall, but it has adapted fully to agile and scrum in the past ten years.

But technology and the firm's direction changed again, and it went back to producing hardware. Interestingly, because of its experience with scrum over the years, the company had no desire to go back to traditional project management, even though the product changed. Telefonica wanted to stick with scrum. So it brought its hardware projects to the scrum framework.

The first issue was relocating the entire facility so that employees could be colocated. The company understood the value that working in close proximity brings and acted to make it happen. Telefonica also created a system where it could easily procure equipment and materials on the very day it needed them: just in time.

The company used scrum teams and fostered cross-functionality. It tested early and often, even using 3D printing and prototyping technologies to hasten the testing. It used lots of open hardware, which it could use for testing. At times, this actually accelerated the company's progress to the point of waiting on the software teams.

Chapter 9

Services

> *"There are more than 9,000 [current numbers have this at 80,000] billing codes for individual procedures and units of care. But there is not a single billing code for patient adherence or improvement, or for helping patients stay well."*
>
> — Clayton M. Christensen, *The Innovator's Prescription: A Disruptive Solution for Health Care*

Scrum within the services industry has enormous potential. We rely on healthcare, education, and public utilities to maintain and enhance our civilized society. Still, there is room for creating lean systems of cost savings and quality improvement. And in many cases, scrum is already being used.

Within each sector, specific challenges arise, too. Unique sets of circumstances exist that need to be dealt with in a tailored way. Many of the outdated systems of development and maintenance arose from simpler times. But as the world grows more complex, so does the need for innovative and flexible project frameworks. Scrum is ideal to deal with new demands. I show you how and with what results.

Healthcare and Scrum

Over the past few years, healthcare and its evolution within the American landscape have been at the forefront of news and talk. Efforts to make healthcare affordable and accessible are often considered a basic tenet of a civilized society. Yet soaring costs, pressure to decrease development time without sacrificing quality, wasted spending, and increasing avoidable deaths have all led to massive changes in the way Americans pay for and receive medical attention.

In 1970, healthcare spending in the United States was estimated to have been $75 billion. In 2012, the figure was $3 trillion, and if current rates of increase are sustained, that figure will be $5 trillion by 2021. As of the publishing of this book, that's just six years away.

Added to this is a healthcare culture where insurance reimbursements are increasingly linked to customer satisfaction. Healthcare technology has an expanded and important influence on clinical outcomes and patient satisfaction. New paradigms exist, and new methods for meeting their needs are required. It should come as no surprise that scrum is being used more and more frequently to address healthcare issues than ever before.

Some of the highest-priority challenges facing the healthcare industry today are

- ✔ Procedural mistakes during healthcare delivery are now the third highest killer in America, just behind heart disease and cancer. A recent Forbes articles states that more than 500 people die each day from "errors, accidents, and infections" in hospitals.

- ✔ Wasted money on unnecessary care. The Institute of Medicine Health claims that a whopping one-third of the billions spent on healthcare each year is wasted money. The American Journal of Obstetrics and Gynecology states that elective deliveries alone cost $1 billion annually.

- ✔ New and increasing regulations require speedy and thorough adaptation.

- ✔ The demand to convert to electronic healthcare records is monumental, yet processes for achieving this are sorely lacking.

- ✔ Research and development into new treatments and medicines need continued funding and creative innovations.

- ✔ Concerns that new medical devices and systems have not been thoroughly reviewed for safety risks, and many of them are designed using traditional methods where design is up front and testing is left for last.

In the following sections, I show you how scrum can help with each of the preceding issues. Remember, improving healthcare is about saving lives. There's no room for error here, and processes that help can and should be implemented. In general, scrum brings the following benefits to the table. Next, I show how it does so in specifies.

- ✔ **Rapid and regular feedback:** Crucial in determining what's acceptable and what's not. This is even more important when the development cycle involves adherence to a regulatory framework. Scrum actually accelerates the point in which internal auditing can happen to better ensure regulatory compliance.

- ✔ **Accelerated time to implementation:** It's about saving lives first — although competitive advantage can be an added benefit.
- ✔ **Faster monetization:** Making quality healthcare profitable will make changes quicker and more likely to stick.
- ✔ **Increased talent retention**
- ✔ **Fewer product defects**

Scrum is needed in the healthcare industry to help foster changes that support clinical decision making within highly effective patient care and business administration. All of this exists while also continuing to be in compliance with the ever-changing demands of regulatory agencies.

Development time for new administrative and clinical systems and products needs to be shortened, and quality and efficiency need to be increased. The current healthcare environment is in flux. Regulations and laws are being changed and refined. Therefore a high degree of flexibility and transparency is necessary to survive in these turbulent waters.

R&D speed to market

Many of the diseases that our parents and grandparents suffered from as children are no longer a concern thanks to the advances in pharmaceuticals and treatments. Aggressive research and progress continue to find cures and prevent both chronic and terminal illnesses. But we want to save more lives, and save them faster.

Customer expectations regarding healthcare and the miracles of science are rising. Payers within the healthcare system are drilling down to find the best value in the medicines and treatments they're buying.

Pharmaceutical companies are under constant pressure to devise new medicines to keep up with the stiff competition. Yet they must do this within a cost-cutting and economizing environment. To compete and succeed, they have to be the fastest, most nimble, and most cost-effective — as in every other industry I've looked at in this book.

Yet big pharma's output has, on the whole, stayed flat. Most pharmaceutical organizations are tackling new situations and technological advances with the same project management frameworks used in the 1940s. They're surrounded by new ways of doing business, yet have mostly stayed within traditional management mind-sets.

Scrum can offer some positive change in the following ways:

- Every experiment begins with a hypothesis. In scrum, this is the release goal.

- To test the hypothesis, a series of premises need to be true or false. Each premise is a sprint goal. The sprint backlog is broken into tasks and experiments needed to fully explore each premise. The definition of "done" for the sprint outlines the type of tasks and activities that must be conducted and accepted for a premise to be considered fully tested and explored.

- At the end of each sprint, the team presents its findings to stakeholders, who ask questions and validate the team's sprint conclusions. Stakeholders should include representatives from regulatory teams. If something was missed, the scrum team knows it early instead of at the end of the entire set of sprints in the release. They can conduct the follow-up activities to address the feedback in the very next sprint if it's a priority.

- After all premises have been validated, the hypothesis either stands or is invalidated. Either way, it's a "releasable" conclusion.

- All the actions needed to test the hypothesis are the requirements on the product backlog and get prioritized accordingly.

- With new products or improvements on old ones, scrum allows you to iterate quickly. The mantra of "fail fast, fail cheap" means that you can be as nimble as you like with trying new ideas and processes.

- Self-organizing scrum teams allow developers to come up with the best research and solutions.

- Customer, business, and regulatory involvement (as stakeholders) throughout the process means constant feedback and direction. Because of this, accountability is shared and engagement rises.

Scrum frameworks have actually been used by several medical-device manufacturers with much success. Abbott Laboratories scored a hat trick when it achieved time-to-market savings of 20–30 percent, cost savings of 35–50 percent, and fewer software defects. Employee morale also increased.

Reducing mistakes, increasing quality

While we have the greatest technology and treatments ever known, we still have room to improve. Incredibly, mistakes during healthcare delivery in America are now the third-highest killer. The actual numbers are nothing short of astounding:

✔ The Journal of Patient Safety recently conducted a study that estimated that over 400,000 people die every single year from preventable mistakes that occurred while they were in the hospital.

✔ According to a 2010 report from the Department of Health and Human Services, 180,000 Medicare patients die every year from preventable hospital mistakes.

✔ In 2011, the Centers for Disease Control and Prevention indicated that 1 in 25 patients gets an infection from their hospital stay, 700,000 of these individuals get sick from their hospital-borne infection, and a tragic 75,000 die.

A report by the Journal of Health Care Finance estimates that these medical errors, if you include lost productivity in the workplace, may total up to $1 trillion annually. In many cases, these errors can result in a device or medicine getting banned forever on a very short notice, resulting in a complete loss to a company that has invested billions of dollars during the development cycle.

While the causes of these errors may vary, the quality assurance built into the scrum framework can ferret out problems and their solutions early. System inefficiencies, bottlenecks in work flow, communication breakdowns, lack of timely feedback — all these can be more easily identified and dealt with while using scrum. Looking at it more closely:

✔ As communication is increased, inefficiencies become visible. Scrum exposes these through daily scrums and sprint reviews; real solutions can be tried, tested, and adapted.

✔ While licensed physicians are the only people authorized to diagnose patients, self-organized teams (of the entire staff) facilitate the necessary treatment, rather than the command and control system of the highest-ranking physician.

✔ Feedback is rapid, and adjustments can be quickly implemented and retested.

✔ As quality goes up, unnecessary risks and wasted costs go down.

✔ As input from all members of staff and key groups is sought after and used, buy-in increases and morale improves. This is hugely valuable in healthcare, where many people are overworked and burnout can be high.

Scrum has been used within the healthcare environment with great success. It starts with administrative buy-in, followed by the implementation of scrum teams and their inherent roles. Then the process begins, following the roadmap to value just like any other scrum project. Follow the stages I've outlined along the way and watch the positive changes unfold.

Cost cutting

Those words alone are enough to perk the ears of any healthcare administrator. And in a sense, every single problem and solution I discuss will help save costs. Avoidable illnesses and deaths, increased efficiency in care delivery and administrative flow, ease in following existing and new regulations — pretty much you name it — can be improved and it will save costs.

Cost savings are a hallmark of scrum. Not only do you achieve an increase in speed to market, which accounts for a large part of the cost savings, but you also streamline processes, remove inefficiencies, and generally make better business decisions. For instance, as reported by the Center for American Progress in 2012, "administrative costs in the U.S. health care system consume an estimated $361 billion annually — 14 percent of all health care expenditures in our nation. At least half of this spending is estimated to be wasteful."

Consider savings in the context of unnecessary care costs. A 2012 study conducted by the Institute of Medicine estimates that we waste $750 billion annually on unnecessary healthcare. The causes range from inefficient and unnecessary services, to overpricing, to excessive administration costs, to fraud.

Some of the ways scrum can help are

- **Sprint retrospectives:** Scrum makes it habit and culture to consistently and frequently ask such questions as

  - What about our claims process is unnecessary?

  - How can we minimize repeat patient visits?

  - What additional steps can we take to reduce patient risks even further?

  - Where are the bottlenecks?

  - What if form XYZ were electronic?

  - What's stopping us from increasing our daily claims processing rate by 20 or 50 percent?

- **Daily coordination of priorities:** During daily scrums, such questions as these can be asked:

  - Is this necessary for this patient today?

  - What's in the way of this patient going home well today?

  - How can we remove that obstacle?

✔ **Transparency and simplicity:** With scrum, you want to maximize the amount of work not done, especially if it's also harmful. This is essential. For example, reducing the number of early elective deliveries (37–39 weeks as opposed to 40) would eliminate up to 500,000 neonatal intensive care unit (NICU) days.

Claims backlog reduction

In 2013, a white paper was written by Availity covering the amazing success that Carolinas Healthcare System had in reducing its claims edit backlog by implementing scrum.

Carolinas Healthcare System began with the following situation: A claims edit backlog of $8 million in unpaid claims, with 600,000 claims being submitted each month. This created cash flow issues, aging accounts receivables, and low employee productivity due to this huge backlog.

Scrum was implemented and the company witnessed the following: The error rate for claims was almost halved. The number of claims requiring edits dropped by 85 percent. And the number of days a claim had to wait for edits was reduced from 40 to 2 or less!

On top of this, where Carolinas Healthcare System originally needed 13 staff to complete the work, given the increased efficiency created through scrum, the company was able to reposition seven of those employees into different roles, with all of those roles of high value to the organization.

Claims processing

In 2012, one of the major healthcare payers initiated a multiyear program for transferring its old legacy system to a modular system that complied with the Medicaid Information Technology Architecture (MITA) framework.

Initially, the program followed the waterfall project management approach. The program team spent more than 18 months diagramming business process flows, gathering requirements, and documenting business rules. The outcome was reams of documents and flow diagrams with no tangible business value.

Project leadership changed the approach and implemented scrum and, with scrum's incremental approach, started seeing the return on investment (ROI) within just a few months. One of the major pieces of the enterprise system was up and running in production within six months. While this book is being written, this program has already implemented its second major release.

All those regulations!

With the changes brought on by the Affordable Care Act (ACA) in 2010, along came a flurry of new regulations. Whether more or less in quantity, they're certainly new, and a huge learning curve lies ahead for healthcare service providers in integrating these new rules.

Whether the ACA, FDA, IEC, HIPAA, or any other alphabet-soup acronym in the healthcare field, these regulations are in place to protect patients and healthcare providers, and each healthcare organization needs to find ways to comply. Implementing solutions to address new regulations can be challenging and even tedious, and with fewer resources to work with, it can be all the more daunting.

Here are some of the ways that scrum comes out on top in regard to understanding and abiding by new regulations in the healthcare industry:

✔ A product backlog can be created and prioritized by business value and risk mitigation. The scrum teams and organization as a whole then have the rationale to make business and resource decisions during the complex times of regulation changes.

✔ Previously, the technical and business sides of healthcare solutions might not have met eye to eye. After all, their mandates were probably different. But as the business side is covered by a product owner, and development teams are formed to design solutions, all of a sudden goals come in line. Scrum team roles are peer roles, working together to facilitate the right environment for aligning goals and purpose, which is ideal for implementing changes to deal with regulations.

✔ Self-organized teams help define the best solutions. When the new regulations are narrowed down and prioritized, it's easier to pinpoint solutions and implement them quickly.

✔ The evolving regulatory requirements can then be built into the scrum team's definition of done. This way, product owners and stakeholders can rest assured that they'll be in line when audits and inspections take place.

Scrum doesn't escape regulations. Regulations have the good of the patient in mind. Scrum is a tool for responding to changes by being tactically flexible while remaining strategically stable, and thereby making sure that the end goal — better healthcare — is achieved.

Electronic healthcare records

Converting patients' medical data into electronic healthcare records (EHRs) is a monumental task. EHR is attractive for making healthcare more efficient and less expensive, for improving the safety and quality of care, and for convenience to patients. But the scope of data conversion is huge, entailing high cost and labor. It's estimated that between 2010 and 2011, hospital adoption rates have risen from 11.5 to 18 percent. But that leaves a significant 82 percent left to go.

One of the problems with EHR conversion is that no set consensus exists of what the end result will actually look like. The benefits aren't clear to everyone involved. Of course, this is where scrum's foundation in empiricism excels. Empiricism asserts that knowledge comes from experience and making decisions based on what is known. We start with what we know, create a product backlog, prioritize it, and begin developing those at the top. With the feedback loop in place, you'll quickly start seeing what works best.

Some of the issues with EHR conversions are as follows:

- The number-one issue within healthcare providers is finding the financial resources to undertake the EHR conversion.

- Significant amounts of data entry are involved.

- Integration issues arise, such as designing software so that EHR software with different standards can communicate.

- Privacy concerns. Many EHRs aren't shared between organizations currently, but the goal is for all healthcare providers and organizations (such as labs, specialists, medical imaging facilities, pharmacies, emergency facilities, schools, and workplace clinics) to be able to securely share information involved with a patient's care. Making this conversion seamless brings in privacy issues and ensuing legal liability ramifications.

- Independent practitioner physicians with varying degrees of loyalty to care delivery organizations have different mind-sets, which make EHR conversion efforts challenging.

Scrum addresses each of these issues in the following ways:

- Scrum reduces costs and budgetary commitments.

- AC + OC > V: Terminate the project as soon as the actual cost (AC) of the project added to the opportunity cost (OC) of not working on other projects is greater than the value (V) you're expecting to get from the future functionality. See Chapter 5.

- With scrum's incremental approach, only the highest-priority requirements are completed first, and therefore can be funded incrementally rather than all up front (for more on incremental funding, see Chapter 13). With this in place, items that don't matter as much, or may not actually be needed at all, are left until last. This alone increases cost savings.

✔ Inspect and adapt. Scrum allows you to identify problems, like unexpected HIPAA privacy concerns or legacy data compatibility issues, early on before they cause reams of damage. The best solutions can then be found and tested again. Identifying these issues early on saves money in fixing them much later.

✔ Common definition of "done." Scrum brings transparency by defining common standards, so independent practitioner physicians can share a common understanding of EHR implementation within an organization. A common language approach referring to the new EHR process can increase the adoption rate for this monumental mandate.

Medical device manufacturing and safety

In line with the pharmaceutical industry's need to produce new and amazing medicines, medical device manufacturing firms have their own set of issues — some of which overlap. They, too, live within highly competitive and cost-conscious environments.

As with pharmaceuticals, many are beset with traditional project management mind-sets. Up-front designing, combined with late back-end testing, means that defects get detected late and the costs for fixing them rise. And that's assuming that the defects are detected before the product hits the market. See the "Pair programming" sidebar in Chapter 4 for the exponentially increasing costs associated with defects.

Risk and issue management

In risk and issue management in healthcare IT implementations, having documented risks and issue tracking in the event of a regulatory audit or legal action is considered crucial.

In traditional project management, this is typically achieved by the creation and maintenance of a risk and issue log that's based on initial requirements determined at the project kickoff.

As requirements change throughout the course of the implementation, these become hard to manage and often become the driver for cumbersome change management processes to be initiated.

In scrum, you can build the risk management into your process. You can just make it part of your definition of done. The requirement is not completed until specifically stated risks are identified, mitigated or accepted, and documented.

Scrum's focus on continual review provides better outcomes than the traditional project management methodology.

With scrum, you can

- ✔ Build product testing into each iteration. Catch those defects early, stamp them out, and implement better designs.

- ✔ Colocate designers with engineers so that they're immediately accessible and can have real-time everyday feedback.

- ✔ Many times the customer doesn't know exactly what they want right at the beginning. Only after the initial high-priority requirements have been developed can they see a fuller picture. Scrum allows for this.

- ✔ Inspect and adapt constantly. Only build what's most important, and test and garner feedback regularly and frequently.

- ✔ Get daily sign-off with the product owner on work done.

- ✔ Receive feedback from stakeholders at regular sprint reviews. This gets them involved throughout the development process.

- ✔ When syncing software and hardware development, the teams can coordinate early and often.

- ✔ The definition of done for both teams can include integration and testing throughout each sprint rather than at the very end.

GE Healthcare

GE's imaging unit found the following ailments in its traditional approach to developing these types of medical devices before implementing scrum:

- ✔ **Predictability:** The company was running 12–24-month projects, usually with significant delays.

- ✔ **Scope creep:** Those representing the business usually pushed to add features beyond the original scope.

- ✔ **Phased gate approach:** Minimal customer interaction until the first round of testing was a major contributor to delays and soaring project costs.

- ✔ **Silo teams:** Artificial barriers existed between functional, technical, and business units in the organization.

Scrum healed these ailments in the following ways:

- ✔ Product owners were an integral part of the scrum teams. This alone significantly broke down silos and aligned priorities across the organization. The whole business began working in unison to release the right product to customers on time.

✔ Short sprints in which actual product increments were completed and demonstrated. The feedback received early on steered the project to earlier project completion than normal.

✔ Senior leadership excitement. Early on, by observing successes at one of their joint ventures using scrum, executive leadership caught the vision of what scrum could do, and their support accelerated adoption.

✔ Due to high regulation of the industry, GE built regulatory steps into the definition of done and acceptance criteria. Development teams adjusted to this level of effort when estimating and executing.

By incorporating scrum into the medical device manufacturing process, costs come down and time to market is reduced, but most importantly, defects are reduced, resulting in less reputational and regulatory risks. The chance of a product actually harming a person goes down because the product has been tested and integrated so many times already. In the end, this is what matters.

Education and Scrum

Throughout the last few sections, I've been emphasizing how scrum can be used in a variety of industries — all of them, in fact. Scrum is a framework for developing products, not a software-specific tool.

Education is one such industry. Children are the future, as their children will be after them. Educating young people, and ensuring that they have the ability to come up with creative, innovation solutions and decisions themselves, should be the top priority of every culture.

Public education was first created in a different landscape — that of basic education for workers. The need was simple as the work world was simple. Today, however, complexity has grown exponentially, as has an individual's choices for jobs and their overall role in the world.

Because of this change in the work landscape, we want education to prepare children to effectively participate. In instances where teachers are still trained to prepare and deliver material in the old way, a better way exists.

Scrum in the classroom enhances how children adapt creatively and flexibly to change, prioritize projects and ideas, and creatively come up with new solutions. Technology and media are changing so rapidly that the information that kids receive from the world around them is always in flux. With scrum, they can learn how to turn this into an advantage.

Challenges in Education Today

Education today faces different challenges than ever before. Curriculum is expanding in scope, underperforming students require more attention, and classroom sizes are increasing.

As you've seen, within these outwardly appearing wheels of chaos, progress can so often be made with scrum. First, I go through three of the main challenges facing education. Next, I discuss ways that scrum is providing solutions for each. Many of the solutions overlap, such that by implementing scrum, the negative impact of all these challenges are decreased.

In many respects, teachers inherently use scrum. However, they use a different vernacular that is perhaps unknown to those outside of the profession. For example: objectives, scaffolding, mini-lessons, modalities of learning, and reflection.

Teachers already set goals for each lesson. They use the standards as the goal, but then set objectives for the lesson, as some standards require multiple steps. These multiple steps are called *scaffolding*. Teachers break the lesson into "iterations" so that students can be successful and accomplish each necessary aspect. Along the way, they use both formative and summative assessments to then gauge and modify the learning. Students and teachers alike reflect at the end of each lesson, like a retrospective.

Next, teachers are trained to use collaborative learning models and to do projects that engage students and get their buy-in. Teachers are virtually trained in scrum, but with different methods and vocabulary.

Curriculum scope increase

Remember the days of "reading, writing, and arithmetic"? The curriculum requirements for teachers have been expanding for decades. More information is required to be covered, and teachers can be overwhelmed just trying to keep up. These curriculum pressures come from three sources:

- School systems and governments
- Parents
- Students

No Child Left Behind (NCLB) in the United States is just one government program that's been introduced over the years. With NCLB's emphasis on standardized testing, teachers were given a new set of parameters to work toward. Over the years, other programs from all levels of government have left their mark as well. Although many of these programs bring high-quality elements to the school experience, each also leaves a new mark, which often means more work.

Many topics and experiences used to be taught in the home by parents. School was for the basics. Now, school systems cover subjects never before imagined in the classroom. A few that were introduced just in the last decade are listed here:

- ✔ Bully prevention
- ✔ Antiharassment policies
- ✔ Body mass index evaluation (obesity monitoring)
- ✔ Financial literacy
- ✔ Entrepreneurial skills development
- ✔ Health and wellness programs

Nothing in itself is wrong with these additional programs. In fact, they look great. However, teachers are being asked to include some of these topics, along with many other new ones, and of course, the old standards of reading, writing, and arithmetic. Yet, they've been given no more actual hours in the day for teaching, and often work with limited resources and funding.

Students themselves arrive with a host of experiences and knowledge that would have been science fiction just a few decades ago. They're often computer literate by their early years, and have been exposed to adult themes and messages through TV, films, and music. While the teaching techniques I mentioned previously are inherently scrum, the actual spectrum of what's being taught has increased. But the overarching goal for everyone remains the same: well-educated students.

Effective prioritization and inspect-and-adapt methods are essential to effectively administer this growing curriculum. Teachers do this as they carefully plan each day and empower students to be self-organizing and self-managing. Rather than following a strict, rigid plan outlined at the beginning of the year, they regularly conduct assessments and adjust their schedule, sometimes spending more time than planned on a subject to help a struggling class, and sometimes spending less time than planned when a class just "gets it" quicker than expected.

More and more, teachers are also recognizing the value of "refactoring." In the old days, you took a test, you got a grade, and that was it. For better or worse, that was your grade, no questions asked. As educators have learned from experience, adaptations have been made to allow students to learn from mistakes and be rewarded for their learning. Continual feedback loops allow for learning, followed by an assessment (a pretest or quiz), with feedback and more learning followed by the final assessment. Rather than the grade being the only goal, students are starting to also understand and appreciate what they learn using these same events as used in scrum.

Moving low-performing students upward

Teachers are hugely instrumental in moving individual students through learning blocks and helping peel them off the lower rungs of performance. However, sometimes teachers work from a structured curriculum that requires them to move on with new topics and subjects even though not all their students may have full comprehension. While they might want to spend more valuable one-on-one time with each student, they simply can't and still keep the overall curriculum moving forward.

Therefore, the individual attention needed to help low- or moderate-scoring students sometimes isn't available due to lack of time. Teachers need to keep progressing in their curriculum. Large class sizes can add to this conundrum.

 According to the National Center for Public Policy and Higher Education, every school day, 7,000 kids drop out of high school. That's over a million each year. In the end, we're producing fewer candidates for high-level careers.

As a result, low-performing students arrive in their next year's class without a full understanding of the previous year's material. Or, they're held back and taught the same material over again without new learning techniques. Evaluations are done, but teaching doesn't necessarily circle back to those weaker areas of understanding.

According to the Carnegie Foundation for the Advancement of Teaching, more than 60 percent of students entering a community college today in the United States need to complete developmental courses before they take normal college-credit courses. Of these, 70 percent fail these developmental courses. This blocks their way to higher-level math and technical courses and stumps their career possibilities.

Success in elevating individual students comes through collaboration among schools, teachers, parents, and students. What if the scrum framework were applied for each individual student, with team members consisting of such participants as the teacher, the student, the counselor, a school administrator, and a tutor? This team could set iterative goals leading to an end goal, with regular feedback loops, all the while inspecting and adapting progress and the process to tailor-fit the student's needs.

Most schools are always trying to get more buy-in from parents and the community. In one school I'm aware of, when the teaching staff wanted to change the discipline plan, they did several iterations of revisions and feedback sessions until finally it was implemented. Following implementation of the new policy, iteratively addressing concerns and changing the behavior of teachers and other staff members were to follow.

Increasing student-to-teacher ratios

Classes are getting bigger, and therefore individual teacher-student attention is dropping. It's a tall order to manage the entire class and the increasing curriculum, and provide student- and subject-specific teaching.

For example, in 2010, Georgia cut funding for its state schools by $1 billion, after which the State Board of Education was forced to lift limits on class sizes. The Board simply didn't have the money to hire enough teachers and keep class sizes down.

Teachers spend time building relationships, modifying a lesson, executing lessons, and helping students one on one. Finding time for this is the most important challenge of education. As funding decreases, but yet teaching methods and systems stay the same, it's inevitable that education in the classroom will suffer. Scrum can help leverage teachers' time and increase adaptability.

I go into how scrum can address these roadblocks in the next sections.

Scrum in the Classroom

The basics of scrum work in education like anywhere else. I'll start with broad, conceptual fits and move down to real examples of scrum in action.

As scrum is based on goals and vision, setting focused learning goals allows students to adapt their learning styles to their speed of learning. By focusing on one learning goal at a time, each subject and level can be mastered before moving on. With scrum, teachers can emphasize high-priority learning items that students then focus on.

Scrum remains effective in large class sizes because smaller scrum teams can be formed for projects. Within limits based on the age and nature of the individual groups of students, these teams can be self-organizing and self-directed in ways to reach educational goals. (See the following example.)

Inspecting and adapting does work remarkably well in learning environments. Studies have shown that students who have lesson plans to adapt to, and can work on those specific areas where they struggle, achieve better comprehension. Iterative teaching models have been introduced to the classroom with remarkable results in the following ways:

- The teacher outlines the unit or project for all the students, and groups are formed (sprint planning).

- The teacher executes daily teaching and guides group work-learning tasks, setting a time goal too (sprint).

- The student and teacher assess student performance at the end of the timebox (sprint review).

- Two choices are created from here. If the student performs above a preset cut-off level, they move onto new material. However, if they perform below this level, the sprint retrospective is conducted.

- Using feedback received at the sprint review, identify the problem topics with each student.

- Form new teams to maximize the teacher's ability to help them by leveraging the common challenges that each student is facing. These teams will work together in increasing their understanding of the topic.

- Revise the material for these new groups (product backlog refinement). Let the students come up with ideas for how they can better learn the subject material.

- Run another sprint.

- Assess student performance and repeat, incrementally improving student performance.

And the cycle continues. In these studies, student performance saw "significant improvement." Students also had fewer mistakes and more confidence, and spent less time actually figuring out the problems.

Remember, student scrum teams do not have to be shifted as they chose to in this study, but can be kept stable. This way, cross-functional teams can be created with students who may have higher skills in some areas than others. Subsequent sprints can use the same techniques as in pair programming and shadowing. By learning from other students, each student gains new skills and advanced students expand their skill set.

State and national standards may dictate certain requirements for demonstrating mastery of subjects (that is, the definition of done), but each school or teacher can enhance the state or national definition of done to suit their own circumstances. What a student learns and how they show that they have learned it are vital elements to the overall success of the sprint. This will vary according to the situation, but the definition of done should be made clear to all, especially the students.

How one teacher approaches scrum

So how does it actually work, this scrum-in-the-classroom concept?

The best part is that kids love it. They become active participants with the white boards and sticky notes and the responsibility of making sure that each bit is in its proper place.

But I want to delve into some real-world examples.

Following is how one teacher approaches scrum in the classroom:

1. Set up a project of one to five day's duration.

   It's effectively a sprint. The teacher has the original plan, but they get class buy-in through listing requirements. If the project is to understand the periodic table of the elements, for example, requirements could be sections of the table. Tasks might be the individual elements themselves.

2. Scrum teams of students are formed, and they decide who fills each of the scrum roles as a team.

   A high degree of autonomy is placed on these teams.

3. A project backlog is created, often utilizing a task board.

   The kids write down the requirements. The teacher facilitates as a scrum master and keeps everyone focused.

4. Using sticky notes on a white board, wall, or blackboard, children get involved with ordering and prioritizing them.

   Children love the sense of accomplishment that comes from seeing things move from to *do* to *doing* to *done.*

5. Each project session begins with a daily scrum. The students are actually using scrum language, like daily scrums, scrum master, and sprint reviews.

6. At the end of each sprint, conduct both the review and retrospective. Buy-in increases, and when appropriate, the students can contribute to the goals for new projects.

Children enjoy the hands-on process and progress. They can quickly see progress and are amazingly flexible in adapting. In short, as you saw in

The Marshmallow Challenge in Chapter 1, kids naturally think in terms of the iterative process. Scrum is just a formalized way of dealing with natural brain wiring.

eduScrum

In a town called Alphen aan de Rijn in The Netherlands, scrum is being used in a high school and secondary educational college. It is called eduScrum and educators using it are experiencing amazing results.

Teachers and students are using scrum in all subjects, and they form scrum teams with all the scrum roles intact. Three teacher scrum masters are leading the charge, each facilitating the process in their respective class. They also conduct daily scrums on the projects, and sprint reviews and retrospectives. They collected data on the results of this process with 230 students, ranging in age from 12 to 17 years old.

The quantitative results were impressive. In The Netherlands, test scores fall in a range of 1 to 10. A score of 5.5 is fine, but students strive for 6.7 or better. The students participating on teams using scrum consistently outperformed those who didn't by a range of 0.8 to 1.7. In terms of percentages, these are significant increases.

Furthermore qualitatively, half the students said they

- ✔ Understood the subject material better
- ✔ Had more fun (hugely important for learning)
- ✔ Could work harder and faster
- ✔ Felt they were learning in a "smarter" way

Teachers also noticed greater engagement from their students and an overall more positive experience. Interestingly, this is often what corporations and organizations report when they incorporate scrum — improved employee morale.

An interesting side effect of scrum in schools was that the students reported just plain having more fun with classes and learning. This made them more eager to go to school and participate. And those shy, quiet types? They flourished as their skills and contributions were noticed in the reviews and retrospectives.

The team atmosphere also came out shining. Well over half the students learned to cooperate better and developed trust in their team members.

They opened up to giving and receiving feedback, and the teachers noticed a more relaxed atmosphere.

Blueprint

Blueprint High School in Chandler, Arizona, is a nonprofit organization that creates and implements special education options. It sees using scrum in its classes as a way to prepare its students for the twenty-first century workplace.

Leaders at Blueprint High School decided that having a high school diploma wasn't enough to prepare the school's students for the twenty-first century. They also needed skills in collaboration, creativity, accountability, critical thinking, and teamwork. Interestingly, these are all qualities that scrum naturally fosters.

One of the key components in teaching scrum was getting students to go from determining the "what" in their projects to the "how."

With Blueprint, the scrum roles were more flexible based on the individual team context. Sometimes the teacher would be the product owner or scrum master, and other times, the students took on these roles. As the teams matured and garnered more experience (as young as fourth-graders), they automatically took over the role of product owner. The teachers simply identified the type of projects to be completed, and then the students took over by developing their own goals, implementation, and reviews.

Collaboration and teamwork skills took off.

While Blueprint didn't conduct the type of quantitative study that eduScrum did, Blueprint experienced many positive anecdotal outcomes:

- ✔ Greater student engagement
- ✔ More fun
- ✔ Greater empathy for each other
- ✔ Independent thinking
- ✔ An overall more positive educational experience

One teacher even said that her kids would even come in if they were sick because they didn't want to miss a single day of school! That really is wholehearted buy-in from students.

The Military and Law Enforcement

Many agile and scrum experts have an appreciation for agile principles and the scrum framework because of their experience in the military. That's been the case for me as well as others, such as Sean Dunn and Benjamin Saville, who shared some of their experiences with me.

Militaries are mistakenly perceived to value strong centralized decision making. However, military strategists have long since known that centralized decision making quickly leads to defeat on the battlefield: A commander cannot possibly see all parts of the battlefield nor communicate fast enough to understand the chaotic and rapidly changing situation or exploit fleeting opportunities. Wise commanders understand that they must empower those at all levels to make timely decisions.

In 1871, German military strategist Helmuth von Moltke (the Elder) sagely observed that "no battle plan survives contact with the enemy." It was his approach to decentralized decision making that today is known to the military as "Mission Command." U.S. Army Chief of Staff General Raymond Odienro describes mission command as

> "... the conduct of military operations through decentralized execution, using mission orders to enable disciplined initiative within the commander's intent. Done well, it empowers agile and adaptive leaders to successfully operate under conditions of uncertainty, exploit fleeting opportunities, and most importantly achieve unity of effort. Importantly, it helps establish mutual trust and shared understanding throughout the force. Mission Command is fundamental to ensuring that our Army stays ahead of and adapts to the rapidly changing environments we expect to face in the future."

The principles of Mission Command are practiced by most western militaries, including the U.S. Marine Corps and U.S. Army. In fact, the U.S. Army operates the Mission Command Center of Excellence to train leaders in the methods of decentralized decision making.

Traditional military consists of huge command-and-control structures. Thank goodness we have had leaders willing to make difficult decisions, and we have had soldiers ready to carry out tough orders. However, more and more military leaders are now seeing that all command and control may not be the ideal approach after all.

In 2007, General David Petraeus reversed the course of the Iraq war by enabling small, cross-functional teams to make decisions that fueled the counterinsurgency on the ground in Baghdad. "Security of the population, especially in Baghdad, and in partnership with the Iraqi Security Forces, will be the focus of the military effort," Petraeus said. In many ways, agile teams are analogous to the special forces teams. They are both small, highly trained, highly professional, cohesive, and cross-functional. Special forces teams are small in size and cross-functional to bring situational-appropriate actions to bear. Cross-functionality, remember, means that every member of the team can do more than one thing, and ideally everyone on the team can do every skill necessary.

Like agile teams, special forces teams are stable and long-lived. Through hard-earned experience, they know how to work together and trust each other, and will all pitch in to do whatever is needed to accomplish the mission. That mission may require fluency in a foreign language, building relationships with local villagers, or even skilled use of deadly force if necessary. The mission may call for any combination of those things, yet carrying out the mission may involve something completely different. Special forces teams know how to learn and adapt.

Another similarity is that both agile and special forces teams create a sense of mutual accountability. In high-stakes situations, whether in business or on the battlefield, the desire to not let down a team member is more important than any deadline.

Like scrum sprints, missions for military teams are normally broken down and can be accomplished very quickly, within weeks at the longest. Longer missions wear out soldiers, deplete supplies, and require significant ongoing support. You find an exponential correlation to the length of a mission and the cost and rate of failure. Short missions provide better focus, team morale, and success.

One of the many examples where a military commander succeeded by changing his command-and-control approach is Admiral Nelson at Trafalgar. Instead of requiring strict adherence to signal flags hoisted on his flagship, Nelson delegated quite substantial authority to ship captains: "In case signals can neither be seen or perfectly understood, no captain can do very wrong if he places his ship alongside that of the enemy."

Cybersecurity and warfare

Cybersecurity and warfare are the new global battlefield. Frequent, fast, and thorough inspection and adaptation to keep up with, and even stay ahead of, attackers will be crucial to a nation's survival.

The United States Department of Defense (DoD) has implemented a series of Information Assurance directives (8570.01 and 8570.01-M), ensuring certification baselines for security essentials. These encompass a broad spectrum of skills and focus areas. These certifications correspond to the individual's level of responsibility and experience, and they all require continuing education to maintain the most current skill sets.

The primary challenge is to always be prepared for an enemy of unknown size and sophistication, who may have unlimited resources and the ever-growing threat of exploitation due to changes in technology. All active participants are constantly striving to be bigger, better, and faster than their adversaries.

DoD components will often assign a tiger team to address an incident that requires immediate attention and requires a collaborative and expedient solution. The teams are small and consist of a combination of specialists and cross-functional members. The primary goal of the tiger team is to run the problem to ground and document the results through after-action reports and repositories for lessons learned (retrospectives resulting in actionable improvement plans).

Like special forces, tiger teams have close parallels to scrum. Although they will usually have a defined leader, they are typically wholly collaborative and are accustomed to flexibility in response to a changing environment as they address their respective incidents.

Scrum and the FBI

Cyberattacks of all sorts, from credit card hacking to government and military security threats, are increasing around the world. Military and cyberwarfare experts agree that controlling this expanding threat is a major concern. Cyberthreat deterrence programs that can adapt to the ever-changing nature of these sophisticated challenges are needed — and needed fast. In many cases, it's an issue of national security.

The FBI has been increasingly active in finding solutions for responding to these cyberattacks on a national and criminal level. Leadership knows that using old techniques for handling these uber-modern threats isn't enough. New ways of applying technology, shaping their workforce, and collaborating with partners are required.

Not surprisingly, they're approaching this conundrum with scrum in mind.

As published by the FBI's Information Technology Strategic Plan for FY 2010–2015, the FBI is in fact creating

". . . an agile enterprise with evolution toward consolidated and shared infrastructure, services and applications. As part of the agile environment, the FBI will sustain a rigid information security management program, implementing tools and processes to enhance utilization of the Enterprise Architecture (EA) through virtualization and abstraction. Strategically, the FBI will focus on fully understanding, adopting and integrating a shared services approach to IT and business challenges."

After the 9/11 terrorist attacks, the FBI began to work on streamlining its flow of information and coordination with all relevant entities. After a couple of false starts, it developed the Sentinel program: a comprehensive software case management system. The goal is to replace a current system consisting of a mixture of digital and paper information flow with a purely digital one.

For ten years, the project was conducted using the FBI's prescribed waterfall methods, including extensive up-front design and fixed requirements. In 2008, a new CIO, Chad Fulgham, started requiring incremental delivery from the contracted developers. Specifically, by 2010, scrum was used officially. Here are some of the symptoms of the waterfall process used up to that point:

- ✔ Only 4 of 18 workflows were live, but with defects.
- ✔ Less than 1 percent of the 14,000+ forms were created in the new system.
- ✔ Cost to date was $405 million, with an estimated $350 million more to go over six years.
- ✔ All delivered functionality was considered optional throughout the organization.

When scrum was implemented, excess staff was cut by more than 50 percent, user stories were created, and 21 two-week sprints were scheduled — an 85 percent decrease in projected schedule.

Healthcare, education, and the military and law enforcement all have one important thing in common — people's lives: our health and well-being, our knowledge and preparation for the future, and our security. Scrum works in each of these areas, in real lives, for real people, and for real changes for the better.

Chapter 10

Publishing

"History will be kind to me, for I intend to write it."

— Winston Churchill

In any disruptive environment, quick and pivoting innovation tactics are needed. Publishing and the news media are going through massive changes right before our eyes. Traditional products and readers are all changing, and no one knows where it will end.

Publishing houses and news organizations need to continue monetizing current products and also finding new sources of revenue. For instance, trying out a new form of native advertising (such as ads intermingled in a feed of news articles) needs a quick turnaround time and a quick response to customer feedback. Promoting a new book through an author's existing social media channels, or developing new revenue-generating ideas for customer feedback, requires a disciplined feedback cycle, focused development, and close interaction with the customer.

Scrum can handle this type of shifting landscape smoothly. When the goalposts keep moving, it doesn't make any sense to aim for where they used to be. We don't know how publishing and news will continue to evolve, so instead we can inspect and adapt along the way. Those in publishing that are most successful are doing just that.

The Iterative Angle

Enormous rates of change are occurring. Brick-and-mortar bookstores are dying and readers have shifted ways of finding new books and authors. Even libraries are receiving less funding, and much of their shelf space is being converted to computers and other media.

On top of this, readers can now choose between reading on desktops, mobile platforms, and less and less, traditional hardback and paperback books. Now, different forms of media are competing against each other for the same content.

In this new publishing environment, traditional revenue models are vanishing. Given the changes in the revenue streams for both advertising and subscriptions, new models are needed, those that can take advantage of this new digital world. But publishers are still working through discovering what that will come to be.

The music industry experienced a similar seismic shift. Traditional "album" buying flew out the door when iTunes flew in. Free, and often illegal, music downloads stirred up a fresh debate on copyright law (enriching scores of lawyers along the way), and avenues for music today are dramatically different from those 10 and 20 years ago. However, music still exists, new songs and albums are created all the time, and musical life goes on. It just looks different.

The same can be said about the future of publishing. For some, massive industry changes are terrifying; for others, opportunity is recognized, flexibility is sought, and inspect and adapt are seen as paramount. A problem that some publishers identify is that because of the rapidity of change, they're not sure which data they should use to form their decisions. The sand is shifting right under their feet.

No surprise to you by now, this is why scrum can help the publishing industry continue to flourish. The very qualities that so many find unsettling — rapid change, shifting consumer needs and desires, uncertain sources of revenue — are the ones in which scrum excels.

Inspection, adaptation, and refactoring

As you've seen, this is the heart of scrum, and it fits the world of publishing more than ever. As with each industry I cover, publishing has its own unique set of challenges and scrum-based solutions.

Changing readers

What a reader expects from a book, magazine article, or newspaper feed is changing. Immediate information and instant gratification are the norm. Unless the author is already a huge bestseller with a wide following, no longer will most readers sit down and finish a 1,000-page tome.

In business books, a standard measurement for correct page count is the time it takes to read it on an LA-to-NYC flight.

Incorporating rapid feedback from readers, via short articles, blogs, and analytical tracking tools for reader click-through rates and responses, a flood of data can be accessed. News media, publishers, and individual authors can quickly see what readers are responding to and adjust accordingly.

Not only does this rapid feedback cycle mean better content, but it also means faster monetization. As you inspect and adapt on the go, you're able to follow those paths that lead to more clicks and hits, and therefore incorporate more revenue streams through advertising and sales.

Changing writers

Hugh Howey broke more than one traditional mold with his New York Times bestselling novel *Wool*. He published the original short story on Amazon for 99 cents a copy and received such overwhelming positive response that he kept on writing.

Howey then wrote and self-published five serial stories, getting feedback from readers with each one, and combined them to create the book *Wool Omnibus* (self-published by Broad Reach Publishing). It landed on the New York Times bestseller list and created a sweet seven-figure revenue stream for him.

Serial stories produced in sprints. Feedback from readers and potential book buyers. Using self-publishing where each detail could be inspected and adapted along the way. The entire success story was an unintentional variation of scrum.

After self-publishing and reaching the New York Times bestseller list, Howey signed a contract with a traditional publishing firm, Simon & Schuster. In yet another mold-shattering move, he sold only the print rights to the publisher, and kept all digital rights and proceeds for himself. This was a previously unheard-of deal.

Changing products

What and how people read are also in flux. Graphic novels, manga, and interactive serials combine with novels, articles, and blogs to create a wide net within which authors place their work. Add to this e-readers, smartphone apps, and steadily decreasing hard copy, and you have an unrecognizable world in front of you.

No author or reader is left untouched by this literary revolution. T.S. Eliot's classic epic poem *The Waste Land* now has its own iPad app. But this isn't just a copy-and-pasted edition of the text. Look at the features that are incorporated:

- ✔ A filmed performance of the poem by Fiona Shaw
- ✔ Audio readings by T.S. Eliot himself, and other greats like Alec Guinness and Viggo Mortensen
- ✔ Interactive notes to help the reader with cultural references and poetic nuances
- ✔ Videos of literary experts providing insight on the masterpiece
- ✔ Original manuscript pages to show the reader how the poem developed under the editorial guidance of Ezra Pound

In short, for anyone into masterpieces, this app has more than any before. The key is to notice how the publishers (Faber and Touch Press) aren't sitting on the sidelines lamenting the good ol' days. They're jumping right in and producing great art in new ways.

For publishers and authors alike, scrum's feedback cycle allows for fast input and therefore an accelerated time to creating products that customers want and will pay for. Those that embrace this change, and incorporate agile frameworks (like scrum) that allow for it, are excelling in this new environment.

"Survival of the fastest to change" is the mantra. See change as an opportunity, and you will come out on top.

Applying scrum

Just like in software, content can be easily and frequently inspected, adapted, and refactored until it's ready for publication. Obviously, for shorter works, this is easier. But it can be adapted to all sizes and lengths.

Blogging, for example, is a natural at inspect and adapt. Write the blog and with analytics you can now see an amazing array of data, such as

- How many people saw it
- What other pages of your website or blog they went to
- How long they stayed
- What links they followed

For longer pieces the process works as well. My first book, *Agile Project Management For Dummies* (published by John Wiley & Sons, Inc.), is a perfect example:

1. I established my vision for the book (a field guide that people who were really doing scrum could use as a reference).

2. I established a roadmap: the book outline.

3. I broke the outline into book sections (my releases).
   Each chapter then became its own sprint.

4. I started with Chapter 1, writing it according to Wiley's *For Dummies* development standards.

   After I sent Chapter 1 to my Wiley editor, I was told that she hated it and why (feedback, feedback, feedback).

5. I implemented that feedback in Chapter 1, identified the lessons learned, and used what I learned to write Chapter 2.

   I sent Chapter 2 to my Wiley editor and was told that she didn't much like it and why (feedback, feedback, feedback).

6. I improved Chapter 2 and used what I learned to write Chapter 3. This time, when I sent Chapter 3 to my Wiley editor, she told me, "It's okay, but it would be better if you . . ." (feedback, feedback, feedback).

This cycle continued until we had synced up with Chapter 5.

Had I written all 20 chapters, sent it all to Wiley at once, and had my editor say she hated it, I would not have a book in the marketplace today.

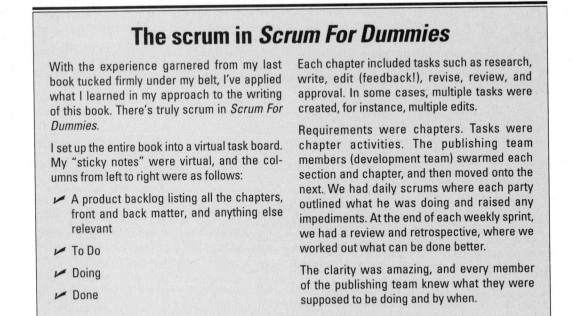

The scrum in *Scrum For Dummies*

With the experience garnered from my last book tucked firmly under my belt, I've applied what I learned in my approach to the writing of this book. There's truly scrum in *Scrum For Dummies*.

I set up the entire book into a virtual task board. My "sticky notes" were virtual, and the columns from left to right were as follows:

- A product backlog listing all the chapters, front and back matter, and anything else relevant
- To Do
- Doing
- Done

Each chapter included tasks such as research, write, edit (feedback!), revise, review, and approval. In some cases, multiple tasks were created, for instance, multiple edits.

Requirements were chapters. Tasks were chapter activities. The publishing team members (development team) swarmed each section and chapter, and then moved onto the next. We had daily scrums where each party outlined what he was doing and raised any impediments. At the end of each weekly sprint, we had a review and retrospective, where we worked out what can be done better.

The clarity was amazing, and every member of the publishing team knew what they were supposed to be doing and by when.

News Media and Scrum

How many people do you know still get a newspaper delivered to their door every morning? How many young people do you know who subscribe to a printed paper?

The news media has experienced a seismic shift all its own. Print has gone online, advertising changes with every new medium (such as print, radio, TV, online, social, and mobile), and a reader's news-gathering experience has metamorphosed.

But remember, in scrum, change is good. Or, at least, scrum helps you harness that change for improvement.

What the industry is experiencing is disruption. Clayton Christensen coined the concept of "disruptive innovation" and describes it as "a process by which a product or service takes root initially in simple applications at the bottom of a market and then relentlessly moves up market, eventually displacing established competitors."

The biggest challenges for traditional print media organizations are finding ways to monetize their current product offerings, as well as going digital — expanding their product offering to digital news products, including digital advertising. Print and digital are two different beasts. Smart media companies that have both a print and digital presence have separated the two sides of their businesses to allow them to each do what they do best. The digital side of these companies, as pointed out in Chapter 7, implement scrum. But what about the traditional sides?

Brady Mortensen, a newsroom veteran and senior director (product owner) of publishing systems at Deseret Digital Media said,

> *"In reality, news organizations have probably been practicing a lot of scrum techniques for many years without realizing it. Daily scrum meetings are not uncommon. With local TV stations or daily papers, the "sprint" length is one day and the end product is a collection of newscasts and a paper. There is also a usable product created at the end of each cycle. Newsrooms live and die by these practices. What would help traditional news organizations is to recognize that what they already do is scrum-like, but to embrace the techniques even more."*

The presses that are flourishing in this new environment are those that have proven nimble — and especially those that have adopted scrum to identify their highest-risk areas at regular intervals, and then pivot (inspect and adapt).

Firms such as The Washington Post, The Chicago Tribune, and NPR all use aspects of scrum in their newsrooms. Some of their specific techniques are as follows:

- The Chicago Tribune begins with asking who are the end users, what are their needs, and what features can we include to fulfill those needs? It then prioritizes features in piles labeled "must," "want," "nice," and "meh." The paper tosses out the bottom two piles and works from feature to feature. When the deadline arrives, it stops.

- The assigning editor is usually the product owner. The development team consists of journalists, designers, photographers, editors, and others related to developing content.

- Scrum helps reduce the number of meetings, which can be overwhelming, especially in digital media.

- NPR uses a two-week sprint cycle, with a two-hour-long sprint planning meeting at the start.

- Stand-up daily scrums are used and last for 15 minutes. Teams coordinate who's working on what stories, and impediments are identified and removed.

✔ The Washington Post has a specific agile technique for developing content for its live blogging platform:

- The Post always begins with a vision — what is the effect it wants to have on the user?

- Daily scrum meetings.

- A development team might be a developer, designer, editor, and reporter.

- Pairing up for work is common, and The Post used it long before implementing scrum. Two journalists sit at the same desk and finish the project. This intensifies the work and limits distractions.

- The goal is to go live with the news as soon as possible, and then get feedback from the users and the group.

- Based on the feedback, adapt and adjust from there.

Definition of done for content

Using scrum to develop nonsoftware products and services, like content for publication, is really quite similar to using scrum for software. The definition of done for content development teams should clearly outline what it means to consider content that's ready for prime time.

Going back to our roadmap to value, a publishing scrum team should have a vision statement that specifically states what their readers' needs are, how the publication meets the needs of their readers and is differentiated in their market and industry, and how this ties in to their corporate strategy (for more on vision statements, see Chapter 2).

The roadmap reflects this vision by outlining the areas of editorial emphasis to be covered by the publication, including any seasonal considerations. The product backlog is a prioritized and ordered list of proposed features, series, and stories to be researched, developed, edited, and published.

The vision is the framework for defining what it means to have "done" content, one story or article at a time. The definition of done might look something like this:

With each article, we have succeeded in fulfilling our vision to [statement of how the need is met and differentiated] after we have

✔ Addressed the who, what, when, where, and why in the lead. Those elements are not buried.

✔ Ensured balance, making sure that both sides of an issue are represented.

- ✔ Ensured that search engine optimization (SEO) standards and requirements are met in article elements such as headline, tags, and body.

- ✔ Cited at least one source for each side of the issue.

- ✔ Checked twice for accuracy to avoid embellishing and bias.

- ✔ Prepared accompanying content for social media posts.

- ✔ Verified that line edits and copyedits are completed.

A newsroom where these criteria are front and center for content curators, editors, and producers to see at all times provides consistency and clarity on what is expected and what success looks like.

A news user story? Often scrum teams and stakeholders that use the user story format for requirements shorten their colloquial reference to them as "story" or "stories." So, this can make for some amusing conversations in a news organization. For instance, "How close to finishing that story are we?" might require a follow-up clarification. Whether it's an actual news story or a user story about publishing news, anything on the news organization's product backlog can be broken down and developed by the scrum team.

NPR uses scrum for developing its content-delivering platforms. Zach Brand, NPR's head of all things digital said, "We found out that an unintended consequence of implementing agile at NPR is that it has begun to break down silos between digital and other departments . . . by involving stakeholders from other departments in the product development process."

The news media scrum team

A content team director for a major regional news site identified the following scrum implementation. This team's role was to curate, edit, and post daily content to the site. Scrum is still applied, but they weren't developing code. Their adoption of scrum covered the following issues:

- ✔ What is the end product? News content customers want to read.

- ✔ What is the product backlog? Potential news stories and associated media posts. This was constantly changing.

- ✔ What is the release? Continuous delivery. Content is delivered as soon as it is edited and approved.

- ✔ What is the sprint duration? The 24-hour news cycle.

- ✔ When is sprint planning? First thing every morning. Discuss the backlog stories that have received editing approval.

- ✔ When is the sprint review? End of each day or before sprint planning each morning, which includes a review of the articles published and resulting analytics for inspection and adaptation for the next sprint's articles.

- ✔ Who is the development team? Content curators, reporters, photographers, editors, graphic artists, and videographers.

- ✔ Who is the product owner? The managing editor.

- ✔ Who is the scrum master? A member of the development team who understands and has experience with scrum, and has the organizational clout to remove impediments for the team.

- ✔ Who does backlog refinement and when? The entire development team and the product owner throughout each day, curating and evaluating proposed news stories, including breaking news as it happens.

When these basic questions are asked, the broader picture comes to light. Each role, artifact, and event can be identified and assigned. It's just a matter of taking the time to see how scrum fits in this industry's model.

Sprint flexibility

Daily sprints in a news organization often provide the flexibility needed for daily news feeds. You can't plan on the news five days from now, but you can plan out a day of story time — most of the time. Breaking and unexpected news stories can be dealt with during the sprint with direct communication between the team members.

Media with longer content cycles, like magazines (online and/or in print form), can have longer sprint cycles for content. Each feature — whether a section, article, chapter, or other segment — can be broken down into requirements and tasks when appropriate.

Part IV
Scrum for Business Functions

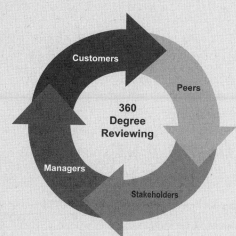

In this part . . .

- ✔ Optimizing project portfolio performance.
- ✔ Scaling scrum across 1,000+ person project teams.
- ✔ Funding projects incrementally and profitably.
- ✔ Developing the right talent for scrum.
- ✔ Maximizing business development and customer service teams.
- ✔ Enhancing IT and maintenance value and efficiency.
- ✔ Visit www.dummies.com/extras/scrum for great Dummies content online.

Chapter 11

IT Management and Operations

Any sufficiently advanced technology is equivalent to magic.

— Sir Arthur C. Clarke

*I*n Chapter 7, I discuss scrum in the software development industry, and you've seen several examples of scrum's power in this arena. Some people assume that information technology (IT) and software are one and the same. But this is way off the mark.

Software development has to do with the creation of software applications that run on computer systems and electronic devices. Information technology is all about computer and telecommunications systems for storing, sending, and retrieving information.

Not every organization has a software development division (although more and more do), but it's rare indeed to find an organization that can survive without a staff of IT professionals devoted to the smooth flow and security of information.

However, IT operations can vary widely from one organization to another. Their roles and responsibilities might differ, and even within an individual group, the type of work done might vary from day to day and quarter to quarter. On top of this, IT is experiencing rapid changes as technology continues to evolve and possibilities are racing ahead.

Like any growing field, challenges abound. When the system gets overwhelmed and services get interrupted, mission-critical work may be delayed, or even stopped, resulting in increased costs, wasted resources, loss of revenue, and even loss of customers. And the backlog of an IT team can fill up as fast as any team out there.

In this chapter, I look at IT management and operations, and describe how scrum, once again, provides time- and cost-saving solutions for modern-day challenges.

Big Data and Large-Scale Migration

The sheer scale of data today is astounding, and even as I write this, it's getting bigger. Trying to get your head around the size of big data is much like trying to picture a huge mathematical phenomenon — like the speed of the expanding universe. It's so big that it goes beyond what most people can imagine.

Consider some numbers:

- Walmart conducts 1 million transactions per hour, which feeds databases of over 2.5 petabytes (which is about 167 times the size of the data in all the books in the Library of Congress).
- Facebook houses over 40 billion photographs.
- eBay handles 50 petabytes of information *every day*.
- To decode the human genome, 3 billion base pairs must be analyzed. The first time, it took 10 years; now it takes one week.
- Cisco estimates that in 2013, the amount of annual Internet traffic reached 667 exabytes.

What's in an *exabyte?* One billion gigabytes, or 10^{18} bytes of digital information. It goes like this:

- 1 byte is the equivalent of a single digital character of text (such as the letter a).
- 1 KB is a kilobyte, or roughly 1000 bytes of digital information.
- 1 MB is a megabyte, or 1 million (1000^2) bytes of digital information.
- 1 GB is a gigabyte, or 1 billion (1000^3) bytes of digital information.
- 1 TB is a terabyte, or 1 trillion (1000^4) bytes of digital information.

✔ 1 PB is a petabyte, or 1 quadrillion (1000^5) bytes of digital information.

✔ 1 EB is an exabyte, or one quintillion (1000^6) bytes of digital information (over 245 million DVDs).

The importance of big data can't be overstated. It's not only huge in quantity, but much of this data is also highly personal and sensitive and can affect lives as well as bottom lines. The challenge is to gather, manage, and interpret data quickly, effectively, and correctly. Additionally, the possible future use for this data as we design these processes for storing and retrieval must be considered. All of this data needs to become useful intelligence, not just data. The old ways of doing this are now insufficient. Big data is projected to grow 800 percent over the next five years.

A significant challenge is that 80 percent of this data is unstructured (such as emails, blogs, spreadsheets, text documents, images, video, voice, and search logs). This unstructured segment is growing faster than structured data. In other words, the majority of data is a huge mess. It is data, not information.

Data security and protecting privacy are more important than ever; at the same time, it's more difficult to ensure than ever. Traditional data management frameworks and processes are just not capable of processing this quantity. Speed, flexibility, and instant feedback are needed (by now I'm sure this sounds familiar). Six months is too long to hope that a new, untested system works. And chances are, by the time six months comes around, the requirements have changed, or even more worrisome, a new gap has not yet been identified.

To deal with this tsunami of data, many firms and organizations are moving to the cloud. Many even have their own in-house clouds or virtualized environments. (See Chapter 7 for details about cloud computing.)

Data warehouse project management

Data warehouse projects are traditionally thought to be difficult to manage. While each segment or phase of the project may have a discernible beginning and end, the data warehouse itself is never finished, but is continually growing and changing.

A *data warehouse* isn't some barbed-wire-fenced building on the outskirts of town. Rather, it's a process or framework for handling data within a firm or organization. It's a knowledge-based applications architecture that facilitates strategic and tactical decision making.

A further complexity is that continuous merger and acquisition activity brings in enterprise-wide data integration issues. New assets and groups are acquired or spun off, and their corresponding data and processes need to be managed. Maintaining diverse legacy applications that don't integrate well can be more costly then conversion projects.

An example of the successful implementation of scrum is that of a multibillion dollar energy company with operations in the United States and Brazil. Frequent mergers and acquisitions created a need for the timely and accurate integration of data. Senior management needed reports created on the new entities and their new products and customers. Specifically, they were focused on energy-efficiency projects to keep a strong hold on that customer segment.

However, the data existed in multiple formats across multiple applications, including budget and financial data in spreadsheets, a customer relationship management (CRM) tool, and data from a variety of cloud-based customer surveys.

Steps in the scrum integration process went like this:

1. Roles were established:

   - The stakeholders were identified as the end users.

   - The product owner represented the stakeholders and sponsors.

   - The project manager became the scrum master.

   - The development team was represented by the data architect, system architect, and an ETL (extract, transform, load) architect/resource.

2. The stakeholders and product owner determined a highest-priority starting point — budget data.

3. Extract, transform, and load (ETL) was the scope of the initial project chunk. As data became available, the product owner worked with stakeholders to identify reports that could be implemented incrementally, and plugged them into the product backlog for prioritization into upcoming sprints.

4. Sprint 1 is executed: Budget data was loaded into the data warehouse. The data was then verified using sample reports.

5. Sprint 2 is executed: CRM data was loaded into the data warehouse. Sample reports were also used to validate the data.

6. A result of the second sprint was that stakeholders identified new requirements in the budget data after comparing it against the loaded CRM data. These were added to the product backlog and prioritized.

7. Sprint 3 is executed: Survey data was loaded and validated with sample reports.

8. From the third sprint, new data sources were discovered and loaded during the sprint.

9. Sprint 4 is executed: Integration of all three data sources was verified with sample reports.

10. In the remaining sprints, reports were written according to priority.

In a matter of months, not years, the entire database migration was finished. The data warehouse was fully functional, and a process was in place for managing new data and changes along the way. Part of the reason for the success of this project was how business and development teams worked together toward common goals.

ETL stands for extract (read the data), transform (convert the data), and load (write the data), which are three database engineering functions used to pull data from one database to put it into another.

The process was also quicker to market because it didn't entail the waterfall approach of loading all possible data from all possible sources and then testing. Rather, the highest-priority data was implemented first, in phases, and inspected and adapted along the way. New findings were incorporated in the very next sprint, and the next-highest-priority data was implemented next.

Enterprise resource planning

Enterprise resource planning (ERP) is a suite of integrated and dynamic software applications that organizations and corporations use to gather, manage, interpret, and integrate business processes, including planning, purchasing, manufacturing, inventory, marketing, sales, distribution, finance, and HR.

Implementing an ERP system usually means doing simultaneous development across various functional areas (such as marketing, sales, inventory, and purchasing) to conduct a specific business transaction. Implementation involves the design and configuration of many modules simultaneously. These modules, while being developed individually, must also be designed for cross-functional application. For example, while designing the sales module, careful consideration is given to both the upstream and downstream processes.

To picture this, think of how sales fits in the overall "end-to-end" process. You start with inventory, and subsequently you need to be able to bill your orders. Therefore, the sales module must seamlessly integrate with both your inventory module as well as your finance module (and your inventory module with your manufacturing and purchasing modules must integrate with your finance modules, and so on).

Unfortunately, the design and build of these individual modules traditionally take years before the integrated testing phase even begins. By this time, any gaps between the two will require even more time to identify and fix. One small gap between sales and finance can result in months of extra work. And it is common that this "fix" may not integrate perfectly with another module somewhere else in the process. With everyone working in "silos" until the integrated testing phase, early detection of gaps and misfits is prevented.

Traditionally, ERP providers handled this interdependency by locking in a specific development sequence. In fact, even parameters that won't be used needed to be specifically configured in the order defined by the ERP provider.

Now, with scaled scrum teams (see Chapter 12), we can do that customization in parallel, with each scrum team focusing on a specific functional area and using automated integration testing to ensure that the business transaction works across the modules. Following agile techniques allows the integration testing to occur every day (from day one) as opposed to months of back and forth, years into the project.

Although it may seem that these modular interdependencies are a liability, they actually make it easier to divide the work into chunks that fit into separate scrum teams running synchronized sprints. Product backlog prioritization is set at the program level, and incremental requirement changes are minimized. Sprint backlog prioritization also falls in line. You maintain the flexibility of scrum and dramatically accelerate the pace of implementation. (Again, I dive deeper into this vertical slicing model in Chapter 12.)

ERP systems architecture is also increasingly becoming more SaaS (Software as a Service, see Chapter 7) oriented, which means that the monolith components are more modular than they used to be for client installations.

Also, the tasks required to configure ERP systems are usually repetitive, so cadence and estimation can be established early on and provide accurate sizing and timing predictions.

In Chapter 12, I talk more about scaling scrum across multiple teams. To tackle more of an ERP implementation project at once to speed delivery, multiple teams may be used to work on each of the business function components at the same time. Effective use of scaled scrum will enable multiple scrum teams to structure their definition of done to include integration, regression, performance, security, and regression testing at the sprint level rather than the release. This will be required because the nature of ERP systems is that after you introduce conflicts into production, they are very difficult to correct. Teams learn early on to be disciplined with their definition of done.

I've also found that scrum works really well with these types of projects when they're focused on delivering business intelligence for the organiza-tion. Visual reports of data have a clear business-focused requirement for the user of the report. The work to prepare the data (such as aggregation and manipulation) makes up the tasks supporting the delivery of a report for the specified user (such as an executive or a manager).

Multiyear ERP implementations used to be common, but organizations cannot wait that long in today's fast-paced market. Organizations need solutions faster and cheaper. It's critical that customers see a return on their invest-ment as quickly as possible, while also improving customer satisfaction.

Iterating, inspecting, and adapting through scrum make this possible.

A nonprofit client of mine recently took on a massive conversion project of several legacy systems into a new enterprise resource planning (ERP) solu-tion. Historically, this would have been a nightmare job. An apt description would have been hammering a square peg into a round hole or herding cats. But even those euphemisms are easy challenges compared to combining diverse data management systems into one.

The roadmap that the client set up indicated an 18-month project life. The vision was an end-to-end solution for the company's management of global real estate resources. The steps it took are as follows:

1. Logistics. One team secured an open space that they organized into a scrum team room, complete with a full wall dedicated to a task board. Another team set up shop right next door within earshot for easy collaboration.

2. With the help of the stakeholders, the product owner determined the first minimum viable product (MVP) — a set of the most common pro-cesses relating to leasing activities. Users could benefit from these right away.

3. The release was planned, including a handful of sprints, with the new MVP as the goal. The team went to work.

4. Developers were added to the team who could set up third-party inte-grations without the need to send that task off to an outside team.

5. Shadowing and pairing were used immediately as the system was new to everyone. They wanted to achieve cross-functionality as quickly as possible.

   They also invited a member of the traditional deployment team to join full-time. He sat with the scrum team and learned the configuration steps during the sprints. This way, when it came time to deploy to production, this came off without a hitch thanks to shared knowledge and up-front testing.

6. The team moved on to integrate new features of the roadmap, while their customers enjoyed the benefits of the recently developed leasing features.

Much was learned from this first release that was incorporated into future releases for different aspects (such as planning, building, operations, and maintenance) of the new system. Through the scrum process, the team was able to get something in front of the customer quickly, enabling them to move forward comfortably on the next-highest-priority features.

The Service-versus-Control Conundrum

The value of an IT group is staggering. They're the heart that keeps information coursing throughout an organization. Technology systems that they manage become more and more sophisticated and complex. Added to this mix is the easy availability of other software applications and cloud resources, and an increased trend in employees bringing their own devices to work (BYOD) or bringing in outside applications (BYOA).

Recall that, BYOD in technology refers to *bring your own device,* specifically referring to the use of outside applications and tools not supported by internal IT. *BYOA* stands for *bring your own application.*

TrackVia conducted an online survey of 1,000 employees and 250 IT workers. It found the prevalence of BYOD and BYOA to be widespread. Some of TrackVia's results were as follows:

- ✔ 46 percent of senior IT employees believe that the use of outside applications is causing data leakage.

- ✔ 40 percent of respondents thought that their company didn't have the financial resources to provide the necessary IT tools and applications.

- ✔ 76 percent of IT workers realized that their outdated enterprise tools weren't giving their clients what they needed.

- ✔ 50 percent of IT workers don't expect employees to only use work devices and apps.

Shadow IT is IT tools and solutions being handled outside the organization's normal IT structure.

If employees don't feel that they have the tools they need from IT, it's a natural for them to seek solutions elsewhere — especially when those solutions are so readily available through SaaS and mobile apps. This loss of control becomes a significant concern for IT teams when nonsupported devices and applications create security risks or interfere with enterprise-approved solutions.

The fact is, a balance can be achieved between providing employees the tools they need to do their jobs and yet maintaining enough control and security. Consider the following:

- IT can't control the personal devices and apps that employees use, but they can control data access. Use scrum to develop apps that securely access the data. The scrum framework will narrow the features so that the MVP is quickly identified and implemented.

- Have IT members participate as stakeholders in other scrum teams' sprint reviews. This way, IT knows firsthand what the development teams are working on and what tools they're using. Questions can be asked on the spot, and needs can be addressed in a more informed manner.

- Likewise, invite department representatives to IT sprint review meetings to get their feedback on the IT roadmap. They can learn what's important to the organization for developing products. In this way, the business comes into alignment with IT.

Scrum provides the speed and customer alignment necessary to reduce shadow IT. Treat the issue, not the symptom, and do this by giving employees the tools they need, when they need them, in the way that they need them. Scrum helps you do this.

Security Challenges

You may have heard some of these terms: bots, worms, malware, phishing, security breach. For some, the Internet and its various manifestations are fertile ground for malicious activities. Major data breaches are making the headlines far too regularly. Following are just a few examples of companies and organizations that recently experienced compromised customer information:

- Oct. 2014, JPMorgan Chase: 76 million people
- Sept. 2014, Google: 5 million people

- Sept. 2014, Home Depot: 56 million people
- May 2014, eBay: 145 million people
- Feb. 2014, University of Maryland: 310,000 people
- Jan. 2014, KB Kookmin Card, Lotte Card, NH Nonghyup Card: 104 million people
- Dec. 2013, Target: 110 million people

Recent headlines have a similar ring:

- Oregon Employment Dept. Reports Breach
- "Mayhem" Malware Exploits Shellshock
- Kmart Says Payments Cards Breached
- Dairy Queen Confirms Card Breach
- Hackers Grab 800,000 Banking Credentials

Too often security is an afterthought. It's sometimes seen as "nice to have" and "we'll deal with it when it becomes a problem" rather than the very real issue that it is. Security risks are increasing and need to be addressed earlier rather than later. This section covers some common practices of how scrum can help expose security-related issues and facilitate improvements in how they're handled:

- Refine your definition of done. At both the release and sprint level, the definition of done is critical. Decide upon security requirements that should be met at each timebox to be considered done. By adding a security task to each requirement to address your definition of done, the costs of mitigating security risk can be spread out over the life of the project. Make it a high priority from the very first appropriate spot.

- As a scrum team member (any role), if security isn't as high a priority as you feel it should be, address it at the next retrospective. The business stakeholders and/or product owner may need to be trained on the issues. Identify the issues and place them in the product backlog.

- Have IT team members attend project team sprint reviews and provide security feedback.

- Consider establishing a security "guild" within the organization that promotes awareness and skill development surrounding security common practices and technologies throughout the organization.

Guilds

Guilds are groups of people across an organization that share common knowledge, tools, and practices. It's like a community of practice, where people engage regularly in collective learning and sharing knowledge around a common set of interests or practices. Examples of guilds might be security, system administration, database, quality, and scrum.

✔ Guilds should be open to anyone interested in mentoring others or learning more, including those who are new to the skill or practice.

✔ The guilds should meet often enough to build knowledge and increase learning and skill levels across an organization.

Consider making sure that at least one person on every scrum team becomes a member of the security guild. This will go a long way in ensuring that security practices are common and that awareness is being built across and throughout teams.

The Retiring-Boomer Gap

It's estimated that beginning in 2012, 10,000 baby boomers will become eligible for retirement every single day for the next 15 to 20 years. That's a lot or people, and many of them are IT professionals.

The entry-level employees taking their place come from a different generational mind-set. Personal growth and ambition are often higher values than staying with the same firm for an entire career. This means that those long-term employees you could always count on to be there will be fewer and fewer. The following common agile practices can help retain and grow newer employees:

✔ Create a mentoring program between those about to retire and their younger replacements. This increases the efficiency in transfer of knowledge as well as increases buy-in and loyalty.

✔ Give new IT employees projects and responsibilities outside their comfort zone. Give them training and new things to learn. This alone increases mental and emotional engagement. Guilds facilitate this process by providing pools of experts in each area. As well, senior- and junior-level developers working together enhances both party's skills.

✔ Build in cross-functionality activities like pairing and shadowing (see Chapter 4).

These activities can also help longer-term employees keep growing. People on their way out of organizations can sometimes resist change as they just want to finish out those last years before they retire. However, guilds can provide a means to tap into their expertise and immense value. Get these employees out of their comfort zones by organizing workshops, "lunch-and-learns," and training.

Lunch-and-learn sessions provide less formal opportunities over the lunch hour for those with specific technical knowledge to share what they know with other development team members and thereby enable cross-functionality across teams. If guilds are organized around certain knowledge areas, all development team members who are interested should be invited to participate in the lunch-and-learn sessions.

Encourage new people to grow, and then empower them with the means to do so. This is what most of us are after. Where boredom and routine can motivate people to leave for greener pastures, challenges, opportunities for growth and recognition, and a sense of purpose help people to stay and commit.

Profit-and-Loss Potential

As I mentioned previously, the business value of IT is immense. Its value needs to be communicated and demonstrated regularly to the rest of the organization. Sometimes, however, this value is overlooked in the face of problems that piggyback on technology. A huge opportunity lies in communicating clearly the value that IT brings to everyone involved — even if these benefits are only in the form of risks mitigated.

The key question to ask is, "Does this task or activity improve our organization's core priorities?" If so, keep it in and prioritize. If not, figure out how to eliminate that function and focus on mission-critical tasks.

Increasing visibility to the organization (through such artifacts as IT's prioritized product backlog and increments demonstrated at sprint reviews) gives insight to the entire organization of how IT works to remove bottlenecks in information and communications flow and provides the tools to enhance productivity. When the entire organization understands the value that IT brings, interactions between IT and other departments become more collaborative and IT's solutions become clear enablers of corporate strategy.

Just like a scrum team increasing their velocity from 25 to 27, all it takes is a small operational cost percentage savings to make a big bottom-line improvement over time.

Energy efficiency is a hot button these days and is one such example of how saving a little bit amounts to a lot over time. A wide array of tools are becoming available to help save costs on energy. Through better monitoring and application of energy-saving products, a few percentage points in cost can be saved; this allows IT to bring in more profits.

IBM estimates that IT and energy costs combined account for up to 75 percent of operational costs and up to 60 percent of capital expenditures in an organization.

It's estimated that a 25,000-square-foot data center uses over $4 million in energy each year. While this number won't be eliminated at once, by using incremental steps to inspect and adapt, costs can be decreased gradually and appropriately. A small percentage savings out of $4 million isn't bad.

Innovation versus Stability

Organizations rely on IT operations for stability, performance, and uptime. Yet they must also always be innovating, which implies the need for changing quickly and often. Stability and change conflict with each other. How can you have both?

This conflict is solved by tightening collaboration between operations and development teams. Rather than developing new technology and throwing it over the fence for operations to support, and vice versa, the operations side of the business builds sandboxes, or sets of standards within which development teams can build.

For instance, every time development teams make code changes in the process of innovation, they can breathe easy knowing that those code changes are made within the set of standards agreed upon between operations and development. Changes to database structures or designs within operational standards avoid the risks inherent in the same changes made in development silos with little or no collaboration with operations.

These standards are incorporated into a team's definition of done. IT can rest assured that within each sprint, the teams are staying in the sandbox with each requirement. When changes to the sandbox need to be made, development and operations consult and establish the new boundaries.

The need for improved coordination is key, especially with software development, and this is where "DevOps" comes in.

DevOps

Development Operations (DevOps, a portmanteau of the two words and also previously known as "agile operations") is a growing solution to a gap in developing software applications. Figure 11-1 shows an example of how DevOps addresses the coordination challenges described previously.

Development Operations (DevOps) stands for the collaboration and integration between software developers and IT operations. Through the DevOps process, developers and operations work together through the entire life cycle of product creation.

Traditional IT tasks are being shifted to DevOps team members. This not only offloads tasks from IT, but it also enables development teams with DevOps team members to take their product development further to production with fewer IT dependencies. Virtualized data centers make this increasingly possible because IT manages the platform, which makes creating new virtualized environments possible by someone with DevOps capabilities on a project scrum team.

What were once IT dependencies can now be done within the scrum team. Higher quality and a faster speed to finish are achieved within the sprints.

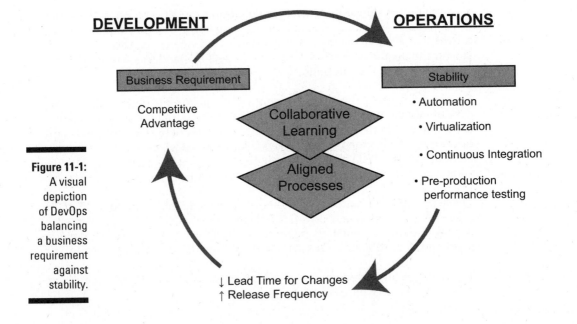

Figure 11-1:
A visual depiction of DevOps balancing a business requirement against stability.

Maintenance

After an application is deployed, maintenance teams provide the support. This can be in the form of responding to support inquiries, fixing defects, and implementing minor enhancements to address functionality gaps in production.

When scrum teams are focused on project work, whether software or IT, triaging operational issues is disruptive. Project and maintenance work are quite different. They require different types of work and effort by developers, which also involves a different cadence. If a project scrum team maintains operational or maintenance responsibilities, development of new functionality will be interrupted frequently, impacting release schedules of new business value and functionality to the customer. (See Chapter 12 for more about the cost of delay from thrashing a development team like this.)

By separating maintenance from the scrum teams' new development efforts, maintenance can be streamlined and new development can progress uninterrupted. I recommend a maintenance scrum team structure that separates these two functions so that interruptions are minimized without increasing overhead. See Figures 11-2 and 11-3.

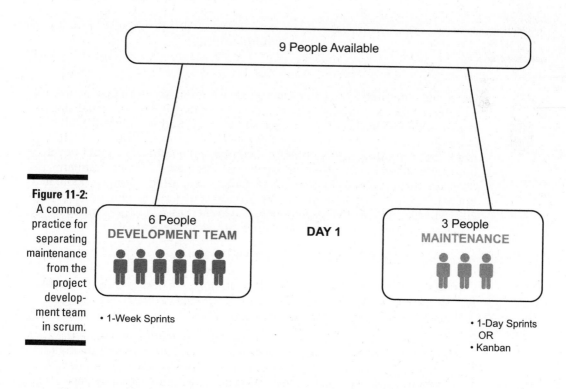

Figure 11-2: A common practice for separating maintenance from the project development team in scrum.

9 People Available

6 People
DEVELOPMENT TEAM

DAY 1

3 People
MAINTENANCE

• 1-Week Sprints

• 1-Day Sprints
OR
• Kanban

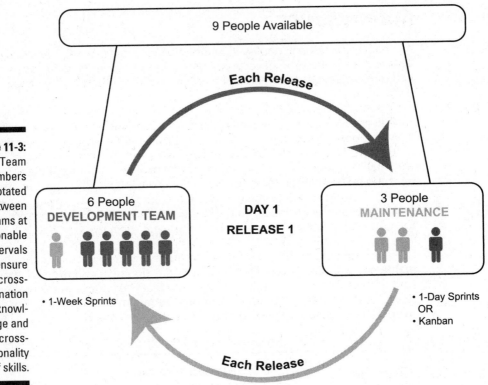

Figure 11-3:
Team
members
are rotated
between
teams at
reasonable
intervals
to ensure
cross-
pollination
of knowl-
edge and
cross-
functionality
of skills.

I introduce the kanban concept of a visual sign for managing a task board in Chapter 6. Some scrum and agile teams use a kanban board for visualizing their workflow. This is not to be confused with the Kanban Method, which is rooted in the Toyota Production System's just-in-time methods, which has become another approach to incremental and empirical product development in software and other industries besides manufacturing. Kanban does this through several practices, including visualizing workflow (kanban board), limiting work in progress (WIP), optimizing flow, making process policies explicit, and improving collaboratively. Whereas scrum prescribes roles, artifacts, and events, kanban is less prescriptive in these areas.

Here's how the process in Figures 11-2 and 11-3 works:

✔ At the start of a new release cycle, split out a small subset of the development team, with enough skill and knowledge to effectively maintain the product, into a maintenance team.

As shown in Figure 11-2, if you have a development team of nine to start with, you could take three developers and form a separate maintenance scrum team, leaving six developers to do new product development work in the existing scrum team. Your team size may vary.

Fewer or more than three maintenance team members may be needed. (Remember that although the existing scrum team is now smaller, they will no longer be thrashing between new product development and maintenance work. Fewer people does not mean less output. Actually, since thrashing has been eliminated, they should be able to significantly increase new product output.)

✔ The maintenance team runs one-day sprints or kanban, to respond to rapidly changing requirements (often changing daily). Each morning the team triages and plans the priorities for the day, executes the work planned throughout the day, and then at the end of the day reviews what was accomplished and clears it for release (release can happen anytime and does not need to happen daily).

✔ Maintenance teams can be smaller than new development teams. The product owner and scrum master for the maintenance team are often the same as for the project team. Thrashing is minimal, if at all, because it is a single application.

✔ At each project team release (or if your team releases often, at reasonable intervals, for example, 90 days), one member of the project team transitions to the operations team to be a full-time dedicated member, providing the necessary knowledge transfer for supporting the release. Again, thrashing is minimized because it is done at the release level, and the team members continue to work on the same product. See Chapter 14 for more about minimizing thrashing to maximize stability and profitability.

✔ At each release, likewise a member of the operations team transitions to the project team to be a full-time dedicated member of that team.

✔ Everyone eventually does both new development and operational work. There is no permanent "I'm on A team" or "I'm on B team" mentality.

✔ Cross-pollination of product and domain knowledge is a key benefit.

✔ Cross-functionality builds through rotations as well.

Kanban within a scrum structure

Maintenance teams typically run daily sprints or kanban rather than one week or longer sprints like project scrum teams. I often recommend running daily sprints instead of kanban because I like the forced product and process touch points associated with scrum's sprint review and retrospective; however, kanban can be effective if done within a scrum structure.

Kanban's practice of visualizing workflow fits right in line with scrum. Limiting work in progress is also something I've looked at in previous chapters that helps teams stay focused and get to done.

Managing flow and estimating based on lead time (elapsed time from the request to delivery)

(Continued)

and cycle time (elapsed time from the start of work to delivery) are also useful for teams using kanban. Scrum teams may find lead and cycle time useful in their planning and communicating with stakeholders, as well:

- ✔ Lead time is the amount of time between receiving a request and delivering it finished.

- ✔ Cycle time is the time between when it gets started and when it's delivered.

(Therefore, lead time is what the stakeholder often cares about.)

Teams using kanban are also aware of the theory of constraints, meaning that the team's system is limited in achieving more by a number of constraints. In scrum, velocity is a constraint, and the scrum master continually looks for ways to remove organizational drag to increase velocity, thus reducing it as a constraint.

Where kanban falls short by itself is its lack of a forced feedback mechanism. It's very easy for teams using kanban to avoid this feedback loop and perpetually communicate among themselves and with stakeholders: "Yeah, we have work in progress, and we're making progress." Sure, their kanban board is visible, but how effective are their inspect and adapt efforts for both the product and the process? Scrum provides that structure to kanban.

In the context of one-day sprints, if you're concerned about the overhead of these daily sprints, don't be. A one-day sprint is one-fifth of a one-week sprint. The time cost works out to be incredibly efficient and minimal. Have a look at the breakdown in minutes:

- ✔ Daily sprint planning rounds up to 25 minutes maximum. Be sure to involve the stakeholders who requested the requirement as needed to help clarify anything the development team will need to understand about the requirements.

- ✔ Daily sprint review becomes 15 minutes maximum.

- ✔ Daily sprint retrospective is 10 minutes maximum. Be sure to inspect and adapt every single day, even if you have an emergency and everyone just wants to go home.

- ✔ Also do retrospectives at macro levels, in sync with the development team's sprint retrospective, as this will allow for larger-scale inspection.

- ✔ Daily scrums won't be necessary because your sprint planning in the morning will take care of coordination and synchronizing priorities. However, impediments will need to be addressed as they arise throughout the day, so the scrum master needs to be vigilant and proactively follow up on known or potential impediments throughout the day.

The key to one-day sprints is splitting the requests so that they fit in a day. This will take practice. In the beginning, our teams did one-week batch releases. When they first transitioned to their new one-day cadence, the number of fixes completed by week's end decreased. However, customer satisfaction still increased because customers went from waiting a week to getting something every day. Waiting and satisfaction are opposing dynamics.

Chapter 12

Portfolio Management

- -

In This Chapter

▶ Prioritizing portfolios with scrum

▶ Applying scrum to entrepreneurial endeavors

▶ Scaling scrum using vertical slicing, SAFe®, and LeSS scaling options

- -

"There is nothing so useless as doing efficiently that which should not be done at all."

— Peter Drucker

Most organizational efficiency problems are not at the execution team level and are not fundamentally efficiency problems; they are effectiveness problems at the executive level. The number-one issue in portfolio management is a failure of leadership to properly prioritize projects and therefore allocate talent appropriately. This failure of leadership is then masked by thrashing people across several projects. Communication fails, priorities get dropped, and the squeaky-wheel syndrome takes over — where the loudest stakeholder gets the most attention and resources.

You only have one way to handle the situation of more projects than talent — prioritize. Effectiveness over efficiency. If an organization is highly efficient, but working on the wrong features, what good does it do? It's far more critical to be effective. Work on only those highest-prioritized projects and those highest-prioritized features within them. Profitability flows from this.

In this chapter, I go through the main challenges in portfolio management — number one of which is prioritization. Then I discuss the scrum solutions that are available.

Portfolio Management Challenges

Four key challenges prevent good portfolio management if not handled effectively. I present these challenges in the following sections.

Portfolio management is the simultaneous coordination, integration, management, prioritization, and control of several projects at once at the organizational level.

People allocation and prioritization

Above all else, not having enough time, money, or people is the biggest constraint on portfolio management. These constraints force leaders to prioritize effectively, to reduce organizational drag (such as thrashing) on talent, or to push the burden down to a level that doesn't have the clout to fight back (that is, the "if I demand it, I'll get it" mentality). Unfortunately, many leaders choose the latter. Prioritizing effectively means choosing only those projects that are highest value and risk and feeding them to stable teams one a time. If you only have one scrum team, feed them one project at a time. If you have five teams, feed them each only one project at a time. If one project is too big for one team, have as many teams as needed swarm around the highest-priority project until it is done; then feed them the next one.

People lose a minimum of 30 percent of time just in the cognitive mobilization-demobilization associated with task switching.

Racing in reverse is a concept that I teach regarding spending too much time on the wrong things. You can see my webinar on this topic at `https://platinumedge.com/blog/video-mark-laytons-racing-reverse-presentation`. Remember how I've discussed being effective over being efficient? If you're not effective, you're racing in reverse. If you're pushing people to work more, put in overtime, and pump out beyond their means, you actually *increase* the amount of defects and therefore future work and cost.

The project prioritization conundrum can be addressed by asking one question: If this project isn't a high enough priority to give it dedicated talent, is it necessary right now?

But it's this gap in prioritization that presents the largest challenge in portfolio management. The "squeaky-wheel syndrome" reigns, where the loudest stakeholder voice is the one that directs the action. Corporate strategy, not whims or the loudest voice, should drive prioritization.

Dependencies and fragmentation

With projects running simultaneously, bottlenecks from dependency issues arise, as do delays because of integration difficulties. In traditional project management, people, money, and equipment are shared. It's not uncommon for managers to allocate each person across multiple projects (50 percent here, 40 percent there, and even squeezing out the last 10 percent for some other project) just to feel like the managers are utilizing every ounce of power available, believing that it's making the organization as efficient as possible.

Historically, project managers ended up trying to do everything all at once, because they're under pressure from business owners to deliver across several areas. They end up racing after different goals, without separating and prioritizing what needs to be done first. Dependency issues end up tying the projects in knots, because the core dependent project wasn't executed first.

Disconnect between projects and business objectives

Most projects begin in line with business objectives, but as time passes, managers continue to brainstorm product ideas and hypothesize all the directions the product could take. This is only natural. But without consistent feedback loops with customers and stakeholders, and without daily coordination with the development team, the scope creeps in many directions and distance in communications increases and breaks down until the project objectives become unknown.

This, in turn, reflects the lack-of-prioritization issue at the core of the problem. With scrum, prioritization (and reprioritization) happens continuously throughout the project (at each of the roadmap, release, sprint, and daily scrum levels). Because of this, the product backlog always has the next-highest-priority items ready to go, and each release is the next most minimum viable product.

No more squeaky wheels, pet projects, or rudderless prioritization.

Shooting the messenger

Being the bearer of bad news to C-level management is no one's favorite task. Even when a team knows that their project is awry, they may hesitate to tell senior management for the perceived negative impact on their careers.

Unfortunately, the longer they wait to deliver the bad news, the worse the problems become.

While early and frequent communication of impediments and problems is the scrum style, traditional project management supports the opposite: the "tell me when it's done" mind-set. This results in the business owners often being removed from even knowing that their project has gone astray until it is too late to correct.

Accountability needs to be in the right place, not assigned to a middle-man project manager who's not doing the work of product creation. Scrum's transparency removes this issue. The product owner has ownership over the business objectives and priorities, and the development team owns how to technically implement and how much they can commit to achieving. The team shares their solutions directly to the product owner every day of each sprint and to the stakeholders directly at the end of each sprint.

The product owner doesn't answer for the developers, nor do the developers answer for the product owner. Each answers for themselves. Scrum provides the opportunity for appropriately placed accountability, transparency, and ownership.

Scrum solutions

Here is a theme to the preceding problems:

- ✔ People allocated across several projects and therefore diluted and unfocused
- ✔ Diluted and unfocused talent whose problems then become shared by all
- ✔ Divergence in development versus business objectives due to lack of communication
- ✔ Fear of communicating problems

Scrum actually conserves resources for business owners by placing high-risk and high-priority items first. If you fail, *fail early, fail fast.* If those business owners don't think the project will come to fruition as they want it to, they have the opportunity to pull the plug early and save precious resources and time.

Effective portfolio managers use the equation I showed you in Chapter 5, AC + OC > V, as a termination trigger. *When the actual and opportunity costs outweigh the value of the project, it's time to move on.*

Scrum removes the diverted focus of talent by having dedicated teams that are cross-functional, but yet not thrashed across multiple projects.

With the scrum framework, a portfolio manager can often determine within a few sprints whether a project is viable. This means that it either moves forward speedily and efficiently or it's removed from the backlog and the talent are freed for higher-priority projects. This way, less stigma is involved in having a project "fail" because the costs of failure have been dramatically reduced up front.

Remember WIP (work in progress) limits for development teams? (See the section on swarming in Chapter 5.) The same applies to portfolio management. You can have as many projects open at once as you have scrum teams. A stable team can swarm on a requirement, a release, and a project until it is done, and then take on the next-highest-priority project. If you have multiple teams, that's great. Align skills with projects, and with each team dedicated and stable, they will get each project done serially faster than if talent is thrashed between projects. That means that *all* projects will complete under a dedicated team model before *any* project completes under a thrashed model. Remember, thrashing adds a minimum of 30 percent more time to projects. It just doesn't pencil.

Figure 12-1 illustrates the difference between running serial projects (dedicated teams) versus parallel projects (thrashing teams), and the financial cost of delay of thrashing.

In this example, a portfolio has three projects, each running in succession (that is, serially). Assume that one unit of value can be produced in one unit of time and each project is able to produce one unit of value ($) after it is complete.

The cost of thrashing the team is a minimum of 30 percent more time to finish each project. For even numbers, say 33 percent for this scenario. Over three projects (99 percent), that's roughly a whole project's length in itself wasted by thrashing the teams around.

So, going only one unit of time past deployment of the serial projects, the parallel projects will have returned $$$ (3$ — one $ for each project deployed) at the end of that time period. The serial projects will have returned $$$$$$+$$$$ (10$ — that's more than three times the ROI).

Which one of these scenarios delivers the projects to the customer faster? Which one produces more profit?

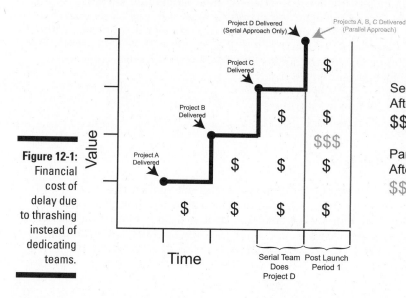

Figure 12-1: Financial cost of delay due to thrashing instead of dedicating teams.

Stop thrashing. Run one project at a time through one team at a time. By dedicating teams, everyone gets their project earlier, plus gets an earlier and higher return on investment (ROI).

As executives start prioritizing to eliminate thrashing, the constant feedback loop of sprint reviews ensures that stakeholders (including the executives) are brought into direct alignment with the scrum team's work. Through constantly communicating the highest-priority items, stakeholders can ensure that they get what they want, while at the same time, developers avoid the "squeaky-wheel syndrome."

Goals are kept in alignment, and strategies and tactics are prioritized. Constant communication means that problems and impediments are brought up early and solutions can either be applied or directions changed. Creative innovation and experimentation can be encouraged without fear of undue waste.

Portfolio management for organizations, both new and established, both small and large, require discipline and effective prioritization. I cover solutions for each of these categories in this chapter.

Startups

Forming your own startup company is no small endeavor. You have all the normal challenges associated with starting a business venture, including use of personal funds to finance the endeavor and planning for success. Yet on the other hand, startups have certain advantages and huge potential. Their small size increases their agility, and decisions can be made quickly, without the weight of corporate bureaucracy. Still, making tough decisions early and getting minimum viable product out the door faster than everyone else is critical for entrepreneurial survival.

Lean Startup is scrum for startups.

Lean Startup

Typical of the waterfall method, many startups begin with an idea, spend time and money on developing that idea into a formal multiyear business plan, and then hope that it's what the customer wants. Many times, startups fail before they even have a chance to show the client the product. Recent data shows that 80 percent of new businesses fail within the first 18 months.

In one sense, an 80 percent failure rate is terrible. Let's face it, those are not betting odds. But on the other hand, all those potential competitors are being swept away on the tide of ineffectiveness. With Lean Startup, new businesses can expand on their advantages and avoid unnecessary pitfalls.

Given traditional project frameworks, the client is often left out of initial planning and prioritizing conversations. This misses the opportunity for needed collaboration and tailoring the project correctly. After all, one size does not fit all, and the end user could remain unsatisfied and unengaged.

With Lean Startup, the same inspect-and-adapt approach used with the scrum framework is applied from the beginning. Critical to this is the concept of the constant feedback loop. Sprint planning, sprint reviews, and sprint retrospectives allow for constant inspect and adapt at the startup level.

With Lean Startup, you don't have to wait for months or years for those valuable prototypes to be made. With the prioritization process of highest value and risk, you'll have products to place in stakeholders and customer's hands within weeks. The feedback gained can then be immediately used for future iterations.

As well, critical yet often overlooked questions can be addressed, such as should this product even be created? Does it work at its most basic level, and if so, is it economically viable? Before huge sums of money are committed, basic questions and answers can be brought to light. Fail early, fail cheap is its own form of success.

Pivoting is a word you'll hear in the Lean Startup world. You pivot when you inspect and adapt, which in Lean Startup terms is to "make a structural course correction to test a new fundamental hypothesis about the product, strategy, and engine of growth" (`http://theleanstartup.com`).

The prioritization process is driven by reality, not hope. As features are developed and feedback is gained, that data is immediately incorporated into new iterations (sprints) and requirements.

The Lean Startup model of build ⇨ measure ⇨ learn is essentially the scrum model:

- ✔ **Build:** The sprint cycle creates the product increment supporting the release goal (MVP).

- ✔ **Measure:** The feedback is received in both the sprint review and sprint retrospective.

- ✔ **Learn:** New requirements get added to the product backlog as a result of stakeholder and customer feedback, and the plan of action for the improvements learned from the retrospective.

Dropbox

Dropbox, a file-storage and -sharing application, was at one time a product most people didn't even think they needed. The company took the concept of minimum viable product (MVP) and used it to get people using its product early on in its development. So how could you sell something that people didn't even know they needed? Henry Ford once said "If I had asked people what they wanted, they would have said faster horses." Lean Startup is a great agile tool for enabling entrepreneurial innovation.

Because developing the Dropbox product involved extensive integrations with computer platforms and operating systems, developing a full prototype just wasn't feasible given the complexity of the engineering necessary. Dropbox solved this dilemma by creating a video targeted to technologically savvy early adopters, showing why they needed it and how easy it was. The company knew that it needed feedback as early as possible, and from those who would give the developers the most knowledgeable feedback. This is where taking a Lean Startup approach allowed Dropbox to drive early traffic and grow its waiting list from

5,000 to 75,000. Literally overnight, the company had validation that its product was what the market wanted. The video was its first MVP and captivated an audience for its next MVP, which would be the highest valued file-storage and -sharing features.

Although with scrum, you only want to demonstrate working product at the end of every sprint, in Lean Startup, decisions are often the product increment.

In scrum, when a decision needs to be made about how to develop a requirement or set of requirements, a common practice is to include in the sprint a "spike" to answer that question. This is when a development team researches and dissects an unknown issue to establish direction on how to address a requirement. This might be something like, "Should we use Oracle or MySQL for this database?"

For Dropbox, its MVP became an opportunity to demonstrate to customers what they didn't know they needed, and to quickly and inexpensively validate or nullify their hypothesis about their idea.

Scaling Scrum

Scrum, in its essence, was designed for decomposed projects that could be started and finished quickly. After all, a scrum team consists of about seven developers, a scrum master, and a product owner. A natural limit exists to what can be accomplished with this size. Some projects are large enough that they require more than one standard scrum team.

Scaling scrum occurs when more than one scrum team is working on a project or portfolio of projects that have some level of affinity. Microsoft's Office Suite application is one such example. One team might have worked on Word, another on Excel, and yet a third on PowerPoint. However, they all had to be integrated and working effectively together to be sold as one package. Many projects are so large that they require multiple teams and projects within them. Scrum has the ability to meet this need.

Scaled scrum can be implemented in different ways. Some examples are vertical slicing, enterprise scrum, SAFe®, and LeSS (you find others as well). While I'm familiar with and certified in many of the scaling models, vertical slicing is the original model and is simple enough to discuss here.

How does enterprise scrum actually work? Remember, wherever multiple teams are working toward a single release package, an enterprise-level scrum model will be required to ensure effective coordination, communication, integration, and removal of impediments.

A vertical slicing overview

With vertical slicing, several scrum teams are established to achieve the overarching program goal. Each scrum team works in synchronized sprints of the same length on a separate portion or module of the overall product, and then those modules get integrated together through an integration scrum team after each sprint. The integration scrum team lags the development scrum teams by one sprint and is its own scrum team, having its own dedicated development team members, product owner, and scrum master.

Figure 12-2 illustrates how each individual team's features feed into the integration team's backlog for architectural and system-level coordination.

The *integration scrum team* handles all system-level development work for the integration of functionality produced by each of the teams that feed into it, and provides architectural oversight to unify the individual scrum teams.

Take Microsoft Office as an illustration:

- ✔ A separate scrum team develops the functionality for "compose/transmit messages" (requirement ID 1.1.1.1).
- ✔ Another team develops the functionality for "grammar/spell check messages" (1.1.1.2).
- ✔ A third scrum team develops the functionality for "search messages" (1.1.1.3).
- ✔ The integration scrum team does the development work to integrate the functionality together into a package that the Email integration team can integrate into the entire Email module.
- ✔ The Outlook integration team then takes the Email modules, along with the Calendar, Contacts, and other modules, to integrate them into an Outlook package that can then be integrated by the MS Office integration team into the entire MS Office suite.

In this example, integration teams operate as separate scrum teams, with dedicated team members for each role.

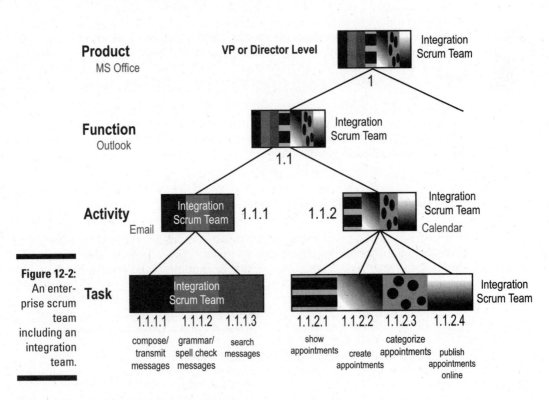

Product
MS Office

VP or Director Level

Integration
Scrum Team

1

Function
Outlook

Integration
Scrum Team

1.1

Activity
Email

Integration
Scrum Team

1.1.1

1.1.2

Integration
Scrum Team

Calendar

Figure 12-2:
An enter-
prise scrum
team
including an
integration
team.

Task

Integration
Scrum Team

Integration
Scrum Team

1.1.1.1   1.1.1.2   1.1.1.3

compose/   grammar/   search
transmit   spell check   messages
messages   messages

1.1.2.1   1.1.2.2   1.1.2.3   1.1.2.4

show   categorize
appointments   create   appointments   publish
                appointments   appointments
                                    online

Scrum of scrums

The scrum of scrums model facilitates effective integration, coordination, and collaboration among scrum teams using vertical slicing. See Figure 12-3. Each role of each team has a daily coordination opportunity with people of the same role in other teams to coordinate priorities and dependencies and identify impediments that affect the broader program team. The scrum of scrums for each role is facilitated by the integration-level person for each role. Thorough integration and release efforts establish a consistent and regular scrum of scrums model.

Product owner scrum of scrums

Each day, following the individual scrum teams' daily scrums, the product owners from each scrum team meet with the integration team product owner for no longer than 15 minutes. They address the requirements being completed and make any adjustments based on the realities uncovered during the individual scrum team's daily scrum. Each product owner addresses the following:

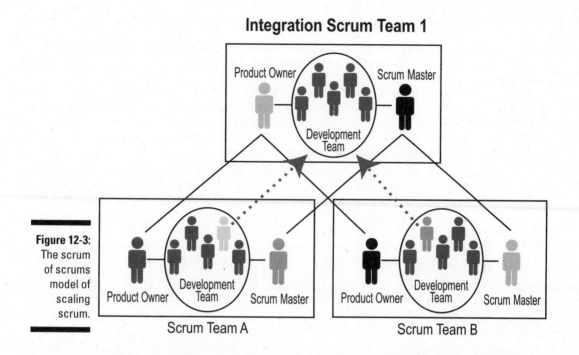

Integration Scrum Team 1

Product Owner   Scrum Master

Development Team

Product Owner   Development Team   Scrum Master

Scrum Team A

Product Owner   Development Team   Scrum Master

Scrum Team B

Figure 12-3:
The scrum of scrums model of scaling scrum.

✔ The business requirements that each has accepted or rejected since the last time they met

✔ The requirements that should be accepted by the time they meet again

✔ Which requirements are impeded and need help from other teams to resolve (such as "John, we won't be able to do requirement 123 until you complete requirement xyz from your current sprint backlog.")

The integration team product owner makes the cross-team prioritization decisions necessary to ensure that the impediments are addressed during the daily scrum of scrums.

Development team scrum of scrums

Here, each day following the individual scrum teams' daily scrums, one development team member representative from each scrum team will attend the integration team's daily scrum and participate with the integration development team members in discussing the following:

✔ What their team accomplished since the last time they met

✔ What their team will accomplish between now and the next time they meet

- ✔ Any technical concerns they have that they need help with
- ✔ Technical direction decisions that the team has made and what anyone should be aware of to prevent potential issues

It's a good practice to rotate development team members who attend the scrum of scrums, either daily or for each sprint, to ensure that everyone stays tuned in to the integration efforts of the portfolio.

Scrum master scrum of scrums

Respectively, the scrum masters from each scrum team also meet among themselves with the integration scrum team scrum master for no longer than 15 minutes to address the impediments that each team is dealing with. Each scrum master addresses the following:

- ✔ The individual team-level impediments resolved since the last time they met and how they were resolved, in case other scrum masters run into the issue
- ✔ New impediments that have been identified since last time they met and any unresolved impediments
- ✔ Which impediments they cannot resolve on their own and need help resolving
- ✔ Potential future impediments that everyone should be aware of

The integration team scrum master then makes sure that the escalated impediments are addressed after the daily scrum of scrums.

With vertical slicing, a single product backlog exists, and team attributes are assigned to those requirements as they move down to the development scrum team. At the top level, a requirement gets numbered, for example, Requirement 75. As it moves to the next level, attributes are assigned to it so that people know which team owns it: 75A, 75AS, 75ASM might be for a requirement that went from the program level (number), to the application level (A), to the section level (S), and to the module scrum team (M). With this model, I can see the overall program but can quickly filter down to my team's piece of that overall program.

A common question that I get during training is "Who is responsible for architecture in a vertically sliced program?" The answer is that it depends on which modules will be impacted by the decision.

Your organization should have existing architectural standards, coding standards, and style guides. This way, each team doesn't have to reinvent the wheel.

Consider an architectural decision that needed to be made, and it was only going to impact module A. The development team of module A would make that decision. If it was going to impact multiple teams, the development team at the integration level that all impacted teams roll into would make that decision. That might be one level up or four levels up.

Vertical slicing is a simple way to maintain the autonomy of each scrum team within a wider program context, but it is just one of many scaling models available. The following examples are other existing models for managing projects at various size and portfolio levels.

Scaled Agile Framework (SAFe)

Scaled Agile Framework® (SAFe®) is a framework for scaling scrum and agile principles across multiple teams and their projects at the portfolio level. The SAFe "Big Picture" is shown in Figure 12-4.

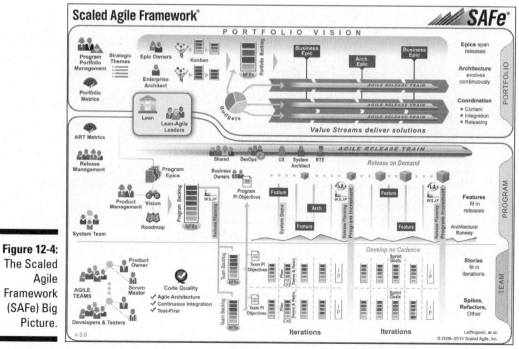

Figure 12-4: The Scaled Agile Framework (SAFe) Big Picture.

Reproduced with permission from © 2008–2014 Scaled Agile, Inc.

While differences with vertical slicing exist, many similarities do too, such as

- ✔ Development is done in scrum teams.
- ✔ The teams are aligned in the sprint lengths and cadence.
- ✔ Scrum of scrums are used to coordinate at the program level.

Within SAFe, you find three prescribed levels of integration and coordination:

1. Portfolio

   Here the vision and roadmap for the entire portfolio are established. Strategic themes are developed to support the vision. Budget, business objectives, and overall architecture governance are managed at the portfolio level of SAFe.

   Three portfolio-level roles drive these decisions:

   - Enterprise architect: Establishes a common technical vision and drives the holistic approach to technology across programs through continuous feedback, collaboration, and adaptive engineering design and engineering practices.

   - Lean-agile leaders: Teachers and coaches in the organization helping teams build better product through the values, principles, and practices of lean and agile software development. This role can be similar to a scrum master or a scrum mentor as outlined in Chapter 2.

   - Epic owners: Epics were introduced in Chapter 3, although SAFe uses a different feature-epic relationship. In SAFe, epics are the largest requirements, broken down into features, which are broken down into user stories. Epic owners usually drive one or two epics from identification through analysis and into decisions relating to implementation with development teams at the team level.

   The portfolio backlog in SAFe consists of both business and architectural epics. The enterprise architect, lean-agile leaders, and epic owners manage this portfolio backlog using kanban.

2. Program

   Within the portfolio, each program has a set of program epics from the portfolio backlog, owned and driven by an epic owner in that program. A vision and roadmap for the program are established, which support the portfolio vision and backlog.

   Here is where release and product management occur. The "agile release train" (ART) model is used, which is a team of agile teams delivering incremental releases of value. The "train" departs the station on a reliable schedule of release opportunities that each program can jump on if ready. If you miss one release, when another one comes along, you can catch it, just like a train schedule. The ART provides a fixed cadence with which the teams of the program align and synchronize.

At this level of integration, the work of the individual teams comes together to form release packages under the direction of shared experts such as DevOps, user experience (UX), system architecture, and release train engineering.

The program product increment (PI) objectives artifact contains summaries of the product's business and technical goals for the upcoming release. During release planning, the team reviews the vision and goals, creates user stories around them, and plans the development necessary for this release. This becomes the team's PI objectives.

SAFe requires two working demos at the end of each iteration showing the working software or product created:

- The Team Demo showcases the product for the scrum team.
- The System Demo showcases it for stakeholders at the program level.

The release abstract showcases what has been released of working, real value in every release. After all, producing working product is the goal of every sprint or product increment.

3. Team

Programs are made up of a certain number of agile teams, and each can only be on one program. This works very much like the first layer of integration that's referred to in scrum of scrums. Agile teams are essentially scrum teams, each with a development team, including testers and a product owner and scrum master. They work on cadence with the other teams of the program, and their team backlogs support and align with the program backlog.

Portfolio managers like the SAFe model because of how clear and visual it is. For larger organizations, it also provides structure for middle management's involvement with scrum teams. SAFe also integrates agile techniques (eXtreme Programming), such as test-driven development (TDD) and continuous integration (CI).

Test-driven development (TDD) is an agile software development process in which an automated unit test is written before coding begins. The developer runs the test and watches it fail, and then develops enough code to pass the test without regard for efficiency. The developer then refactors the code to remove as much coding as possible, while still passing the automated unit test. This is sometimes referred to as *red, green, clean* — the test fails, the test passes, the code is clean. TDD dramatically minimizes waste in code, maximizes unit test coverage, and enables more seamless merging of the developer's work into the main body of work through continuous integration.

Continuous integration (CI) is a practice that code developers use where they continuously integrate new code into a shared product. Each time code is added, it's automatically tested to ensure seamless integration.

Code quality is one of the core values of SAFe. Any organization's ability to quickly create quality functionality requires reliable code. This has three parts:

✔ Agile architecture abstracts help organizations solve complex problems based on the nature of their large project needs. These are proven solutions for set problems and underline the importance of software architecture in any large-scale project.

✔ Continuous integration at the team and system level, incorporating code from the many development teams.

✔ Code is tested at every increment to ensure working software at every release.

Each iteration delivers working software within a strict timebox.

As technology and customer needs change, so do the products required to fulfill those needs. Refactoring is done to ensure not just delivering current business value but future value too.

Safely transitioning from waterfall

A big data company with offices in the United States and India recently made the transition from waterfall to SAFe. Market challenges existed for them including increased competition, changing technology, and long lead times to bring new product to market.

The company's waterfall process was so full of documentation that 25 to 40 documents had to be signed by up to ten stakeholders to get anything approved. Then multiple ongoing projects created thrashing and low visibility and prioritization. The firm was floundering beneath its own bureaucratic weight.

Within 22 months of introducing SAFe into the organization, the company achieved the following results:

✔ Regrouping over 500 employees into over 60 agile teams

✔ Decreasing the time to market by an incredible 27 weeks

✔ Decreasing the time to fix errors from months to hours

✔ Increased customer satisfaction and employee morale

Initially, the company was hesitant to bring in the scrum framework. It believed that scrum was only for small companies, and it would never fit the needs of the company's much larger, multinational presence. SAFe provided a scaled scrum solution that was a good fit for the company:

- The company began with a few pilot teams utilizing scrum, and after working out some organizational glitches, achieved success.

- It brought in agile and scrum coaches to help it integrate the scrum framework into the larger organization.

- It began to inspect and adapt with the scrum process itself. Using pilot teams, the company started with three scrum teams, then added a couple more, and eventually were running many scrum teams concurrently. So rather than leaping in with every penny and person, it incrementally scaled scrum with SAFe.

- Given success with the preceding steps, the company did a full-scale SAFe rollout. It brought in more experts, created in-house scrum training programs, and kept senior management fully in the loop.

The company's scaling issues were dealt with in the following way:

- Verticals were formed to leverage product owners, management, and development.

- Cubicles were redesigned into agile pods, facilitating colocating and team collaboration.

- Release trains were established, facilitating ongoing product releases, coordinated across each portfolio.

The complete conversion to SAFe took just 22 months, resulting in increased effectiveness and time to market, fewer errors, and increased customer and employee satisfaction.

John Deere

Several years ago, John Deere's Intelligent Systems Group (ISG) scaled using SAFe within its projects. As with the preceding example, this didn't occur overnight but entailed an incremental process. Key challenges were

- Hundreds of developers would need to be involved.

- Fixed delivery dates existed, requiring vehicles to leave factories on schedule.

- Complex and embedded systems were already in place, such as displays, receivers, and guidance systems.

- A need existed for increased speed to market, but yet without an increase in costs.

The first of these steps were a couple of smaller scrum projects to test the water. Just within these test projects, scrum was able to decrease the product delivery time from 12 to 18 months, to an incredible two to four weeks. This new framework lopped off months and years in getting the company's products into its customer's hands.

So while senior management still brimmed with questions and concerns about scrum, the hard data served to justify a much larger scrum rollout. The initial planning went like this:

- ✔ Management needed to be fully on board. The company solved this by educating management on the quantitative benefits of scrum through a two-day scrum workshop, and what scrum could specifically do for the ISG part of John Deere.

- ✔ Get the developers on board. The company worked with team leads and project managers to get their buy-ins because these titles would not exist under a scrum model.

- ✔ John Deere couldn't begin with only a few teams; the company needed all 200+ developers on board. It formed release trains to help everyone sync up to get on board.

- ✔ Establish a training plan and budget — quickly. Literally hundreds of people needed to get up to speed on SAFe and scrum immediately.

After the preceding modifications were established, John Deere moved ahead:

1. Management established the "domain" (that is, who and what was involved). They decided on a brand with about 130 employees.

2. Management formed the scrum teams, over 12 of them, and educated the team members that they would only be working on one project at a time now — not as many as five that they had previously been assigned to!

   Testers now needed to be colocated and integrated as part of the scrum team, because testing is an early and ongoing activity of scrum.

3. The scrum masters and product owners were selected. The new roles and responsibilities were established and explained.

4. Management then launched the scrum training and release train planning.

So while the story ends with a beginning of sorts — the portfolio now being developed within scrum — a whole lot of background took place first. The results were astounding:

- ✔ Field issue retention time went down by over 40 percent.

- ✔ Warranty expense dropped by half.

✔ Time to production was reduced by 20 percent.

✔ Time to market was 20 percent faster.

Plus, customer satisfaction and employee satisfaction were significantly raised. While these types of results are common with scrum, they are still excellent results overall.

Large-Scale Scrum (LeSS)

As you've seen, scrum can be used for more than small businesses and projects. Large-Scale Scrum (LeSS) is one more way in which the scrum framework can be scaled into massive projects.

What's meant by *Large* in LeSS? Products have been successfully developed using LeSS with as few as four to five small teams up to products being developed by 1,500 people and spanning half a dozen countries. In other words, how big would you like large to be? LeSS can scale scrum up or down to work in many environments.

The key to scaling up scrum is to begin with a firm foundation. A thorough knowledge of the basic scrum team of about seven individuals is then amplified into many teams, in many locations, with a process of coordination. This is LeSS.

LeSS defines two frameworks: "LeSS" and "LeSS Huge." The difference lies in the size of total teams involved. I look at them both.

The smaller LeSS framework

Figure 12-5 illustrates the basic or smaller LeSS framework. Here, the number of scrum teams varies, usually between five and ten scrum teams of eight people each. Eight teams is usually the upper limit seen in practice.

One product owner covers up to eight teams, and this is where the size limit comes in. Eventually, the product owner won't be able to manage effectively. Too many teams and too many features will be in the product backlog for one person.

The idea of having one product owner for multiple teams goes against what I've said previously about dedicated roles per team. The product owner should start working with area product owners (analogous with the product owner "agent" practice in Chapter 2) when the product owner feels that they are spread too thin (such as when they are working with more than one team). This is an element of LeSS and why basic LeSS is limited in size. Naturally, colocation is a significant contributing factor for success in this framework, as well.

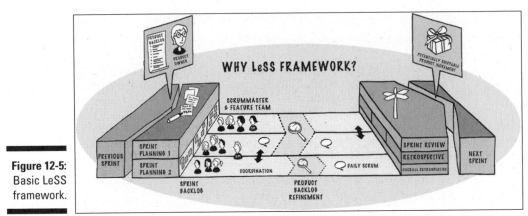

Figure 12-5:
Basic LeSS
framework.

While much of LeSS remains true to the scrum framework, the differences are important:

✔ Sprint planning (Part 1) is still limited to one hour per week of sprint. Although not all developers are required to attend, they aren't discouraged, and at least two members per sprint team attend, along with the product owner. The representative team members then go back and share their information with their respective teams.

✔ Independent sprint planning (Part 2) and daily scrum meetings occur, and members from different teams can attend each other's meeting to facilitate information sharing.

✔ Coordination meetings take place daily during each sprint as required. LeSS does not prescribe a specific format for this meeting, but daily scrum of scrums (discussed earlier in this chapter) are one of several common practices used in LeSS.

✔ Backlog refinement is done for the overall product backlog with representatives from each development team and the product owners. Individual team backlog refinement also takes place at the individual team level.

✔ Sprint reviews are done with representatives from each team and the product owner.

✔ Overall sprint retrospectives are held in addition to individual team retrospectives. Scrum masters, product owners, and representatives from development teams inspect and adapt the overall system of the project, such as processes, tools, and communication.

LeSS Huge framework

With LeSS Huge, the sky is pretty much the limit as far as overall project team size goes. A few thousand people could work on one project.

The scrum teams are divided around major areas of customer requirements, called "requirement areas." For each area, you have one area product owner and between four and eight scrum teams (a minimum of four teams in each requirement area prevents bloat of having too much local optimization and complexity). So now you have one overall product owner with several area product owners forming the product owner team. Figure 12-6 illustrates the LeSS Huge framework.

As in scrum and in smaller LeSS, you have one product, one definition of done, one (area) product owner, and one sprint. LeSS Huge is a "stack" of basic LeSS for each requirement area all together. Each requirement area uses basic LeSS, and the set of all requirement areas is within LeSS Huge. Some of the differences are

- ✔ A product owner planning meeting happens before the sprint planning meeting.

- ✔ Area-level meetings are added. Sprint planning, review, and retrospective meetings are done at the area level, and area-level product backlog refinement occurs.

- ✔ Area product owners coordinate a limited number of individual team product owners.

- ✔ Overall sprint reviews and retrospectives involving all teams are also done. This coordinates the overall work and process across the program.

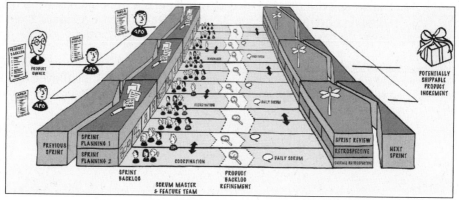

Figure 12-6: LeSS Huge framework.

Used with permission, Craig Larman and Bas Vodde.

LeSS allows for the implementation of scrum and scaling in a way that, for the most part, holds true to the agile principles. Some elements of the scrum framework are upheld with empirical learning, short feedback loops, self-organization, and effective collaboration and coordination.

Leadership tools also exist in LeSS for good decisions to maximize ROI, deliver value to customers, and create happy, sustainable teams.

JPMorgan and LeSS

Large in the context of JPMorgan means over 3,000 employees working in multiple international locations. In 2013, the company decided to convert to LeSS. As you've seen with other case studies, it began first with smaller pilot projects to get the feel for it. The results, which you can imagine were impressive, motivated the firm to get scrum rolled out at a much grander scale.

The company began by choosing a single division to pilot — securities — and then working on solutions to create a more customer-centric approach from the previous individual component approach. Customers needed families of components rather than individual ones. This hugely simplified planning and coordination, because groups were planned rather than individual components.

One of the issues that the firm came up against was choosing who the new product owners would be, because with its waterfall approach, business wasn't involved with development. The company solved this by choosing willing participants from both the operations side and R&D.

JPMorgan then formed requirement areas (as shown previously for LeSS Huge). Each team was given a project, and a product owner was chosen. The teams were encouraged to develop cross-functionality to reduce bottlenecks and the risk of losing a critical person. HR eliminated job titles such as Business Analyst or Tester, and they all became Developers. Even team leads were morphed back into the generic title of Developer.

At the end of the initial rollout of LeSS within the securities division, increased effectiveness, customer satisfaction, and employee morale were realized. LeSS helped scale scrum up to this size of operation and continues to be used today.

Chapter 13

Human Resources and Finance

"When the winds of change blow, some people build walls and others build windmills."

— Chinese proverb

Baby boomers are retiring at a rapid pace, new generations of employees are taking their place, and human resources (HR) has taken on high-level organizational value. Wasted funds due to failed projects indicate that a smarter way must exist to finance projects. As in so many business functions, the old methods of achieving goals are becoming outdated within the new and continually shifting landscape.

As you'll see, those companies that are able to recognize the core HR and finance issues, and then apply the scrum framework to their solutions, are those that are staying ahead of the pack. Many opportunities exist to increase human potential and financial effectiveness through the application of scrum.

In this chapter, I guide you through the challenges and solutions in these critical organizational areas.

Human Resources and Scrum

In a recent survey, conducted by the Society for Human Resource Management (SHRM), two core challenges highlight the world of HR today:

✔ Retaining and rewarding the best employees

✔ Developing future leaders

These two concerns are really the same thing. Your best employees often become your future leaders. When the surveyors asked what would be the largest investment challenge facing organizations, the number-one response was "obtaining human capital and optimizing human capital investments."

I always encourage organizations I work with to refer to people as people or talent rather than capital and resources. People aren't commodities. They have individual skills, experiences, and innovations. The term *resources,* when referring to people, is a relic of the past. Start seeing your people as people and seeing their creativity and talents as the irreplaceable value they bring to your organization.

That said, the point made by the SHRM survey is still crucial. Different types of leaders are needed. We need leaders to make the hard product owner decisions discussed in portfolio management (see Chapter 12). And we need servant leaders who work collaboratively to enable and empower teams, such as scrum masters (see Chapter 2). These individuals empower and enable self-organizing teams to come up with the best solutions. They value iterative approaches to building products based on rapid and regular customer feedback, and know how to pivot and respond to that feedback quickly.

We need leaders in development who excel by learning new skills and mentoring others as they grow. We need collaborative leaders who can work in the dynamic environment of scrum. Egomaniacs need not apply. Cross-functional swarming scrum teams are what companies need to stay competitive. In other words, we need leaders who embrace the value of change.

Reducing risky single points of failure saves money for all the reasons I've discussed so far in the book. Teams that work to collaborate on solving the immediate reality of a problem rather than throwing issues over the fence to each other will get quality products to market faster than by using traditional methods.

Creating the Right Culture

In Chapter 4, I discuss what motivates employees the most. It wasn't money, but rather giving them the autonomy and trust to do the job, opportunities to grow, and a sense of purpose. People want what they do to mean something, and they want to work with other people who are growing and engaged in what they do.

The fruits of self-organization and self-management are the creation of an organizational culture that attracts and retains the best and the brightest. If you refer back to Chapter 1, you'll find that these are agile principles 5, 8, 11, and 12.

Creating the right culture has many facets. The number-one thing I look for in an effective scrum team member is versatility. Give me someone who is intellectually curious and has what I call a "contributor personality," and I'll have success with them. I can teach them technical skills. Give me a prima donna who thinks that this thin slice of development is the only thing worthy of their time and they will taint the entire team. What is the most important job on a scrum team? It is the job necessary to ship the product. Sometimes that is coding, sometimes it's QA, and sometimes it's documentation. Whatever that task is, it is the highest-status, most critical job of the entire project.

Crucial to the creation of an attractive organizational culture is the attitude of executives. What qualities do they embrace and how do they invest in their people? Like a magnet, leaders will attract those people who respond to the culture they provide.

While broad organizational culture is obviously important, so are tactical team skills necessary in creating the right culture. Cross-functionality within teams, thereby fostering the ability to swarm, is critical. The key is skills not titles. A cross-functional, self-organizing team is the perfect environment for skill development. And as employees grow, they can become more engaged in the organization's goal and purpose.

Technology changes too fast to get stuck in the single-technology "specialist" mind-set. The standard tech choice of today may be totally different than what's needed tomorrow. The specialty of tomorrow is the ability to learn and adapt quickly. You need team members that recognize this.

As skills are emphasized over titles, a culture is created where you don't have to hire one person for each skill. Expertise (not "specialist" . . . there's a difference) leadership is always needed. It's just that you don't need a specialist in every seat.

Situational leadership is important. For example, if Jim has expertise in .NET, I'll probably defer to Jim when I'm facing a .NET problem. Carol may have expertise in QA. When discussing QA, I may do the same thing. Sam may have just come back from a .NET conference, and while Jim might be strong in .NET, Sam may have learned something that Jim doesn't know.

The following sections describe two ways to examine HR and scrum.

HR and existing organization structures

Here I look at several key HR issues for how to organize and manage current employees within a scrum structure. Each issue can actually be turned to an advantage using scrum.

Incentivizing

Forced ranking and competitive incentive structures promote competition between individuals. Scrum is team-centric. The team receives praise, and the team receives suggestions for improvement. Incentives should be on this team level too. If the team succeeds, the team gets the prize.

When a football team wins the Super Bowl, who gets a ring? Every single person on the team, whether they played that day or not. That's team-centric. If a development team has a good year, everyone on the team might get a 15 percent bonus, not just a few select individuals. Depending on your seniority, 15 percent could be insignificant or very significant.

In larger teams, this may not work. But with scrum, development teams are 7 +/– 2, and so it is difficult for one or two team members to fly under the radar and unlikely that the team will allow it to happen very long. A self-organizing and self-managing team will demand the contribution of every team member so that the prize will be earned by all in the end.

Compensation

If everyone is cross-functional, and no titles or specialists exist, how do you create status? Individuals will create status through knowledge and being the go-to person on a subject. Being a heavy lifter on the team is shown by the number of tasks with your colored dot being in the Done column of the task board. It's by people wanting to pair with you and shadow you on tasks.

Seniority and relative compensation is established by a combination of skill depth and breadth.

Each member of a development team has at least one skill. If you know how to do one skill, you are a Band 1. Now you can be a junior-level Band 1 or a senior-level Band 1, but you are a Band 1.

If you know how to do two skills, you are a Band 2. Now you can be a junior-level Band 2 or a senior-level Band 2, but you are a Band 2. Three skills, you are a Band 3, and so on.

Each new skill gives the developer another band. As the team matures through shadowing, swarming, team pairing, and knowledge sharing, each team member should be adding skills (becoming cross-functional). As higher levels (such as Band 2 and Band 3) are achieved, the pay scales rise accordingly.

It's a true win-win situation because an organization can both pay you more *and* save money by having teams of cross-functional individuals rather than an army of sharp shooters who only know how to do one thing.

By incentivizing developers to learn more skills and therefore increase their status, you also give them the opportunity to design their own educational and therefore career path. Often, the skills they develop will be those they're most interested in or have a natural inclination for. As well, they may be introduced to skills that they never would have tried before, but find they have an aptitude for.

The team is incentivized to gain more skills, and the company is benefited by being able to pay fewer people higher rates and developing scrum teams that are more effective and efficient.

Underperforming team members

If anyone on a self-organizing, self-managing team isn't pulling his weight, scrum exposes this fact quickly so that the team can correct the issue. In Chapter 4, I discuss the Hawthorne effect, which shows how a worker's performance improved when someone was watching them. Visibility and performance are directly proportional. Scrum also utilizes information radiators, such as the task board and the burndown chart, which raise visibility and hence performance.

A client of mine actually had multiple flat-screen TVs in his lobby. They were split into quadrants and showed the day's burndown of four projects at a time, refreshing with new projects every 20 seconds. Every person walking into that lobby (including suppliers and clients) could see the status of every project that the company was working on. That is a high-visibility situation for each scrum team and each team member.

Lack of transparency in goals and expectations can also play a role in underperformance. If a person doesn't know exactly where they're headed, it's understandable that they can get off course.

Underperformance in scrum can easily be identified from the burndown charts when daily tasks are marked as either accomplished or not accomplished. New code is comprehensively and automatically tested every night through the automated tests of continuous integration (CI). With this type of visibility, and as the entire team is accountable as a single unit, any lapses are easily found and solved.

Under a traditional model, if a developer wanted to hang out on Facebook for three hours each day, it was easy to do. They could take a 45-minute task and tell the project manager that they needed four hours to do it. If the project manager said that they could do it in less time, the response might have been, "Really? Show me how." Because the project manager probably didn't have the coding skills necessary to fully understand the task at hand, his only option was to let the developer get on with whatever they was doing.

The rest of the team members figured that as long as they were doing their job, it was an issue between that developer and the project manager. However, under scrum, everyone is held accountable as a single unit. So if a developer spends three hours on Facebook, his teammates will hold them accountable for not doing their share.

Here are some other ways that scrum can expose performance issues:

- In the daily scrum, before any escalation of an issue is needed, team members can suggest that a troubled developer join them in shadowing or pairing on a task. This is the team's call and sometimes is all it takes.

- Sprint retrospectives are excellent times to identify gaps in skills and possible solutions. Root causes of the underperformance can be unearthed, such as team dynamics, the environment, and misunderstandings.

- In sprint reviews, the team can encourage the struggling person to engage in the demo. In preparation for this, things might come to light that prompt ideas for the retrospective.

- If all the developers know that one person isn't carrying his weight, but are perhaps uncomfortable bringing it up themselves, a good scrum master will facilitate the interactions to address the issue.

Bottom line: Under scrum, your job is my concern because we'll be held accountable as a single unit.

HR and scrum in hiring

When you make organizational changes and adopt scrum practices, hiring new employees will be different than before. Consider the following when hiring for each scrum role:

- Developers:
  - Remove titles from the job descriptions and base your searches on skills. You'll not only filter your search results based on skill keywords that candidates decide to include in their profiles, but you'll also naturally filter out those candidates who are more interested in touting their past titles than skills.

- Search for candidates with curiosity and a desire to cross-train — those who have demonstrated an ability to work outside of their comfort zone.

- Search for people with broader skill sets and experience in moving between different skills.

✔ Product owners:

- Look for that key characteristic of decisiveness.

- Find people who have demonstrated working collaboratively with developers and stakeholders.

- Seek the soft skills of communication and proactivity. Providing effective and timely clarification is critical to a scrum team's success.

✔ Scrum masters:

- For the scrum master, you want the soft skills, such as facilitation of conflicts and demonstrated impact on previous teams' performances.

- Don't advertise for a project manager hoping to convert them to a scrum master. The project manager role does not exist in scrum, and it may not be the right fit.

✔ In general:

- Search for those with previous scrum and/or agile experience.

- Regularly review job descriptions and update them with appropriate scrum role terminology and agile principles to attract candidates who prefer working with scrum.

TIP

Holacracy is a system of organizational governance consisting of self-organizing teams rather than a traditional hierarchy. It can be thought of as a hierarchy of circles where each circle is a self-organizing team run with democratic principles. In 2013, Zappos was the largest organization (1,500 employees at the time) to embrace the ideal of holacracy with success.

John Bunch, one of the transition leaders at Zappos, said, "One of the core principles is people taking personal accountability for their work. It's not leaderless. There are certainly people who hold a bigger scope of purpose for the organization than others. What it does do is distribute leadership into each role. Everybody is expected to lead and be an entrepreneur in their own roles, and Holacracy empowers them to do so." For a visual depiction of holacracy, check out Figure 13-1.

Ideally, he says, holacracy is "politics-free, quickly evolving to define and operate the purpose of the organization, responding to market and real-world conditions in real time. It's creating a structure in which people have flexibility to pursue what they're passionate about."

Holacracy is scrum's concept of self-organizing, self-managing, cross-functional teams applied at the organizational level.

After you have your new scrum-focused hires, performance reviews can be team based. Reward individuals based on their contribution to the team, shifting the emphasis away from the individual to the team.

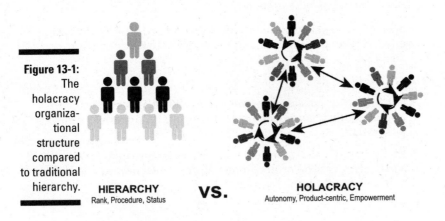

Figure 13-1: The holacracy organizational structure compared to traditional hierarchy.

HIERARCHY   **VS.**   **HOLACRACY**
Rank, Procedure, Status   Autonomy, Product-centric, Empowerment

Performance reviews

Team-level performance reviews are a natural for scrum. Given the high visibility inherent to this framework, daily assessment is given through peers, and team output is consistent and tangible.

However, formal individual annual reviews are for the most part artifacts left over from traditional project management frameworks and have been proven to be ineffective. Some of the reasons why are

- ✔ People need and want regular feedback, not just a one-time review at the end of each year. Instead, regular coaching is the key.

- ✔ It's difficult to assess an entire year's performance, with all its nuances and situational factors, in just one review. By its very nature, the review will be incomplete.

- ✔ Poor performers should be coached and mentored early on, not after an entire year has passed.

- ✔ Positive, constructive feedback is much more effective than the appraisal format of annual reviews.

The most logical and straightforward way to provide feedback for helping team members improve is the 360-degree review given by each of a person's peers. With scrum teams, this is scrum team members, stakeholders, and customers. See Figure 13-2. Instead of being a formal performance review, a 360-degree review is a feedback tool. Each member of the team can understand the effect of their work on every other individual involved. This holistic view can then be used to see how the employee is performing within the entire work environment.

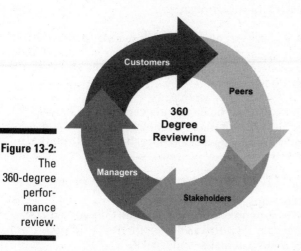

Figure 13-2: The 360-degree performance review.

Use 360-degree performance reviews not just for determining compensation, but more importantly for helping team members inspect and adapt ways to improve in general. When used only to satisfy HR requirements or determine merit increases, the full power of 360-degree reviews is missed.

Some of the benefits of a 360-degree review are

- ✔ Viewing an employee's performance from different angles allows for a greater understanding of which skills need improving and which are outstanding.

- ✔ Growth depends on having quality and frequent feedback. When done often, the 360-degree format ensures this.

- ✔ Starting points can be identified for improving skills.

- ✔ A baseline can be set from which improvement is measured.

- ✔ By having this robust view, blind spots in an employee's behavior can more easily be identified.

Parexel Informatics

I've shown you how scrum influences how we hire and develop talent to optimize the power of scrum. Scrum can also be used to take on hiring and onboarding projects themselves.

Kelly Anderson, associate director of technical publications at Parexel Informatics (a global biopharmaceutical and medical device solution provider), used scrum for a major hiring push.

In May 2011, Parexel took on a large-scale, multimillion-dollar project. It would last approximately one year and required 21 new hires, trained and ready to go. The project was significant — it would double the size of the Southern California–based satellite office.

Developers, database administrators, business analysts, and technical writers were needed. From the start of the recruitment process to the project start date, they had only seven weeks to find, hire, and train these individuals.

On average, U.S. companies take 25 working days (five weeks) to hire a new employee. Firms with 5,000+ employees take 58 working days (over 11 weeks). And this is just to hire the new people, not including the onboarding activities. Given these averages, Parexel (with 15,000+ employees) did pretty well to hire and train their new people in just seven weeks.

Initial challenges were extensive:

✔ No onboarding process currently existed.

✔ No formal new-hire program existed.

✔ The current recruiting process was inefficient.

✔ No dedicated training department or content existed.

✔ New equipment was needed, such as workstations, phones, and computers.

Parexel incorporated the scrum framework for managing this project. To start, the product owner (the HR director) gathered together all the hiring managers, the IT manager, and the HR staff for a one-day planning meeting. They identified everything they would need to do and who would do each part, such as

✔ Gather and create content for corporate, product, and industry overviews; agile development and software overviews; and IT and HR orientations.

✔ Create a week-long, on-site training program utilizing the manual.

- ✔ Establish the new facilities.
- ✔ Purchase equipment and network and software tools.
- ✔ Recruit internal trainers (subject matter experts and managers).
- ✔ Gather and format current material that existed in various forms.

From this single day of planning, they were able to establish roadmap features and product backlog epics for

- ✔ The training program manual
- ✔ IT equipment procurement
- ✔ IT software, licenses, and credentials procurement
- ✔ Setup of the new facility
- ✔ Process for hiring new employees on time

For recruiting the new employees, they also identified the needs for

- ✔ A portal and process for reviewing resumes
- ✔ An interview schedule
- ✔ Standard tests and interview questions

The managers used one-week sprints, and each week everyone demonstrated the progress on his portion of the manual and gathered feedback from each other. IT showed their progress in the facilities and equipment needs. They created the next week's sprint goal and went back to work.

The weekly touch points with IT were important. Several times, impediments were identified on the spot, and therefore could be resolved to keep IT in line with the deadlines.

Hiring managers gave feedback to each other on the content of the training material. This way, they didn't need an exhaustive edit at the very end. By the time the training came, they knew that even if they hadn't had time to review the entire manual, their content had been inspected and adapted along the way and was already quite refined.

In this case, daily coordination was done by email. Face-to-face discussions would have been better, but at least they had daily visibility of progress and impediments. A whiteboard was used for a task board to show each item and its status.

Sprint retrospectives were held each week, and the outcome often involved plans for improving coordination and issues with the hiring portal vendor. Issues were fixed in a timely manner because attention was given weekly.

As well, someone was given the task of addressing any issue as part of the follow-up action plan.

Within this organizational framework, the hiring process was incorporated. An onboarding company provided a portal for managing candidates through the pipeline. This portal provided visibility for each stage of the hiring process they were in, and helped with scheduling rooms and moving candidates from one interview stage to the next.

During training, a whiteboard was placed outside the training room where trainees could post questions. Any employee passing by could post an answer. This way, a crowd source and collaborative culture were introduced right away while everyone was new.

Parexel saw astounding results from their coordinated scrum framework:

✔ All new hires received the same training. Whatever department the individual was hired within, their big-picture understanding of their role was complete. Great employee satisfaction resulted in this shared and unified knowledge.

✔ Onboarding was completed all at once within a one-week time frame.

✔ The entire team was enthusiastic about the project.

✔ This same program is still being used three years later.

After this first wave of hires, inspect and adapt was applied and improvements were made to the system. Overall, the inspect-and-adapt cycle so inherent to scrum, combined with the swarming of each feature, meant remarkable success in a potentially nightmarish hiring project.

Training, developing, and evaluating your employees under a scrum model will likely require changes to how you've been doing these things. You will get the same results that you always have if you continue to stack-rank team members, give attention to titles more than skills, or focus performance improvement activities at only one time of the year by only one supervisor. If you want different (that is, improved) results, change your inputs.

Likewise, how you fund projects under a scrum model requires some tweaks.

Finance

In the end, the goal of business is to make money to continue providing and improving its products or services. Therefore, finance lies at the heart of any successful project. However, increasing competition and tightened budgets require making tough and wise funding decisions.

Billions of dollars are wasted every year in projects brought to market that failed, or died somewhere along their protracted and painful development. Here are just a few examples:

- Ford Motor Co. abandoned a purchasing system *after deployment,* resulting in a $400 million loss.

- J Sainsbury PLC (UK) abandoned a supply chain management system *after deployment,* resulting in a $527 million loss.

- Hewlett-Packard experienced a $160 million loss due to problems with an enterprise resource planning (ERP) system.

- AT&T Wireless experienced problems with a customer management system upgrade, resulting in $100 million lost.

- McDonald's canceled its innovate information-purchasing system after already spending $170 million.

These aren't small numbers, and yet they're only a few examples among many of the types of preventable financial waste that's prevalent today.

A recent survey conducted by KPMG on global IT project management unearthed some startling findings. When respondents were asked about their experiences in delivering value in projects after receiving funding, this is what they found:

- 49 percent said they'd experienced at least one project failure in the last 12 months.

- 2 percent achieved their targeted benefits with every project in those same 12 months.

- 86 percent stated that across their entire project portfolio, they'd lost up to 25 percent of targeted benefits.

My guess is that most of this was preventable.

Incremental funding

Not surprisingly, more and more frequently, companies want to fund an initial deliverable before they make the choice to keep funding more of the project. In scrum, where product increments are produced every sprint and packaged for release every release cycle, incremental funding is easily incorporated.

Incremental funding is a financially driven method of funding projects. It focuses on maximizing returns by delivering sequenced and portioned customer-valued functionality to maximize a project's net present value (NPV).

What used to happen in corporations is that the business team would go before a funding committee with a proposal and return on investment (ROI) numbers that they believed were necessary to get their project funded. If they were successful, the team would spend every nickel of that funding and then either deliver the results or ask for more funding. Few would look at the original ROI numbers from months or years back, because the company wasn't going to get that money back anyway. Sunk costs meant that companies had to move forward at all costs.

In scrum, what happens is that the product owner goes before a funding committee with his vision statement and monetized product roadmap. They might say, "I need $3 million to implement all of these features." The funding committee can then respond with, "Okay, we'll allocate $3 million for your project. But first we'll give you $500,000. Show us that you can deliver the ROI promised for your initial release, and we'll give you more money. But if you can't deliver on a little bit, you can't deliver on a lot."

Net present value (NPV) is the present value of future incoming cash flows minus the purchase price and any future outgoing cash flows.

Many companies prefer to use incremental funding for their projects, with or without the accompanying scrum practices. It just makes more sense. Incremental funding is used to

 ✔ **Mitigate risk:** Stakeholders and product owners are able to test the projected ROI at minimal cost and see whether they hit it.

 ✔ **Reduce cost:** A minimal investment is used at the start.

 ✔ **Maximize returns:** (More on this later in this chapter.)

Another way of looking at this is in terms of MVP (minimum viable product), which I introduce in Chapters 5 and 12. The MVP should be able to be monetized — that is, explicit ROI. If the MVP realizes the projected ROI, fund the next MVP.

Incremental funding creates an opportunity at every release for product owners and stakeholders to examine their ROI. At each release if problems exist then depending on their size and complexity, stakeholders can either choose to invest in fixes, or terminate the project before more money is wasted.

Revenue itself can be started earlier. It's not just less waste but earlier return — and earlier return means higher return. Value is delivered to the customer earlier and his buy-in increases because of it. Controlling risk and cost is important, but so is providing value. Rather than planning on revenue in year three, if distinct features can be identified for generating revenue, these can be chunked out and delivered first. As revenue comes in, the initial costs get offset earlier, and the overall revenue and profit over the life of the product are higher.

Historically, a project's ROI is projected, and funding is received based on that projection. Projects are rarely canceled because testing and customer feedback are left until the end of the development cycle. Even if problems are discovered, it's difficult to take money back after it's already been allocated. Not surprisingly, ROI projections are sometimes inflated to get funding.

With incremental funding, the ROI is kept honest because it needs to be proven at each release. If the increment fails to deliver, no more money is invested.

This lower cost of failure allows developers to nurture their creativity and even form an intra-preneurial culture. Fresh ideas can be tested, and if the ROI is met, they can be continued. Company cultures change as trust is built through tangible delivery and the intra-preneurial spirit is nourished.

Intrapreneurship is behaving like an entrepreneur within a large organization. This type of thinking helps companies innovate and gain a competitive advantage. Organizations that have encouraged their employees to express new ideas and try new things outside of their assigned projects are the sources of some of our most useful products today, including Lockheed Martin's ADP, GORE-TEX fabric, Google's Gmail, 3M's Post-its (my personal favorite), Sony's PlayStation, and Facebook's "Like" button.

Failure no longer exists, and it is instead replaced with consistent learning toward the next success when costs are low and innovation is encouraged. Self-organizing teams now have the freedom and motivation to come up with their own best designs and solutions.

Following are a couple of accounting standard practices that fall right in line with this incremental approach to financing.

Statements of position (SOP)

The American Institute of Certified Public Accountants (AICPA) publishes statements of position (SOP) on accounting issues. SOP 98-1 defines at what point in an internal software development project costs are expensed (that is, capitalized). Under SOP 98-1

✔ Expenses in the preliminary planning stage are expensed in the period they occur.

✔ Expenses incurred during development can be capitalized or split up to be included in the overall price of the software asset and then amortized as costs during the life of the product.

Scrum allows for more costs to be capitalized after planning and throughout the project, because planning and overhead are lower and value-added activities are higher. Most of a sprint is spent doing value-added activities, whereas a traditional model has as much time in planning and analysis as it does in the development phase.

Scrum allows the cost of doing business to occur in increments, as opposed to expensing the entire project up front. Profit can be realized much sooner when you spread initial expenses across the life of the project. The sooner you deliver value to the customer, the sooner the revenue comes in. This capitalization approach means that profit is realized sooner rather than later. This SOP adds value.

Scrum and budgets

Traditional budgeting methods, especially with private companies, entail creating a budget for the entire fiscal year. This budget is meant to capture all expenses and revenues into the future for that year.

Management commits, tracks, and rewards based on this estimated budget projection. If a manager or product group exceeds the revenue estimates or spends less than the estimated expenses, they're rewarded. If they fall short of revenue goals, or exceed estimated expenses, questions have to be answered, but all of that is done in hindsight.

Organizations should only accept a year-long budget for what it is — an estimate. Only the next quarter's estimate should be the actual target and what teams are measured against. It's this one quarter that they try to meet or exceed.

Subsequent quarters are still considered estimates and treated as such. Teams can now incorporate what they learn in the current quarter into the next quarter — inspect and adapt in finance.

In fact, this is how Wall Street works with company estimates. Companies will publish their current quarter's estimates and establish those for the future. However, those further out have less impact than the current one.

Chapter 14

Business Development

· ·

In This Chapter

▶ Improving marketing agility with scrum

▶ Increasing revenue

· ·

"It is not necessary to change. Survival is not mandatory."

— W. Edwards Deming

*B*usiness development, often referred to as sales and marketing, is fundamental to the growth and health of most any organization. After all, getting the word out for what you do, and then finding prospective clients and converting them into sales, is what keeps the motor of business running.

What's the difference between marketing and sales? Marketing is delivering information to find prospective clients to convert through the sales process. Marketing constantly changes as new angles and methods are devised to create product or service exposure to as many people as possible.

Sales is an ongoing conversation between two or more people. It's understanding the needs and wants of that specific individual or organization, and explaining how your product or service fills those needs and wants.

Marketing is the sky over the sales funnel.

In this chapter, I cover how scrum works within the vital roles of marketing and sales.

Scrum and Marketing

Given waterfall project management, sometimes when products are released, it's not clear that they're what the customer actually wants. Little to no end-user feedback has been sought after along the way, so it's anybody's guess as to whether this will be a big success.

Here's the catch: Organizations traditionally have a fixed annual marketing plan (much like the annual budgeting process I visited in Chapter 13). So firms come out with a product that they don't have a clear idea of the success of, yet the marketing for it is often planned out a year in advance.

Additionally, markets change frequently. With the speed of technological advances today, this is even more so and shows only signs of increasing. So even products that have been vetted and proven to be what the customer wants, companies might need to have their marketing angle changed along the way.

I have a good friend who's an Apple product nut. When he heard that the iPad 3 was coming out, he actually slept out on the sidewalk near the store to be one of the first in line to buy it the morning it was released. What did he find out a few days later? The iPad 4 was coming out just five and a half months later. Do you think Apple didn't plan this next release well in advance? It's all part of its speed to market and agility in appeasing customers.

As I mentioned before, sometimes customers don't even know what they want until they get it in their hands and use it. So despite the best of intentions, there remains a mystery to how and what to market.

On top of this, a firm may be dealing with millions of customers and their varied tastes and desires. How many different styles and models of cars, clothes, and gadgets are sold in any one year? And each year, they vary and new ones come out. For every single buyer, marketers want to appease an individual set of tastes.

So while the future is impossible to predict, this is exactly what traditional marketing asks people to do.

Marketing evolution

Just like with most industries and business functions, the world of marketing has evolved. As Anna Kennedy, author of *Business Development For Dummies* (published by John Wiley & Sons, Inc.) shared with me, some of the key changes in marketing recently have been

- ✔ Prospects are able to self-serve information to the extent that two-thirds of the buyer's journey happens before any formal engagement exists with the company.
- ✔ Marketing has shifted to being responsible for generating leads. If as a chief marketing officer (CMO) you're not doing this, you'll soon be out of a job.

- Automation (technology) has allowed marketers to assess where prospects are in the buyer's journey and nurture them on a one-to-one basis.

- Social media provides a forum for conversations between brands and their influencers, prospects, and customers.

So, given those trends, how can scrum help marketers embrace the changes and develop agility in responding to this shifting world?

In a nutshell, these four key changes all relate to each other. Perhaps customers are able to research more on their own before engaging with a seller, which may at first seem like a challenge from the seller's point of view. However, a marketing scrum team that makes its marketing materials trackable can use the analytics to iteratively inspect and adapt its marketing to fit the instantaneous feedback.

This access to feedback (potential customers' actions and interaction with the marketing materials) enables a scrum team to respond and pivot (Lean Startup is addressed in Chapter 12) more frequently and quickly than before. This feedback doesn't require a customer's attendance at a sprint review. A product owner has access to this feedback in real time, thanks to marketing analytics technologies.

Recently, CMG Partners, a strategic marketing consulting firm, released its sixth annual CMO Agenda survey, appropriately entitled "The Agile Advantage." The firm interviewed CMOs, marketing leaders, and agile experts.

Not surprisingly, CMOs had overwhelming agreement on the idea that long-term, highly crafted marketing plans are a thing of the past. Now, speed and agility are key tools. Marketers need to be able to respond to both changing economic landscapes and the shifting desires and needs of customers.

CMOs need help designing solutions that fit the pace and depth of change surrounding them. Increased collaboration and feedback, and then the ability to adapt this information effectively into their campaigns, are priorities.

The survey found three key benefits to specifically using the agile framework within marketing campaigns and projects:

- **Business performance increased.** This arrives in the form of faster speed to market and increased prioritization and productivity.

- **Employee satisfaction increased.** Self-organizing and self-managing teams, combined with transparency and empowerment, lead to happier people.

- **Adaptability increased.** A hallmark of agility and scrum to begin with, this came to the forefront when marketing teams adopted agile frameworks. This adaptability is what was so sorely lacking in waterfall.

More from "The Agile Advantage"

CMG Partners' survey "The Agile Advantage" also produced the following results, showing the need and impact of agility in marketing:

✔ While only 40 percent of the respondents saw themselves as "agile," 63 percent thought it was a high priority to be so.

✔ An impressive 93 percent said introducing agile practices increased the speed to market, and allowed them to make those quick changes they so needed.

✔ Those marketing departments that defined themselves as agile claimed that they were 300 percent more likely to significantly grow their market share.

✔ Introducing agile methods made 87 percent of the teams more productive.

✔ Fantastically, 80 percent of respondents said agile practices both improved prioritization and delivered a better end product.

It's clear that using agile and scrum in marketing allowed greater collaboration between the end user and the marketers. The product brand could then evolve with the customer in hand, rather than hoping that at the end a fit existed.

Cost can be reduced because fewer plans fail with the new fine-tuned approach. With this increase in success rates, customer and employee satisfaction also rises.

Using scrum in marketing

Before I go into specific examples of scrum in marketing, I look at some of the specific ways that it can be adopted. For starters, like with the annual budgeting plan in Chapter 13, the annual marketing plan is seen for what it is. It is a guess that will be refined throughout the year as you empirically learn and adapt.

With scrum, marketing plans can be monthly, weekly, and even daily. After each iteration, inspect and adapt is applied based on feedback from sprint reviews and retrospectives. Now, marketing plans can be adjusted, change can be thought of as progress, and the customer can be marketed to in a way that speaks directly to their changing needs.

New marketing strategies can be tested with actual end users before they're released to broader audiences. In the same vein, brands can be tested within sprints. This is huge cost savings because branding is developed together with the customer, rather than just presented to them at the end.

Agile in marketing

A formal movement exists to apply agile principles in marketing. A set of recognized agile marketing principles has been published, named "Agile Marketing Manifesto," and all of these align with the agile principles I've written about throughout this book. All are scrum in nature.

Some of the key values, which all will sound familiar, are

- Validated learning over opinions and conventions

- Adaptive and iterative campaigns over big-bang campaigns

- The process of customer discovery over static prediction

- Flexible versus rigid planning

The principles are equally applicable, which include

- Our highest priority is to satisfy the customer through early and continuous delivery of marketing that solves problems.

- We welcome and plan for change. We believe that our ability to quickly respond to change is a source of competitive advantage.

- Great marketing requires close alignment with the businesspeople, sales, and development.

- Don't be afraid to fail; just don't fail the same way twice.

- Simplicity is essential.

Scrum in Action

Scrum in marketing is being widely used today, and with astounding success. For all the reasons I mentioned previously, scrum fits this wild and wooly world of shifting customer needs and technology. In the following sections, I discuss three examples of scrum and marketing. Each is real, and each shows the amazing success that's within reach.

Carsurfing

This is a startup app that helps people find and give rides to events such as concerts. Carsurfing facilitates rides finding each other and then setting up the actual arrangements.

After implementing scrum, the marketing team at Carsurfing came up with several lessons learned. For example, each iteration combined the marketing, technology, and creative processes. They built in the look and feel for the customer journey, and added the acquired knowledge of the customer persona into each iteration of design. (See Chapter 3 for my discussion of personas.)

In a beautiful example of inspecting and adapting, the team noticed through analytics that a specific event, the Nevada art festival Burning Man, was getting a huge amount of traffic. The nimbleness of flexible budgets and short sprints allowed them to act quickly and focus all their attention on this one peak of demand. They didn't need to wait until the product had been developed in its entirety with all the functionality on their wish list to drive traffic to the app. Instead, they were able to focus only on one existing feature (matching drivers and riders for a single event). With only an alpha version of the app, marketing was able to recognize a trend of high traffic to a single event. They targeted potential customers for Burning Man and organized 800 rides for that event, a number sufficient to generate viral demand and secure a starting customer base to kick-start their growth.

CafePress

CafePress is a firm that sells themed gifts and merchandise that a customer can customize, such as mugs with pictures and/or memes, or other cultural or current trends.

Yet another layer of versatility was uncovered in CafePress's scrum implementation. The legal implications of customizable products meant that marketing needed a closer alliance with the legal team — one that would facilitate quick response to legal inquiries and concerns. The marketing team needed to be proactively and completely aware of what they could and couldn't say to avoid taking on unnecessary legal liability.

Rather than viewing "legal" as merely a stakeholder, the legal department became integral in Café Press's marketing scrum team, making sure that marketing could get a 20-minute turnaround time in answer to any queries.

CafePress's strategy of bringing legal in more closely is a great example of the benefits of aligning business with development. Sometimes the two sets of goals can seem to be at odds, but with scrum, they're directly aligned with making a better product and creating more satisfied customers.

Building in this close collaboration between business and marketing was vital to the success of the company's marketing team. It saved both time, in getting the right answers quickly, and money, in not taking on any unnecessary legal liability. As these different threads of the business pull together, an effective and efficient business is built.

Xerox

At over 100 years old, Xerox is a household name, usually associated with office photocopying. Ever heard the expression, "I need to Xerox that"? Over the years, this massive firm has branched into many other products and services, such as IT, document management, and all the software and support needed for their printers and other services.

The original photocopy process of making paper copies from documents and visual images is called *xerography*. Electrostatic charges are used on a light-sensitive photoreceptor to transfer powder onto paper, thereby copying the images. Heat then seals the deal, literally. Who invented xerography? A company called Xerox.

Xerox's global, interactive marketing team integrated scrum into their business framework. Their need was to simplify and prioritize the massive amount of demand from customers and marketing teams throughout the world. They knew they had to respond to the changing market and their customers' changing needs, and they needed to be able to respond as fast as their newer, somewhat smaller competitors who could naturally respond and pivot more quickly. Scrum provided the framework to self-organize, iterate, inspect, adapt, and deliver more often.

Similar problems existed as in portfolio management (see Chapter 12), where projects weren't prioritized, so developers were thrashed from project to project and the loudest stakeholder was the one who received his product first. When new initiatives came along, they weren't able to pivot quickly enough to take full advantage of the potential benefits.

The teams would either thrash employees across multiple projects or else one project would get stopped midway, to reallocate people to a new one.

What saved Xerox was segmenting the type of work to be done into three separate queues: new development, creative projects (that is, artwork), and rapid response (service issues that take eight hours or less). Short sprint cycles and the inspect-and-adapt process enabled team members to focus each sprint on only one of the queues, rather than all of them at once.

Thrashing should be avoided. If complete avoidance isn't possible, it should be minimized to every extent possible. The Xerox marketing team was thrashing between each sprint, but at least they were no longer thrashing within each sprint. This focus during each sprint enabled them to frequently deliver increments across the three queues and prioritize those that were most important. Speed to market increased because the teams didn't get sidetracked before being able to complete a project. Employee morale also increased through less thrashing, and customer satisfaction improved by customers getting what they wanted sooner and better.

A hierarchy of thrashing

Here and in Figure 14-1, I describe the many faces of thrashing. However it looks in your organization, apply scrum to minimize the impact of it. Just remember — the more stable your team, the higher your profitability.

Team is stable for project duration: Here the project is stable with no thrashing because the team is focused for the entire project until AC + OC > V (see Chapter 5). This is the most efficient structure. It will quickly produce the best quality possible and maximizes profitability.

Team is stable for release duration: The team is focused on project A until they have something releasable to customers. They then switch to project B until they have something releasable for customers, then they switch to project C, and so on. This is worse than project stability.

Team is stable for sprint duration: The team is focused on project A for the entire sprint. They then switch to project B for a same-duration sprint, then switch to project C, and so on. This is worse than release stability.

Team is stable for the day's duration: The team spends Monday working on project A. They then switch to project B on Tuesday, project C on Wednesday, and so on. This is worse than sprint stability.

Team is stable for blocks of hours: The team spends every morning working on project A, the afternoon on project B, and so on. This is worse than day stability.

Minute-by-minute team thrashing: This is the most common portfolio management approach. Individual team members get started working on project A; 45 minutes later, an emergency occurs on project B, which takes them until lunch. After lunch, they attempt to restart project A, but something comes up on project C that takes the afternoon. On the next day, they are back to square one with project A because of mental remobilization time. The process continues until a project close to an influential executive is so late that the team is forced to spend their evenings and weekends working on just that project. This is the worst-case scenario.

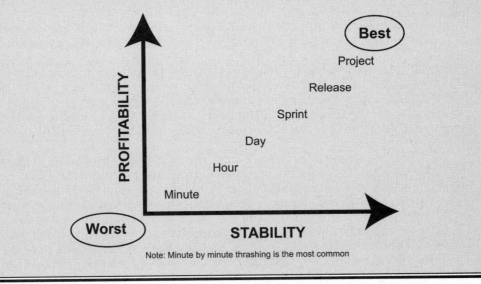

Note: Minute by minute thrashing is the most common

Scrum for Sales

Sales is not an island. It is part of a business development cycle that starts with defining what the market needs and the product and service that will fulfill that need. Then, it goes through marketing, sales, delivery, and evaluation, to leveraging the customer for repeat sales and advocacy.

In traditional project management frameworks, sales is the classic, individualistic, pioneer-style role. Individual quotas must be met and ideally are exceeded, and pay is meted out based on the sales quota results. Salesperson of the Week, Month, and even Year are coveted accolades. Competition is fierce, and in every organization, a few star individuals rise to the top.

While the term "Sales Team" may be used, "team" typically loosely refers to the overall staff of the department and not to the department working as a unified team, while each salesperson is individually responsible. Yet sales and the inherent amount of rejection can be a roller coaster ride both emotionally and professionally for the best of salespeople. When sales are low or an important call goes bad, it can be a challenge to remain engaged. Even skilled and experienced salespeople struggle to maintain an even keel with the rise and fall of good and bad sales days.

Harvard Business Review recently blogged about a change in the trend between individual and team sales approaches. In the ten-year period from 2002 to 2012, the impact that an individual had on unit profitability decreased by nearly 25 percent. However, his "network performance" (defined as "how much people give to and take from their coworkers") increased his impact by over 25 percent. Network performance is 44 percent of a person's impact on their unit's profitability.

Microchip, a leading semiconductor firm, shifted its pay structure away from a traditional, variable compensation plan to one that added a small variable based on company and unit performance. Employees would now be paid a bonus based on their immediate team's performance, as well as on how well the overall firm did. The result was "record growth and profitability, increased rep engagement, and near-zero attrition."

In other words, the best salespeople have been found to interact with others on the sales team and coordinate for the best overall results. Collective skills and even crowd sourcing were cited as ways they excel. Star managers are using team brainstorming with their reps, and even borrowing ideas from other areas of the company. It's as if the trend is to naturally lean toward a scrum framework.

The scrum solution

The sales process of converting leads to closed sales is also known as the sales pipeline or funnel. Figure 14-1 outlines the basic sales funnel.

Figure 14-1:
A classic sales funnel depicting the sales process from beginning to end.

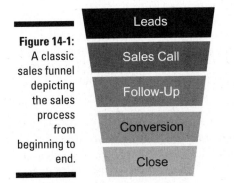

Leads

Sales Call

Follow-Up

Conversion

Close

Scrum, as we've seen before, takes the traditional approach to sales and turns it on its collective head. Here are some of the ways how this happens:

✔ Scrum by its very nature is focused on team success. You might think of a sales team as a group of salespeople pounding the pavement with the same pitch. A sales team, especially with scrum, is much more than that. Just like with a cross-functional product development team, consisting of such developers as designers, engineers, and testers, a sales team needs different skills too, like marketing, sales enablement, sales engineering, subject matter expertise, contracts, legal, and finance. The entire sales team has goals. If the team fails in its goals, the individuals can become open to working together to find solutions for achieving goals.

✔ Along these same lines, rewards are team based. See Chapter 13 for more about the dynamics of team compensation. The type of sales team described previously (all salespeople and no one else) is driven by competition, all working as silos. A team structure incentivizes all team members to "swarm" around a lead to get to "done" (close).

✔ Scrum is all about results over the process to achieve those results. It's focused on reality-based inspect and adapt. What works for one team or client may not work for another team or client.

✔ Results still count. The burndown and burnup charts that I discuss in detail in Chapter 5 can be used in sales. Rather than tracking how much has been done, sales are tracked by how much is left to do in that sprint (burndown). Likewise, tracking the cumulative sales (burnup) shows real-time progress toward the sprint sales goal.

> ✔ Standing daily scrum meetings work well, because nobody wants long meetings. If impediments are discovered outside the team, an outside person can be invited to the daily scrum and partake in an after-party removal of the impediment (see Chapter 6 for a brush-up on after parties).

The product backlog becomes your sales funnel.

A sales manager from an agile-based organization implemented a backlog item task board. Columns included the stages of the sales funnel, such as Leads, Sales Call, and Follow-Up. The entire sales team and management now had an immediate visual of where the team was in the project. Sales estimates were now able to be inspected and adapted based on reality. See Figure 14-2 for an example of the sales funnel as a task board.

In addition to burndown and burnup charts exposing progress, a visible funnel in the form of a task board is quite valuable. The sales funnel in Figure 14-1 becomes the task board shown in Figure 14-2 as follows:

RELEASE GOAL: SPRINT GOAL:

                                              PBI = Product Backlog Item

RELEASE DATE: SPRINT REVIEW: Task = Task

LEADS	SALES CALL	FOLLOW-UP	CONVERSION	CLOSE

Figure 14-2: A sales task board with columns representing the sales funnel stages.

✔ Each row ("swim lane") represents one lead.

✔ **Leads:** This is the sprint backlog of sales opportunities. Leads arrive from a variety of sources and methods, but they all land here and get discussed, vetted, and prioritized before initiating the sales call. This is increasingly becoming a function of marketing (taking somewhat qualified leads and turning them into sales-qualified leads that are ready to buy). Scrum can also help bridge the traditional divide between marketing and sales through this visibility and coordination of the sales team format described previously.

✔ **Sales Call:** An initial sales "call" is made (it could be via any medium, such as door-to-door, videoconference, phone, email, or mail) to further qualify the lead (that is, define the prospect's "need" and position the offering as the solution). This stage involves various tasks to accomplish this, which would have been outlined during sprint planning while in the Leads column. After being qualified, the lead moves on to Follow-Up.

✔ **Follow-Up:** The lead has responded and expressed interest in the proposed solution to his need. A series of steps and tasks are coordinated, timed, and executed by the team.

✔ **Conversion:** Obstacles and impediments to closing the sales are identified, and the team swarms to overcome them.

✔ **Close:** The contract is won and clearly documented why and how.

How is all of this done more effectively as a team? Look again at the skills required to make a sale: marketing, sales enablement, sales engineering, subject matter expertise, contracts, legal, finance, and others.

Ideally we do want cross-functional team members who can do everything. But, having one person who can do everything well is unusual. Having a team of individuals that can do everything well is even less likely. However, having a cross-functional team of members who can self-organize, devise plans, and swarm around a prospect, event, or contract will produce higher results than if one person tries to do everything alone. Because scrum focuses on continuous communication between all parties as to what's needed and what can be done, the scrum sales team will have a clearer understanding of what their prospective clients need and want. They can then present their sales ideas in a way that directly impacts those prospects.

The scrum sales process

Successful salespeople are exceptional listeners and have keen observation skills. One of the basic goals is to discover problems and issues that prospects have, and then show how the salesperson's product or service solves the prospect's problem or issue. To make this connection, the salesperson needs to establish a relationship based on trust — people buy things from people they know and trust.

Scrum selling is about gaining that trust through teamwork. The supporting players may include any of the following: presales, business development, account executives, field engineers, installers, inside sales and support, and service people. Any combination of these people can make up a scrum team and swarm to synchronize communication to support the effort of getting the client to ink a deal. Swarming activities might revolve around

✔ Trade show event preparation

✔ Trade show lead follow-up

✔ Time-bound proposals to develop potential solutions for a sales pitch to out-class the competition

✔ Saving a sale at risk through brainstorming and prioritizing action items

Selling today involves content marketing, webinars, trade shows, social media marketing, and other "pull" strategies. Buyers are more sophisticated and educated given fingertip access to online research, Yelp, Angie's List, and Google.

Sales cycles are more successful when a potential consumer or business is *pulled* toward a product or solution as opposed to a pure outbound "cold call" approach. Push versus pull models are discussed in Chapter 5.

A scrum sales process would mirror the roadmap to value as follows:

1. Vision: Grow our gross sales in Dallas by 20 percent this fiscal year by increasing our social media presence and analytics and following up with a personal phone call or email to everyone who provides their contact information. (The vision model I present in Chapter 2 is for product development. For sales and other nonproduct development projects, it's appropriate to tweak that model based on reality.)

2. Product roadmap (high-level) and product backlog (broken down): A high- and low-level list of changes is needed to make the vision a reality, such as

   • Sales strategy development

   • Acquisition of tools

   • Development of collateral

   • Sales process development and fine-tuning

   • Execution needed for specific deals in the process

   • Assigning key (detailed) social media sites to a team member

   • Finding a tool for tracking sales funnels that the team will use

   • Defining such reporting processes as analytics workflows

3. Release planning: Prioritize the backlog items by month and/or quarter.

4. Sprint planning: As a team, create tasks and assignments for the backlog items.

5. Sprint: Daily stand-ups to coordinate swarming tasks for the day and identify impediments.

6. Sprint review: Demo to the stakeholders (for example, the VP of Sales) that the sprint is complete (for example, the Facebook page is operational or mailing lists of past customers are compiled).

7. Sprint retrospective: Review what worked well and facilitate knowledge transfer. (For example, service/installation folks are learning how new customers are being acquired, and this helps them continue the company messaging that leads to the sale.)

As you can see, the scrum sales process is high touch and common sense.

iSense Prowareness

iSense Prowareness is an information and computer technology consulting company (ICT) based in the Netherlands. In 2010, it adopted scrum throughout it sales processes. The problems that the company had been experiencing were diverse and based on a huge lack of transparency:

✔ The system tracked individual progress, but only the manager looked at this. The number and size of each deal were all the data that was shared, and each rep's progress was measured by these metrics alone. Every week, each individual estimated his numbers for that week, and at the end of the week, reported what they had actually achieved.

✔ The company had no way of knowing how individual efforts were impacting the overall team sales.

✔ No process indicators existed. The only measurement was the amount sold. The number of phone calls could be tracked; however, the closing rate based on these was unknown. Management had limited ways to help their sales team as they didn't know what and where the individual impediments were. The only input was to work harder, as they had no way of determining what "working smarter" meant.

✔ The sales reps worked hard on improving their numbers, but no structured time was spent on reflecting or on the establishment of a system to improve.

Given this quite typical sales background, iSense began implementing scrum. It hired outside consultants to help with the transition and began with

- Weekly sprints from Monday through Friday.

- Quarterly sales targets, which included 13 sprints to each "release."

- Each week, salespeople adapted what they learned from the daily scrums and sprint reviews and retrospectives.

- A scrum task board was created with a burndown chart and orders taken.

- Standing daily scrums were held in front of the task board.

The results? After the completion of the scrum integration, revenue doubled, half of which sales managers attributed directly to scrum — an excellent return on investment for the transition to scrum.

Interestingly, important lessons learned included the ability to assess which sales tactics were working and which weren't delivering total value. Scrum's transparency made abundantly clear that there is no value to an organization being unable to fulfill a closed sale. When the sales team increased their hit rate as a result of this team-based approach, their pool of service providers had not increased to fill demand. The sales managers recognized a way that they could help recruiters fill the demand through temporary contracts, which bought them more time to permanently fill those positions.

This experience has also led to the sales managers promoting cross-functional teams in which sales, recruitment, marketing, and consultants take part all together.

The team just presented would cold-call to gather attendees for events highlighting the products. At the event, attendees would be turned from cold leads into warm ones, and then follow-up contact would result in some of these turning into hot leads and eventual sales. Through analyzing the process and results, the team found that they were only converting 10 percent into actual sales. This allowed the team to discuss and identify gaps in the sales process, refine the sequence, and increase sales. Before long, they doubled that conversion rate.

Through the integration of scrum, the iSense sales team made another important discovery: Making the sale was just the beginning. To truly complete the cycle, the company had to deliver on the product. Sounds simple, but through the process of sprint reviews and retrospectives, where employees from different parts of the company shared information, this gap, too, began to narrow, and the customer benefited.

The sales teams realized that instead of their primary focus being on creating new business, they had more to win with existing contacts and customers. The customers they had already done successful projects with could be used as a starting point for more business. They could become promoters of projects to other companies.

Parts IV and V of *Business Development For Dummies* (Anna Kennedy; John Wiley and Sons) are a great resource if you're new to building marketing and sales departments.

Scrum in marketing and sales works beautifully. Increased transparency with customers and across organizational divisions, regular and frequent feedback from clients and prospects, and prioritizing projects to reduce thrashing have led to amazing successes. Scrum is the framework. Teams apply it.

Chapter 15

Customer Service

· ·

· ·

Get closer than ever to your customers. So close that you tell them what they need well before they realize it themselves.

— Steve Jobs

C ustomer service is one of the most critical aspects of any organization. Positive experiences give us reason to go back or refer friends and family. Yet this is the very area that many customers and clients state is the most problematic part of the experience. They like the product, but its perceived value decreases with poor service.

Remember, customer service equals sales. A happy customer tells their friends and family, and they go back themselves for more services and products. Knowledge about customers equals knowledge-based marketing. Finding new customers becomes that much more effective. Therefore, managing accounts for customers can actually be thought of as an extension of sales and marketing.

In short, customer service is a huge opportunity to increase sales and therefore revenue. Looked after, this one department can propel a firm to new heights. However, neglected, it can affect a company's reputation and goodwill.

The Most Crucial Stakeholder

As far as number of complaints go, Internet service provider (ISP) customer service ranked second highest on Angie's List in 2011. Customer service from phone companies ranked eighth on the most complained about. It seems that where customer options of service providers are limited (add local utilities to this list), customer service is commonly (although not always) weaker than in other industries, with longer hold times, frustrating service, and labyrinth automated service menus. Yet the customer is the most crucial stakeholder in any business. Without them, there's no business.

Comcast has recently gone through a spate of bad press regarding the quality of its customer service. Instances of customers unable to get refunds for bogus charges, wait times forced until closing, and an inability to cancel subscriptions are just a few of the claims.

It's not just in technology companies either. Have you ever been given the runaround in high-pressure sales situations (such as car dealerships and timeshare presentations) by an overzealous sales representative who wants the sale more than your satisfaction?

Angie's List is a national, subscription-based web service where subscribers rank and review rankings for all kinds of household services, from lawn care to Internet service providers to healthcare. More than 2 million households across America participate.

The Federal Communications Commission (FCC) states that in the United States, over 300 million wireless subscribers exist, millions of whom need customer service every year. Cable TV service centers handle over 60 million customers per year, and satellite TV providers over 24 million.

So while the need for service is enormous, as you can see from the preceding numbers, the quality is often lacking and millions of people are willing to spend the time to make others aware of their experience. Customer complaints about the handling of their service calls abound.

How can such service-centric firms be missing out on providing timely and effective solutions to customer problems? The following sections break it down further.

The service conundrum

Perhaps the number-one failure in service is that according to customers, half the time their issues aren't even solved by the agent. Now that's a problem. Customers need and expect service representatives to be able to answer questions and solve problems regarding their own product. Unfortunately, all too often, the training in companies fails to provide this.

The service representative might not understand the problem due to the customer poorly explaining it, and/or the representative simply doesn't understand where the customer is coming from.

The cost of losing a customer is far more than their annual subscription rate. While customer service divisions are often thought of as cost centers, in fact, they save and make their firms huge amounts of revenue. Check out these stats:

- ✔ It's over six times as expensive to gain a new client than it is to keep a current one.

- ✔ 78 percent of customers have foregone a purchase or transaction due to poor service.

- ✔ Loyal customers are worth up to ten times the amount of their initial purchase.

- ✔ Twelve positive experiences are needed to make up for one negative one.

- ✔ For every customer who takes the time to complain, 26 others tell their friends instead.

- ✔ In 2010, 67 percent of customers actually hung up the phone because they couldn't speak to a real person.

Information overload

In this day and age of massive amounts of information, too much data is quoted as a source of call center failures. Too much information can actually paralyze the effective functioning of a service representative. Service representatives can become overwhelmed with too much data that's hard to use, and many centers haven't managed this information so that it's useful to representatives.

Have you ever been on a call with one representative and transferred to another, only to find that you have to explain the issue all over again? Oftentimes, a client's historical data doesn't get fed to the rep proactively. It's frustrating for the customer to rehash his situation or to hear those ominous words, "I have no record of your claim here."

Getting the right information to the right people is part of the issue. In fact, 60 percent of customer service centers say they aren't even able to get certain pieces of customer information (for example, portions of customer history) to service representatives. On top of this, more than 30 percent of representatives don't gather and record customer satisfaction data.

Sometimes data isn't consolidated between organizational divisions, or the data is there and it's just hard to find. So while firms are experts at gathering information, it's the timely and effective distribution of that knowledge that's the problem.

It'll cost me what?

Have you ever heard something like this? "I know you didn't do anything to change your system, but in order to fix it, we need to send out a technician next Thursday between the hours of 1 and 5 p.m. and it'll cost you $100."

Or how about those surprise fees that show up on your bill when you didn't order anything new or change your service in any way? The company may have a legitimate need to charge more because of a service upgrade or more features, but still, it's frustrating to see fees appear out of nowhere without clear explanation.

These are all situations that arise out of new technology and paradigms, stuck within outdated project management frameworks.

When service calls are assessed, management often measures efficiency over customer needs and satisfaction. The most collected metrics are

- ✔ 79 percent gather average handle time.
- ✔ 75 percent measure abandonment rate.
- ✔ 71 percent measure average speed of answer.
- ✔ Less than 50 percent actually measure customer satisfaction.

While these are some of the current problems vexing customer service, the following sections look at scrum solutions.

Scrum and Customer Service

Most of the high-level issues listed previously can be tied into and improved by implementing scrum basics. While these problems seem daunting, and we've all likely experienced one or more of them, they're not insolvable. On the contrary: Scrum offers solutions.

Inspect and adapt through feedback

One of the basic tenets of scrum is the feedback loop that facilitates inspecting and adapting. In customer service, feedback is received from customers daily, hourly, and even by the minute. This is feedback not just on the product, but also on the customer service department itself. This is a structure that is perfect for the "per-call" sprint cycle.

In each of the sprint events, customer service teams can ask themselves whether the data they have is what they need to provide the best customer service:

- ✔ Do the tools they have best serve the customer?
- ✔ Is the knowledge they have enough to answer most problems?

The answers need to follow the roadmap to value:

- ✔ **Vision:** The vision for a service call is simple — to provide the customer with quality support that ends with the customer feeling better about the company than before they called.

- ✔ **Sprint planning:** For each call, tangible steps toward solving a problem can be inspected and adapted. For example, each sprint might involve representatives asking customers a certain question during the call to test their progress toward solving the broader problem. If call data shows that hold time is long, an example might be to briefly ask the customers something like, "Do you feel that your hold time was reasonable today?" Collecting these "yes" and "no" answers each call can help validate whether progress is being made with existing processes or whether changes are required to solve the problem.

- ✔ **Sprint review:** A team of service representatives may not find it efficient to reconvene after every call for a review. However, inspecting and adapting at the end of each shift will provide the team and the next-shift teams with real-time feedback for dealing with the realities of the day. Here the team can assimilate the information gathered from the sprint call. What did they learn? What questions should they ask in the next sprint? Based on what they learned, how can they improve the customer experience?

- ✔ **Sprint retrospective:** Again, at the end of a shift, the team can ask whether a better way exists to gather information from the customers. For example, do the existing questions bait the customer to provide a certain answer or are they truly objective? How well did they assess their findings? How well did they document them? What aspects of their process should they inspect for improvements?

✔ **Team daily scrums:** If service teams run daily sprints, the daily scrum naturally becomes the sprint review and sprint planning. But if sprints are longer than a shift or a day, individual issues and impediments can be raised for the broader customer service team to solve in a daily scrum. For example, if a rep is having a hard time transitioning into asking the research question during the call, perhaps another service representative can offer to sit with her for a few calls a day.

Many service centers will involve enough representatives to require multiple teams, in which case vertical slicing or other scaled scrum models would be implemented (see Chapter 12) to enable coordination and integration of activities and shared knowledge and learnings. A scrum of scrums each day would be the natural place to share these lessons learned and coordinate in a quick and focused manner.

A customer service product owner would also naturally be a key stakeholder to a product development scrum team creating the products that they're supporting.

Customer service provides the perfect opportunity to get direct feedback from the most important stakeholder — the customer! When applied to each of the scrum events, and then shared with the product owner and stakeholders, this allows for greater transparency and hence greater effectiveness.

Customer service product backlog

Training knowledgeable customer service representatives is the most important factor in creating satisfied customers. This training isn't a one-time event. New products and services will require additional training as will refreshers on how to handle complaints and miscommunication.

By making it incredibly easy for customers to provide feedback, a product backlog can be generated that contains issues that need to be resolved. These issues can then be prioritized and addresses based on the highest priority.

For new product development scrum teams, release planning (see Chapter 5) is the point at which customer service can mobilize for what representatives need to be trained on while a product is being developed, based on the upcoming inspect-and-adapt changes.

Seventy-eight percent of customers state that their good customer service experience was due to the knowledge the rep had, while only 38 percent said it was due to personalization. Knowledge matters. Training development for representatives is a high priority. Preplanned answers don't carry the weight of true depth of knowledge.

For customer service scrum teams, if a consistent customer need arises, finding a preventative solution can be placed in the backlog and given a high priority. This helps shorten the triage cycle as much as possible. Instead, customer needs can be discovered and addressed in real time. Prioritizing these needs and swarming on their solution help overcome customer service product backlog obstacles.

Customer service should be considered a crucial stakeholder for product development teams. Representatives' feedback should be considered just as reliable as (if not more than) any market research. If customer service representatives aren't represented as integral stakeholders with product development scrum teams, how can product owners be sure that they know what the customers want?

Customer service definition of done

The definition of done for customer service teams should clearly outline what it means to consider whether a customer is satisfied with his level of service. The definition of done should include more than just call length and abandonment statistics.

Going back to the roadmap to value, a customer service department should have a vision statement that specifically states what their customer needs are, how the team meets the needs of their customers, and how their role helps differentiate their organization in the marketplace and ties in to their corporate strategy (for more on vision statements, see Chapter 2).

The vision is the framework for defining what it means to be "done" when providing quality customer service one customer at a time. The customer service definition of done might look something like this:

With each customer, I have succeeded in fulfilling our vision to [statement of how the need is met and differentiated] after I have

✔ Fully solved the customer's problem

✔ Added the problem and solution to product documentation

- ✔ Thoroughly reviewed customer history before offering a solution

- ✔ Updated customer history

- ✔ Searched each of the following knowledge bases for answers (ABC & XYZ)

- ✔ Sought out subject matter expertise from fellow representatives and/or supervisor as needed

- ✔ Kept my cool

- ✔ Helped the customer keep her cool by [stated methods used by the organization]

- ✔ Followed up on promises I made to the customer

Representatives need to understand what's expected of them to provide clarity on what success looks like.

Consider what the definition of done is in providing service representatives what they need to support a product or service. Is this in the form of documentation, additional training, or some preestablished metric? Whatever it is, clarify it and then communicate it.

Inspect and adapt in practice

Historically, emails are lower priority than calls for call centers, so it's common to hear complaints about lack of response to written inquiries. This call center priority makes sense in the context of agile principles — customer service professionals understand the value of voice conversations over written conversations. Still, customers shy away from calling if they don't feel like they have time to hold to speak to a live person. So, their options become email or live chat.

A customer service center that is truly inspecting and adapting would be looking for operational and procedural ways to make written service more successful and integral with call inquiries. After all, one rep can handle multiple chats concurrently while they can only handle one call at a time. At least one study claims that a service rep can handle up to six chats for every call.

Promptly answered voice calls that are competently handled are better than chats for providing great customer service, but chat is better than email because it provides instant response.

Alistair Cockburn is one of the signatories of the Agile Manifesto (refer to Chapter 1). Alistair studied the most effective methods of communication — a key aspect of any scrum environment. Figure 15-1 lists methods of communication from worst (paper and email) to best (face to face at a whiteboard). This underscores the effectiveness of collocation in increasing the quality of communication.

Figure 15-1:
Alistair Cockburn's modes of communication chart.

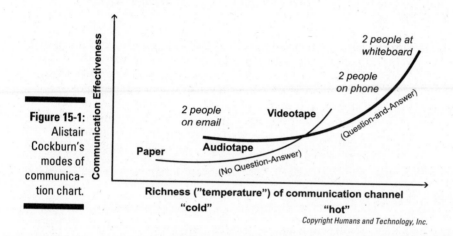

Copyright Humans and Technology, Inc.

As I mention in Chapter 4, Albert Mehrabian, Ph.D., professor emeritus of psychology at UCLA, proved that 55 percent of meaning is conveyed through body language and facial expressions; 38 percent of meaning is paralinguistic, meaning conveyed by the *way* we speak; and 7 percent of meaning is conveyed in the actual words spoken.

The importance of quality of communication simply can't be overstated. Face-to-face interaction allows for real-time questioning and clarification, cued by body language and nonverbal signals. Lack of interactivity leads to misunderstandings. Misunderstandings lead to defects, and nothing is more damaging to schedule and budget, and consequently to bottom-line profitability, than defects — whether that be product defects or customer service defects, the cost is significant.

Misunderstandings aside, the same conversation that takes days of back-and-forth responses may take as little as five minutes by standing up and walking across the floor to another office or cubicle. With customer service, constraints may only allow a service representative to put on a headset and dial a number to have a voice conversation. Voice to voice will be much more effective than chat to chat or email to email.

Perhaps something about voice to voice should be included in your definition of done for quality customer service. For instance, adding something like the following to the previous bullet list might make sense:

- Called an email customer after two passes back and forth to avoid further misunderstanding
- Followed up with a customer by phone instead of email whenever possible

Fortunately, face-to-face conversations are at the heart of scrum. Colocated team members can collaborate with one another every day, throughout the day. Minor issues get resolved before they turn into major ones. With this continual face-to-face collaboration comes a greater understanding of the individual personalities and strengths of each team member. This in turn facilitates increased cross-functionality, improved self-organization, and effective self-management. This is how teams become high functioning.

Scrum in Action

Many companies are already using scrum but just haven't applied it to their customer service departments. These firms could greatly improve their customer service, and therefore bottom line, if they utilized scrum across the board. In fact, if scrum is already utilized within an organization, there should be enough experience and knowledge to be shared for getting started in other departments.

Making this happen isn't that difficult. I previously discussed several ways of adapting scrum through events, definition of done, and the product backlog. Integral to this, is making sure that a customer service rep is present in every sprint review for product development scrum teams. Transparency and awareness stem from this.

Service representative scrum teams can now plan training and other process improvement activities during sprints. Additionally, service representatives can learn from the product development sprint reviews and share this information with their scrum teams.

L.A. Dept of Water and Power

The Los Angeles Department of Water and Power (LADWP) actually implemented the scrum framework, while not calling it scrum. The goal was to enhance customer satisfaction in their net meter Solar Incentive Program. LADWP wanted to reduce delays, streamline the overall experience, and increase transparency.

To increase transparency, the company implemented two dashboards, called Mayor's Dashboards, so that customers could stay abreast of changes and improvements:

- One dashboard included weekly updates on metrics, which included the status of rebate checks.

- The second dashboard displayed the Feed-in Tariff (FiT) 100-megawatt program, which the city uses to purchase third-party solar power. The time and process involved in processing FiT contracts was displayed, and both dashboards displayed issues, solutions, and response times. In other words, a huge increase in transparency occurred.

These were both sprint backlogs made available to all stakeholders and customers. As well as these dashboards, the department also consistently inspected and adapted its process to streamline the process for reviewing applications. Results of this inspection and adaption included

- Increasing staff to handle applications and hotline service

- Removing dependencies between rebate payment and turning on service

- Reducing review time of lease agreements through a lease compliance form

- Automating routine email communications with customers and contractors through an off-the-shelf software solution

The main improvements were in streamlining existing systems and increasing clarity. These two steps alone, and very scrum indeed, improved the overall customer experience. By enhancing the customer experience, customer service was greatly increased. So the company targeted the root causes of issues and set about to fix them with scrum principles.

Part V

Scrum for Everyday Life

5 = LOVE IT!
4 = Good idea.
3 = Yeah, I can support it.
2 = I have reservations, let's discuss further.
1 = Opposed. Do not move forward.

In this part . . .

- Developing fulfilling relationships.
- Planning personal and family projects without stress.
- Achieving financial goals.
- Maximizing education opportunities, from kindergarten to doctorate.
- Visit `www.dummies.com/extras/scrum` for great Dummies content online.

Chapter 16

Dating and Family Life

. . . .

. . . .

"I don't want perfect, I want worth it."

— Unknown

It's easy to say the world has changed. And it has. As you've read through each chapter, I have shown how scrum can help in any business industry to let businesses grow and adapt along with the changing realities of the world.

In the next few chapters, however, I'm going to walk you through some areas of your life where you can implement scrum that you may not have considered. Talking about aspects of your personal life using scrum terms may seem to lack emotion on the surface. But our personal lives are all about prioritizing and making critical decisions with imperfect information and an unknown future, just like in business.

As you read this chapter and Chapter 17, keep the following in mind:

✔ In business, the product backlog applies to a product being developed — a software or hardware product, a service, or some other "done" deliverable to another customer. In family and personal endeavors, a "product" may be a vacation or wedding plan, a relationship, an education, or a retirement plan.

✔ Likewise, when I speak of customers in business, I'm talking about someone who is going to use the product. In personal and family endeavors, a customer may be yourself, your family, your teacher, or your future self in retirement.

Don't let the terminology throw you off. It works.

In addition to the benefits of scrum in the business world, scrum can help you to develop personal relationships and to make time to do the things you love in your daily life. Almost everyone will tell you his or her family or significant other is the most important thing in his or her life — and scrum can help you prioritize them to be so.

Finding Love with Scrum

People have a very real drive to seek love and relationships. Even if each person has a different kind of ideal relationship, we almost all seek out a loving long-term relationship. But the truth is that while dating can be fun and adventurous — finding a lasting, loving, healthy relationship can be difficult.

Relationships have evolved. In modern relationships, people are seeking more honest connections — it's no longer about being married because of societal expectations or ensuring that you don't grow old alone. People now seek out more fulfilling, satisfying relationships based on communication and compatibility.

Although technology has played a huge role in opening dialogue in dating and providing new ways to find potential matches, it hasn't necessarily eliminated all the challenges. In spite of these technological advances and conveniences, it can still be an uncomfortable subject for some to discuss, or even to think about.

I want to show you how scrum can make dealing with dating challenges more comfortable and provide a framework for taking steps that you may have never thought possible in your pursuit of happiness. Here are a few of these dating challenges in detail:

- **Life, even without a family, is busy.** Life is about how you spend the finite amount of time you have each day. Singles have careers, ongoing education, side jobs, personal goals, hobbies, friends, and other nondating activities. It's easy if you're the single person to stay late at work, or take on that extra side job or project. So while many people *want* a relationship, they simultaneously haven't structured their life to have time for one. Making room for dating is about priorities.

- **Communication:** In modern dating, communication has frequently devolved to email or texting most of the time. These amazing technological advances that facilitate making connections can also be a hindrance in strengthening relationships when used to replace face-to-face interactions that are so crucial for minimizing misunderstandings and resolving conflict. No wonder that email and texting make it harder to get to know someone on a deeper level, or so easy to get into a fight.

✔ **Finding the right person:** That's really what it is about isn't it? Finding the right person is just difficult and feels like mysterious luck half the time. But really it can be broken down into something simple: Most relationships don't work out because of a reason from one of two very simple categories:

- Attraction and chemistry

- Personality and values

The problem is finding someone that you not only have a genuine attraction and chemistry with, but also someone whose natural personality and values fit in with how you view life. These two categories oversimplify a variety of factors that impact compatibility that include things like finances, selfishness, and intimacy — all of which contribute to overall potential relationship success.

You might look at those problems and think that they have no correlation with scrum. Modern dating is too complicated! Ironically, that is exactly why scrum works for finding love; scrum is about simplifying and working toward the vision:

✔ Responding to change (such as acceptance, rejection, love, heartbreak, connection, and embarrassment)

✔ Failing early and fast (that is, wasting as little time as possible on someone who isn't compatible)

✔ Inspecting and adapting (that is, tweaking and becoming the right match for someone else and refining what the right match is for yourself)

Even though love is complicated, making decisions based on prioritization and empirical evidence is what scrum can do for your love life.

Almost everyone has been through heartbreak (with the exception of the lucky few who meet the love of their life the first time around, a toast to them!). For some, heartbreak has led to levels of bitterness or introversion to protect from further heartbreak. However, every layer of attempted protection only prevents us from getting closer to the goal of love. Love is an offensive game, not a defensive one. I'll be clear: Inspecting and adapting based on frequent empirical evidence are your keys to finding happiness.

The following sections take a look at how you can put down the complications of modern dating and focus on finding love with scrum.

Setting a vision

The roadmap to value (or in this case, roadmap to love) begins with setting a vision (see Chapter 2). Just like in business, you need a vision to guide you toward your goal.

This is another area that has changed dramatically in the last few years. The only purpose of any kind of romantic relationship used to be that you got married and quickly had children. Even though this is the ideal vision for some people, it is not for others. Define a vision for what it is that you are pursuing when you pursue a relationship. Someone who defines all his interactions by the vision, "I just want to have fun with someone I'm attracted to" is going to approach dating in a radically different way than someone who has the vision, "I want to get married to someone I both consider my best friend and soul mate."

Keep in mind that visions may change as your circumstances and stages in life change. Regardless of what your vision is, your actions and thus outcomes will be perfectly aligned with it. For instance, you may desire to eventually get married, but the thought is so frightening to you at the beginning and seems so far away. So, instead, you set out to date with the vision of having fun. In that situation, is it likely you'll find marriage anytime soon? No, you will have a lot of fun, but it will not necessarily lead to a place of long-term commitment or marriage until you adjust your vision accordingly.

Vision statements are forward looking and internal statements. It's how you see yourself at some point in the future, not where you are today.

Having fun isn't a bad goal! But it is a bad vision if you ever want something else as an end state. Visions are not met instantaneously, and simply having the goal of wanting a life partner does not mean that the next person you go on a first date with is the end of the road. But it will absolutely change your interactions during dating by knowing what you are pursuing in the long run.

Dating in layers

Relationships evolve over time. You should know and clearly define what each stage of a relationship is for you. Look at it this way: If you have a vision of finding a life partner, there will be a series of steps toward that goal along the way. In scrum, this is your roadmap, and each major milestone can be identified as release goals. Here are some examples of release goals on a roadmap working toward a vision of finding a life partner:

- ✔ Launch yourself into readiness for the dating world (for example, update your wardrobe, start a fitness routine, change your hairstyle, or buy wine glasses).
- ✔ Create a short list of must-haves versus like-to-haves in your ideal partner.
- ✔ Start dating compatible people.
- ✔ Get into a relationship (as defined by you).

✔ Become committed long-term (dating exclusivity, polyamorous agreement, engagement, or personal equivalent).

✔ Intertwine lives (cohabitate, joint major purchases, marriage and/or kids).

Each of these release goals requires that you engage in tasks and activities that help you move from stage to stage. The first release goal alone can take some time! The world of dating has changed, especially with the use of online dating and technology. In 2014, a study conducted by the website Plenty of Fish revealed that people who use the word *love* in their profile are more likely to find it. I would argue that this (knowing the right words) could be the natural benefit of having an explicit (that is, written), longer-term vision or direction, even while working in the present.

If you can define what each stage of dating looks like, you can determine what release goal you are working toward. Use a definition of done. A definition of done for readiness into the dating world might be accepting invitations (and bravely showing up) to parties where you can meet new people, along with opening new dating profiles on reputable dating networks and actually updating its settings to be viewed publicly. Each layer of a relationship should have a clear definition of done as set by you.

The Pew Research Center released a study in 2013 that showed that one-third of online daters never went on an in-person date with anyone from the site. A definition of done for using online dating profiles that requires you to arrange and go on at least one in-person date (ideally more than one) would be a reasonable definition of done if the goal is to move forward and find someone for an in-person relationship.

A definition of done allows for clear communication and boundary setting in your dating life. One of the most complicated transitions in dating is from dating to relationship, but you can eliminate some of the confusion by clarifying for yourself what the difference is between dating and a relationship. When you have dated someone to the point where the connection has evolved and has all the characteristics of your definition of done for "relationship," it's time to validate that you're in it. But the best part of using scrum to date is that it is no accident to end up in a relationship; you are an active participant consistently moving toward your goal.

Not everyone in the dating world will have the same definition of done for each stage of a relationship. This is where open communication and connection must be used to build trust. As you move through each release goal for yourself, you will have to be open with those you date about what you are currently seeking and how you define each stage of a relationship.

Discovering companionship and scrum

With your roadmap spelled out, you also have the framework for your backlog of requirements: the activities that you'll plan and take part in to accomplish your release goals and vision, starting with your initial release goal.

Part of your product backlog in preparing yourself for the dating world may be the exploration of activities and hobbies that you enjoy. A lot of value exists in spending this time building community and finding companionship while doing the things that you enjoy. This is the best part of inspect and adapt. During this phase, most of the discovery is about you. What kinds of people you connect with, the community of people you build around you, and the community you find while you are doing the things that you enjoy will build relationships that may connect you to people to date in the future. It will also give you a chance to safely connect with potential dating partners without the pressure of a dating "setup."

Use existing companionship and friendships to identify and refine your product backlog of what you are looking for when you move forward into dating and relationships.

Often, just by putting yourself out there socially can evolve from friendships to dating in these communities. It happens naturally when meeting and spending time with people with whom you share interests. Keep in mind that relationships work in phases. A difference exists between friendships in communities and dating one on one, although the former can lead to the latter.

And don't forget to communicate! It is easy to begin spending time with someone as a friend, and then when it evolves, forget the need to communicate about the shift in the relationship. To strengthen your ability to have good timing with these always potentially awkward situations, use your own definition of done to identify the difference between spending time with someone as a friend and recognizing when you have decided to move on to dating or even a committed relationship. Planning to have that discussion may be an example of a dating backlog item.

Be cautious about spending time with someone with all the intimacy and connection of a committed relationship — but identifying it as a casual friendship. If you struggle with this line of communication, use it as a learning opportunity to inspect and adapt how you can better prepare yourself to move from the release goal of "getting ready to date" to "dating" to "relationship." Poor communication is damaging to both parties and a prescription for the kind of dating drama that most people try to avoid. Use empirical evidence to refine what kind of relationship you are looking for, and use dating retrospectives to ensure that you are moving in the direction of your goal:

- ✔ What is going well?
- ✔ What do we want to change?
- ✔ How can we tangibly implement that change?

Scrum and dating

The benefit of scrum is multifold — the structured approach toward a goal, the empirical evidence, the inspect-and-adapt factor, and saving time. Life is full, but if you can accept that you want a partner in life, you must first be willing to accept that you will have to make room for it. Every single person has heard the excuse (or used it themselves) that they would love to find a relationship, but they just have no time for it.

The good news is this: Your life is in your control. In the early stages of dating, this will always mean making time for dates. In the later stages of dating, this will mean making room for a relationship to grow. Relationships don't happen in petri dishes. You won't find a quick way to go from having no room for a relationship to in-love and having a wonderful work-life-love balance.

Consider your life like a product backlog. If your priority for love-related roadmap and backlog items is always at the bottom, it will always be pushed off for something else. If you decide that it is a higher priority, you will create space for it.

Continuing on the roadmap to value and using scrum to date will include

- ✔ Short sprint cycles
- ✔ Inspect and adapt
- ✔ Improvement for future sprints

In dating using scrum, each date is considered a sprint. This creates a very short sprint cycle meant to continuously work toward your release goal. Because you may not have a date every day of the week, this gives you ample time in between to reflect (inspect) and plan changes and improvements for the next one (adapt). This is your opportunity for backlog refinement and process improvement.

The inspect part of inspect and adapt will focus on how you see yourself and your date together, such as

- ✔ Does this person have the qualities I am looking for?
- ✔ Do I have fun with this person?
- ✔ Do they meet my must-haves?
- ✔ How do I act when I'm around them?
- ✔ What are my thoughts and feelings about them when we're not together?

The adapt portion is up to you. You may adapt what you are looking for (for example, your vision), or you may adapt who you are dating (for example, not going on another sprint with the same person). You may also need to adapt your interaction and try another sprint with the same person based on your review. If, for example you want to try something "more fun," try a date with more lighthearted activities or something that you enjoy to see whether that connection opens.

The best part about scrum and dating happens during this inspect-and-adapt process. You and your dating partner get to form your own unique version of "us" — or not. Just like businesses, the ability to cut something short based on early empirical evidence that it will not fit your vision of a relationship saves not only time and money but also potential disappointment on both sides.

Win as a team

In scrum, the members are all a part of a team. You plan as a team, you execute as a team, and you are accountable based on the success or failure of the team. Even though in dating you may feel like you are a team of one, you are on a team of two. Unfortunately, modern dating is full of examples of game playing, which typically pits people against each other. This mentality in dating overcomplicates interactions and closes down communication. With scrum, you can rise above the nonsense and avoid the games altogether. The best thing you can do for yourself is to embrace scrum's concept of being a team with your date and working for the team to succeed rather than engaging in a contest against your date.

Honest communication is needed for any team, and especially for any successful relationship. A common pitfall in contemporary dating is to test dates through "loaded" questions or actions. Scrum is all about simplifying communication. Using scrum in dating means asking genuine questions and viewing the other person's answers as a chance to get to know her for the purpose of that sprint. An example of testing questions might be to ask a date what they think of a recent news event — one that you believe corresponds with your moral views and then judging her morals based on her thoughts on the event.

This is a poor test. Your date may not be as well informed about this event, or her opinion on the event might be an anomaly to other values that they hold.

To utilize open communication, use the event as an icebreaker to open dialogue by sharing your own views and asking her thoughts. As you plan your date "sprints," plan questions to ask that are genuine and encourage honest answers that help you determine whether this person is the right fit.

To work as a team, avoid putting your date in a situation where you expect a certain behavior from her, but they have no way of knowing what the target is and will often try to answer or behave the way that they believe you want them to, many times missing the mark.

Here are some examples of behavior tests to try and generate what tends to be skewed "data":

- Either party suggesting a date activity that you consider to be extreme (or even just intentionally uncomfortable) just to see how the date will react and judging the date solely on that reaction.

- A woman who believes that a gentleman should pay for a date offers to split the check, but if he accepts her offer, she will no longer be interested.

- A man who believes that physical intimacy should wait until a specific time in a relationship (a timeline defined by him but unshared) but still pursues being physically intimate, and if she accepts physical intimacy, he will no longer be interested.

In these examples, I used some frequent gender norms, but various types of tests exist, and they are by no means limited to these. Each of these are opportunities to ask open-ended questions and share your own thoughts, such as introducing your love of adventure and asking about hers, or sharing your thoughts on the expectations of dating and learning hers.

To use scrum in dating means to work as a two-person team, opening dialogue and building trust and respect from the beginning. This is the most important foundational aspect of a successful relationship, no matter how long it lasts.

Focusing finds love; multitasking finds chaos

Scrum is a focusing tool. One of the biggest reasons that scrum is so successful is that it edits out the noise of trying to do everything all at once. Instead of doing all projects poorly, scrum focuses to do one project at a time, with a higher level of quality than if thrashing around.

The following quote summarizes a recent study from Stanford: "Multitasking in meetings *and other social settings* indicates low self- and social-awareness, two emotional intelligence (EQ) skills that are critical to success at work." (Italics emphasis added.)

The study was examining how multitasking lowered effectiveness in a work setting — but emotional intelligence is a life skill. It will be hard to find love if you diminish your self- and social-awareness skills.

The way this applies to dating is when you date a handful (or more) of people at the same time, your mind and emotions are more distracted by the kaleidoscope of multitasking than focused on the ability to discover whether someone is a good match. Multitasking in dating may also apply to trying to rush through multiple phases of a relationship at once.

Modern dating has taught everyone to date as many people as possible for as long as possible to keep all the options open. This attempt to mitigate the risk of one relationship not working out almost guarantees the risk of numerous or all relationships eventually not working out.

This is not to say that you shouldn't date multiple people. That's a good thing to increase your chances of finding what you're looking for in the early stages. If your vision is aimed at finding the one to settle down with, many different relationships at once won't be a good fit (but will be for the "having fun" vision).

Limit your pool of potential dates using work in progress (WIP) limits (see Chapters 5 and 6).

Rounding out the end of the roadmap to value takes you through the date (that is, the sprint itself) and to the finish line of sprint review and retrospective. As you finish each date, take time to inspect the date itself, that is, your sprint review: Did you like this person? Did you like yourself with this person? Then move into a retrospective for possible process changes, such as the way that you went about planning for the date, the questions you asked during the date, and the tactics or tools you used to evaluate whether your date was a good match. Your definition of done should be specific and clear enough to make it very easy to inspect whether your sprints were successful and help you adapt your backlog for the next sprint.

When potential relationships end or do not move forward into the next release, another product backlog item (potential mate) can take their place. Just as in business, pivoting should not be seen as a bad thing, as long as you pivot early to minimize investment (in terms of time and emotional drag as much as money) and doing so tangibly moves you closer to your vision.

Planning Your Wedding Using Scrum

If you have already found love and are in the middle of an engagement — congratulations! Weddings are one of the biggest celebrations of life and meant to weave together our families and friends and acknowledge the beginning of a lifetime between a couple. Wedding days are full of so many positive experiences, but leading up to the big day can put a strain on the couple trying to plan.

Use scrum for what it was built for — to execute an important project. Weddings are the ultimate project. In wedding planning you have a set date and (hopefully) a very closely set budget. Setting priorities and making decisions accordingly are necessary to have the kind of wedding you want. Planning a wedding successfully with scrum involves the following components:

- Setting a vision. Talk about the ideal must-haves as part of your wedding and the experience that you want to take away.

- Setting a schedule (wedding day) and budgetary constraints.

- Establishing and prioritizing wedding requirements (such as venue, invitations, and cake) into a roadmap.

- Establishing release goals (such as venue acquired, officiator scheduled, friends and family notified, decorations and place settings lined up, and photo shoots established).

- Organizing your first sprint to address the highest-priority backlog items, breaking them down into tasks and swarming those tasks to completion.

- Executing sprints, and iterating on new requirements discovered in each sprint.

- Using sprint review to inspect and adapt (not only priorities, but also product backlog items such as remaining budget) and making new decisions moving forward.

When examining a wedding backlog, you may immediately see what needs prioritization. For instance, some locations will allow outside caterers, while others require you use a specific one. Locations also frequently have very strict time sensitivity rules. Given that location can affect a multitude of other backlog items, it may be considered a "high-risk" item (if not the highest risk) to begin addressing in an early sprint. After that item is set, it may change your existing backlog. You may also make decisions toward big-budget items that you have prioritized early on to know what the remaining budget is for other items.

Toward the end of wedding planning, most couples feel the pressure of long lists of small items to do. Try using a task or kanban board to move small items forward and visualize what still needs to be addressed.

One thing about weddings is that they are expensive. Just as discussed with release planning (Chapter 5), portfolio management (Chapter 12), and financing projects (Chapter 13), using incremental funding and doing the highest-priority requirements first ensures that you have the most critical features even if the money runs out before you've completed the entire backlog. With the venue and food already taken care of, it might not be as big of a deal if a few party favors have to be left off the list.

Families and Scrum

Busy. That is the defining word I hear from families everywhere. Life is on a time crunch, and between the multiple levels of commitment from work and school, it is difficult to find the time to genuinely connect as a family. Without the ability to relax and de-stress through connecting with our families, our stress levels will remain high and lower our effectiveness in many areas of life, including work. Connection and recreation with our families are vital links to overall mental and emotional well-being.

Families can be easily caught up in a cycle of short-term communication via texting and long "to-do" lists. Each family member tends to work on his own lists as if they were an island instead of part of a family. The family misses out on maximizing the amount of support they could be giving one another because of lack of communication and coordination.

The challenges facing families today are as diverse as families themselves, but I want to examine the following universals:

- **Conflicting family priorities:** One member of the family wants a vacation, while another wants to buy a car or needs help paying for college, and yet another wants a home renovation. Just like in businesses, family goals cannot all be met at once. And just like in successful businesses, plans and coordinated decision making are vital to the success of achieving a goal.

- **Communication:** Short texts. Conversation cut short by a call from work. Faces buried in mobile devices sharing photos on social media during meals (and I'm not just talking about the kids on this one). A rushed "report" on chores done (or not done) while running out the door ("Did you finish your chores?" "Yeah, bye Mom!"). Communication is more vital to families than even our work relationships, but it is exactly the place where exhaustion and busyness deplete the vitality of real conversation.

✔ **Conflicting schedules:** Just having the time to be in the same place at the same time has become a luxury. Who is involved in what activity and when create scheduling conflicts to connecting.

✔ **Personal responsibility and accountability:** How can the family work as a unit without burning out or overburdening one member? Every family copes with the pressures of simple daily life, such as chores, cleaning, errands, and paying bills. Oftentimes, one parent can feel unsupported or overburdened, while on the other hand, one child can potentially feel too much or too little responsibility in participating in the needs of the home. And for single parents, this is compounded.

With the challenges of modern life constantly tugging at the bonds between family members, it's important to find innovative ways to stay connected and grounded in the home. Stability and healthy relationships within the family affect everything we do outside of it, from school to career to friendships. In the following sections, I show you concrete examples of scrum implemented into daily life through

✔ Simplifying the means of communication to reconnect

✔ Using a family vision statement to unify as a team

✔ Prioritizing a family backlog to meet goals together

✔ Reducing bickering by making decisions as a team

✔ Increasing responsibility through visibility and ownership

Family dynamics are changing quickly. Families are no longer defined by two opposite-gender parents and their children. Single parents, same-sex parents, blended families, and adopted and "just like family" structures and households may or may not run differently than "traditional" families, but they still grapple with these same issues. As our definition of family has evolved, our methods for dealing with these dynamics of family life require innovation as well. That is the great thing about scrum — its agility and the ability to adapt to the realities of the day.

Setting family strategy and project visions

The biggest challenge in making family decisions can come from conflicting priorities. In ancient times, families frequently had mottos or sayings that defined the character and context of themselves, and I suggest that it is time to bring this back with a modern twist! Wouldn't it be nice to be able to address conflict inside and outside the home by first recognizing that the behavior does not fit the family strategy of how to live out values?

A clear and defined family strategy or mission can provide the outermost boundaries of behavior, values, and structure to guide a family in all its decisions. Family strategies work especially well when all family members have ownership of the strategy statement. Ownership starts as a family defines it together rather than having it dictated by a parent.

In Chapter 2, the vision is where the roadmap to value begins. A vision statement for a project must support the overall strategy or mission, or a disconnect occurs between project direction and overall business strategy. It's no different for families. As families plan projects together, they start with a vision of what the end result of the project will be, and that vision ties in directly to the family's strategy.

Planning and setting priorities

Most families take it a day at a time and, in some cases, an hour at a time. It's all about survival. But to realize the bigger goals that families have, it takes a little more planning and priority management than that. It can be overwhelming, but scrum helps overcome that feeling and provides a framework for breaking it down and enabling progression.

As families define their strategy and decide on projects and activities that carry out their strategy, the projects and activities become clear and more easily prioritized and planned. Scrum's iterative approach to planning, executing, inspecting, and adapting leads families to success.

Following the same structure as in project planning, release planning and sprint planning outlined in the first six chapters of this book also work for families.

Project planning

Families establish a strategy (if they haven't already) and then define the vision (see Chapter 2) for the project goal. Each family member gets to brainstorm the ideas to achieve the project vision, which becomes the roadmap for that family project. The family then estimates the effort and complexity of each one, and then prioritizes and orders the ideas based on their effort, complexity, value to the project, and risks involved. That's the roadmap, and it's owned by the family team.

Family estimations may not need to use the Fibonacci sequence. Estimating is simply a way for the family to get an idea of the relative effort to complete things so that they can plan accordingly. Using T-shirt sizes may be all you need. (See Chapter 4 for more explanation on estimating requirements.)

Release planning

Families can identify minimum viable product (MVP) "releases" (see Chapter 5 for more on release planning and MVP) leading up to completing a project and plan each in detail one at a time as each one is completed. For instance, when planning a wedding, the first "release" may be to select a location and reserve it. Before knowing the venue, you don't really know all the details of what you'll be able to do for the wedding. But when you know the location, you can take such actions as sending out invitations, choosing a caterer, finalizing colors, and selecting decorations.

Always use a definition of done when tackling each sprint and release. If a family product backlog item is vague enough that no one knows how it can be considered done, it shouldn't be considered ready to execute in a sprint, or at least should be redefined or broken down so that it can be determined to be done or not. Vague or open-ended backlog items that make it into a sprint tend to sit in the "Doing" column for a long time. If your family backlog has items such as the following, you know that you need to break them down and quantify how they can be considered done before considering them ready for prime time:

- ✔ "Clean the house." (This could take days depending on what type of cleaning and what portions of the house need cleaning.)
- ✔ "Save money for trip to Yellowstone." (This tells nothing about how much money is needed or what means will be used to earn or save the money.)

Sprint planning

When you know the long-term goal (vision) and you have a roadmap of how to get there, and when you know the big steps needed to get there (releases), breaking the work down into sprints becomes easy. Week-long sprints are a natural cadence for families as well as businesses. For most people, work and school schedules are fairly predictable, and one day of the week usually serves as a starting or end point with a logical place to reset, plan, and review. Even if you don't have a consistent break in routine, one can be established. The family can decide.

Sprint planning for a family doesn't need to take long. With a task board, a family can quickly identify the items from the backlog that can be accomplished during the week. Each family member can identify how they can help with each backlog item. Members move the items from the backlog to the "To Do" column and then talk about tasks that will be required for each item in the sprint backlog. Then they identify when in the week they'll be able to accomplish those tasks. (See Chapter 5 for a refresher on the two phases of sprint planning.)

Then you have hugs, kisses, and high-fives all around as family members agree on the plan and go to work throughout the week. Later in this chapter, I describe how to implement this type of planning into existing or natural family interactions.

Visibility and transparency are every bit as important for families as for businesses. Create a family task board just as you would in a business. Tangible is best. Children love the satisfaction that comes with moving a sticker, magnet, sticky note, or 3x5 card from one column to another every bit as much as adults do. Families can effectively use virtual task boards as well. Find what makes the most sense for your family, but make sure that it's easily accessible and visible. You'll be referring to it and updating it every day.

Daily scrums

This should seem pretty clear by now. Giving family members an opportunity each morning or evening to tell what they did, identify what they'll be working on next, and identify what help they'll need from other family members to accomplish their tasks can happen quickly and greatly improve the chances of success for that day.

Use swarming techniques to move sprint backlog items to the Done column. What better way for older children to learn leadership and service by pairing or allowing a younger sibling to shadow an older sibling to learn a new skill. What better way to increase unity and teach cooperation and collaboration than to encourage family members to work together on backlog items by dividing and conquering on tasks. Teenager Johnny is going to work on weeding the flower bed today and says to younger sister Susie, "I could use your help holding the bag in helping me clear away dirt around the big weeds today."

One of the greatest accomplishments of scrum is the fact that scrum teams are cross-functional. Embrace the concept of shadowing and pair programming in your home by teaching each other new skills when appropriate so that responsibilities can be shared. If one person is responsible for all the cooking — cook together! For the cooking project, one of the children might be able to take on the product owner role by prioritizing and ordering the tasks to be done for the rest of the family to carry out, and then practice her decision-making skills by accepting or rejecting the work along the way. Parents can guide them throughout the process.

Not only are these projects opportunities to bond, but they are also the best opportunity to pass along vital life skills and give each member of the family the ability to take on certain tasks.

Thrashing applies to families as well as businesses. Families are similar to large organizations in that they will frequently have many projects going at the same time. Remember the effects of trying to do too much at once (see Chapter 14's discussion on the hierarchy of thrashing). Planning a big family vacation, plus a family reunion, plus a home renovation project all on top of preparing a child to leave for college is too much for a family to plan at once. Consider the discussion from Chapter 12 on portfolio management. Just as in business, family leadership must make decisions on which projects are the highest priority to ensure their success. You might have pressure to do all projects at once, but you don't have to. As a family uses scrum's planning structure to counsel together consistently in determining what projects to take on, taking the time to assess the effort and complexity and then determine what bandwidth they actually have will force prioritization and ordering, and the big-picture view will allow them to make better-informed decisions.

Thrashing on multiple projects at once (parallel) will take at least 30 percent more time to complete these projects. Working on one project at a time (serial) will actually get you all your projects faster than trying to multitask. Chapter 12 shows the details.

Families love scrum for the same reasons that businesses do. It's a framework of activities that provides discipline and structure to planning the right things at the right times. If you think that adding these scrum events to your already busy schedule is just more overhead, keep reading to see how to do it without that perceived added overhead.

Family communication using scrum

As you have discovered, scrum provides ways to increase critical communications, even when the demand for time is minimal. Scrum uses a variety of tools to accomplish this, one of which is to prioritize face-to-face communication whenever possible. On a scrum team, major decisions are not enacted via text or email. This one simple change can dramatically revitalize the dynamics in your family. Parents more than anyone know that when the tone and body language are present, actual word meaning can dramatically change!

To put it in simple terms: Put down the mobile device in your home and try to talk face to face. An even higher step up is to make it a house rule that if a conversation is being had, neither participant should be watching TV, playing a video game, working on a computer, or using a mobile device. A family's mantra might be, "Look up when we're talking."

Face-to-face communication only works if both people are participating in a focused conversation. Reduce your miscommunication and length of conversations by quitting the habit of conversational multitasking.

To put this face-to-face communication to good use, some existing family activities can provide a natural forum for sprint planning, daily scrums, sprint reviews, and retrospectives — in particular, family mealtime. It's a great forum to hold these events. (And, if you're not already doing it, I'll follow with more reasons why now might be a good time to start.)

In Bruce Feiler's TED talk on "Agile programming — for your family," he discusses the dramatic change that his family achieved in minutes a day using a daily scrum model. Think about the value that a daily scrum could add to your family in a simple 15-minute timebox!

✔ Hearing updates from every member of the family about what is happening in his or her day

✔ Sharing plans or goals for each person's upcoming day

✔ Listening to current challenges for each member of the family

✔ Providing an opportunity to problem-solve as a team, or support one another through challenges

✔ Celebrating accomplishments on a daily basis

Though it is traditionally thought that family dinner time is the necessary time slot for a family meeting, recognize that those crucial 15 minutes can happen anytime during the day. A family daily scrum over breakfast, over dinner, or even prior to a certain TV show — as long as the time slot is consistent and committed to any 15-minute increment — will work. What is happening in each other's lives no longer has to be a mystery. Daily scrums are not long enough to resolve all the issues from daily life, but they do accomplish the task of opening the lines of communication and establishing trust and support. That way, if greater challenges arise, the family support foundation is already in place.

Family meals

Cody C. Delistraty, a writer and historian, published an article in The Atlantic about the benefits of daily family meals. Benefits not only involved family relationships but also success in school and health-related issues like reducing obesity.

After his mother died and his brother went away to school, he said, "The first thing that really felt different was the dinner table. My father and I began eating separately. We went out to dinners with our friends, ate sandwiches in front of our computers, and ordered delivery pizzas while watching movies. Some days we rarely saw each other at all."

After they started having daily family meals (even just the two of them), he noticed, "It was therapeutic: an excuse to talk, to reflect on the day, and to discuss recent events. Our chats about the banal — of baseball and television — often led to discussions of the serious — of politics and death, of memories and loss. Eating together was a small act, and it required very little of us — 45 minutes away from our usual, quotidian distractions — and yet it was invariably one of the happiest parts of my day."

When we eat on the go for convenience, it's rushed, we tend to eat less healthy, and because we're rushed, we don't take the time to talk, share, or listen. Plus, when we eat alone, it is an alienating feeling. Sometimes a quiet meal alone is good, but as Delistraty describes, "The dinner table can act as a unifier, a place of community. Sharing a meal is an excuse to catch up and talk, one of the few times where people are happy to put aside their work and take time out of their day."

From studies conducted on this subject, Delistraty highlights the following benefits of family meals together:

- **Truancy at school:** "Using data from nearly three-quarters of the world's countries, a new analysis from the Organization for Economic Cooperation and Development (OECD) found that students who do not regularly eat with their parents are significantly more likely to be truant at school. The average truancy rate in the two weeks before the International Program for International Student Assessment (PISA), a test administered to 15-year-olds by the OECD and used in the analysis as a measure for absenteeism was about 15 percent throughout the world on average, but it was nearly 30 percent when pupils reported they didn't often share meals with their families."

- **Obesity:** "Children who do not eat dinner with their parents at least twice a week also were 40 percent more likely to be overweight compared to those who do, as outlined in a research presentation given at the European Congress on Obesity in Bulgaria this May. On the contrary, children who do eat dinner with their parents five or more days a week have less trouble with drugs and alcohol, eat healthier, show better academic performance, and report being closer with their parents than children who eat dinner with their parents less often, according to a study conducted by the National Center on Addiction and Substance Abuse at Columbia University."

Inspect and adapt for families

Sprint reviews and retrospectives are just as important for families as they are for businesses. For busy families, it may make sense to review the accomplishments (sprint review) and then review the processes and tools used as well as communication, relationships, and discipline techniques being used (sprint retrospective) during the same meeting time just prior to planning a new week (sprint planning).

Sprint reviews may include results from the school week, the progress made toward planning the next family vacation, and sharing other successes with sports, music, and other activities. It's also a time to review the upcoming calendar to identify items for the backlog to help prepare for them, like a birthday party or getting the house ready for extended-family guests who will be visiting.

For weekly family meetings, the questions follow scrum's sprint retrospective model:

- ✔ What worked well this week?
- ✔ What didn't work well?
- ✔ What can we all agree to work on next week?

You might be surprised at the kinds of feedback coming from each family member. During the family meeting, the family should choose two or more improvements that they can all agree to work on for the following week. This is called a team agreement in the agile space.

The family may also choose what kind of consequences occur if rules are broken or if one member of the family does not meet his or her commitments. Again, rather than the traditional model of consequences following the action, in a scrum model, the team (the family) agrees together on the lessons learned and how to improve them prior to taking on the new sprint goal. They also agree to the benefit or reward of meeting new goals. The reward for participating and achieving the family goal is a wonderful motivator.

Making chores fun and easy

Wouldn't it be wonderful if instead of chores constantly escalating into parent-child arguments, chores could simply be done? More and more parents are discovering the way to do this is to empower their kids to self-motivate themselves through chores using personal task or kanban boards.

Human beings have an innate need to feel accomplished. Most adults make to-do lists, but let's be honest — we like the items that are really easy to accomplish quickly so that we can cross them off the list! Kids crave this same sense of accomplishment and visibility toward completion of important responsibilities. In fact, kids of all ages need to know that their contribution is important. Participating in the household is absolutely essential for kids to know that their place in the family is valued. Choosing age-appropriate ways for kids to participate in the running of the household molds the family together as a unit. Task boards are a no-brainer success factor for kids' participation.

The Agile School (http://theagileschool.blogspot.co.uk) blogger Chris Scott has a brief video of his five-year-old daughter using a very simple task board to get herself ready for bed. Each of her tasks are represented on a piece of paper with a picture that helps her remember what the task is. Prompted by her father, she looks at the "To Do" column and chooses the next task, which is indicated by a photo of a puppy (representing "wash feet"), and moves it to the "Doing" column. She then turns to her dad and tells him it's time to wash her feet! This is a great example of how even the youngest of children are capable of understanding the basics of scrum and have fun moving themselves through their responsibilities. I know so many families that struggle with resistant young children at bedtime, but by using the task board, a young child can practically parent herself to bed!

If kids are struggling with larger chores, treat the larger chore as the "user story" and help them by breaking down important tasks. For example, if they struggle to accomplish "clean your bedroom," have "clean bedroom" be the user story with several smaller tasks, such as "organize books," "put dirty laundry away," "make bed," "wash bedroom window," "put away toys," and "dust bookshelves." That way, they can have the user story "clean bedroom" under the Doing column along with other smaller tasks until all are complete, and they can ask for assistance with larger, more difficult tasks until they learn how to get them accomplished.

Just like in business, family task board requirements (user stories) should be accomplishable within a sprint, and tasks should be able to be completed in a day or less. For younger children, perhaps tasks should be an hour or less to better set them up for success.

In another example from Bruce Feiler's "Agile programming — for your family" TED talk, Feiler gives examples from his own and other families of moving through task boards to address morning routine and chores in order to leave the house. Utilizing task boards reduced the conflict, pressure, and yelling between the parents and kids and allowed for more peaceful morning connection in those quiet early moments.

Saving time and stress creates more room for happy and positive connections. You can find no better benefit from using scrum than to give more loving time to your family.

Chapter 17

Scrum for Life Goals

"If you have built castles in the air, your work need not be lost; that is where they should be. Now put the foundations under them."

— Henry David Thoreau, Walden

The universal applicability of scrum is more than likely starting to become clear by now. Scrum is simple enough to be applied to any business or personal goal, and adaptable enough to work for any important project you want to address.

Everyone has goals in life that end up feeling so big and too distant to approach. That is the best part of scrum — to take the overwhelming and break it down into manageable pieces.

Getting to Retirement

The reality of life is that ultimately a time will come when you will no longer be able to work full-time, but retirement can be defined as anytime you reach enough financial freedom where your passive income — the income you do not actively work for — is enough to cover your expenses. If retirement is defined in this way, it becomes a goal to work toward at any age, and your product backlog of items and release goals support reaching the vision of financial freedom. The further out in the future retirement is, the harder it can be to focus on the things you can do today to reach those important financial goals, as in-the-moment financial needs crop up.

According to a 2008 study release by EBRI.org, 86 percent of respondents in a Gen X and Gen Y study felt that they should do better at saving for a rainy day. The same study found that "... two-thirds of young Americans feel they are behind schedule in having general savings or in saving for an emergency (67%) and nearly as many say their retirement savings are behind schedule (61%). More than four in ten suggest they are behind when it comes to their debt level (46%)."

A big challenge among younger generations is how to cope with rising costs of living while salaries are not rising at the same rate. You can use scrum to address this challenge and progress toward financial security each year.

Using the roadmap to value in developing your retirement vision, building release goals and your backlog, using sprints to work toward each goal is the best way to bring a long-term future goal into the present.

Saving for emergencies

Your first release goal toward the vision of financial independence should include saving for financial emergencies. Emergencies are bound to happen and may come at a significant financial cost. Medical bills, a job loss, home or car repairs, and divorce or family issues causing unpaid time off work can cause financial strain. The only way to protect your future financial safety is to plan for emergencies now by developing a savings fund that covers emergencies, bears interest, and is not locked in to penalties if you have to withdraw for an emergency.

An emergency fund is one release goal working toward your vision of financial security. Sprints should include ways to adapt your budget, focusing on setting money aside.

The most common financial goal for emergency savings is to have the equivalent of six months of expenses in savings. To support this release, you decide sprint lengths (no more than a month) and work on backlog items each sprint that support building a savings plan.

Your income less expenses equals surplus. Surplus generating interest over time equals wealth:

$$Surplus \times Interest \times Time = Wealth$$

If you have little or no surplus at the end of each pay cycle, you need to examine your budget and reorganize your backlog of priorities to either increase your income or decrease your expenses, or both. Keep in mind this motto: Live free before living well. It might be nice to have expensive things, but not if it costs you your financial freedom or future security.

When building your savings, resist the urge to use emergency funding for nonemergency reasons. It's the surest way to back-pedal your progression toward your goal. Create a separate savings account for discretionary purchase goals (like travel, a new pair of skis, or a new car) to help avoid dipping into emergency savings. Acknowledging the need for pleasure purchases is an important step in having a sustainable plan for savings. The key is to balance short-term fun purchases against long-term security goals.

Your sprints should consistently focus on ways to open up your ability to create surplus toward savings. Review the outcome of each sprint to inspect, adapt, and make changes earlier than later. For instance, don't let yourself get stuck sprint after sprint in a passive income endeavor that isn't achieving your goal. Sprint and release goals, and your definition of done, should help you define backlog items that are specific and clear about what success is. Don't be afraid to move on with increased knowledge from your mistakes. The Lean Startup (see Chapter 12) may be helpful to you if you decide to take the entrepreneurial approach to increasing your income.

Building retirement

After you have a safety net, you should shift your savings to building for retirement. This portion of your goal progression will remain in progress even as you move on to other release goals. Your sprint cycle will include examining your options to get the greatest return on investment. For example, at the end of the first sprint, if your benefits package from work includes some matching funds, your product backlog should be updated with items that get you the maximum possible matching point.

When running sprints to save for retirement, focus on how to safely achieve the maximum return on investment. If you're further away from retirement, don't be shy about being more aggressive with your investments in the beginning years of your saving. Several retirement resources are easily accessible to determine your age and how much you should be saving to have a balance between your future vision and your current budget. Keep in mind when using these tools that I have defined retirement as the point in which you can stop actively working because your passive income is enough to support your expenses. While most online tools and retirement advice calculators will suggest an age of 55 or 60, your retirement age is actually defined by you and your vision.

Section 72(t) of the United States tax code allows investors to take money out of their retirement plan penalty free prior to age 59½ for income, but you'll have to take substantially equal periodic payments over time. It can be spread over your life expectancy but needs to be at least five years. This is an example of the inputs that you'll use to determine the age and account balance target for your personal retirement goals.

Securing financial freedom

After you have reached both release goals of emergency savings and actively saving for retirement, your next release goal will be building assets. I'll use a simple definition for assets and liabilities. An asset is anything that will bring money to you, while a liability is anything that will cost you money. Building assets is a personal decision and may require several sprints initially to research and increase your knowledge to support your high-level vision of where you want to be. In Chapter 12, I talk about "spikes" as a product backlog item to research and dissect an issue to answer a question.

Some examples of early sprint goals to consider would be

✔ Structuring your budget to allow and automate a set amount of index fund purchases each month

✔ Identifying ways to increase income by 5 percent doing something you enjoy

Your sprint goals would continue to be broken down to the requirement level such as

✔ Create a budget

✔ Set up an index fund auto-purchase

✔ Establish a home page for your online business

Another example of a sprint goal would be to determine whether purchasing a home will create an asset or a liability. Product backlog items would involve steps and activities for discovering whether the purchase of a home is the best use of your money, such as

✔ Conducting an analysis of whether the home will bring a sufficient return on investment

✔ Determining whether another place or investment would bring a higher rate of return

By this same measure, a large expansive house might be nice — but it brings greater liability if it can't be easily sold at a profit. Research carefully and use early sprints to inspect and adapt toward the release goal of building assets. Building assets is about building passive income to support your vision to retire.

Houses are liabilities (they cost you money) until they generate income through a rental or are sold at a profit. Your primary residence is likely not an asset — you need to live somewhere.

In using scrum for building financial freedom, you will use empirical evidence and the inspect-and-adapt process in the same way that a software project would. Am I tangibly moving toward the goal? How can I achieve the release faster? What roadblocks are in my way, and how can they be removed?

A perfect example of asset building and addressing roadblocks is considering academic education. If your educational status prevents you from moving forward financially, examine the potential asset outcome against the liability. Some questions to consider are

- How much will the education I am considering cost (actual cost + opportunity cost)?
- How much income will it generate after I am finished?
- Does the income it will generate greatly outweigh the cost of getting the education?

Just like with purchasing a home, getting additional education should have a clear financial asset outcome for you before embarking on it.

Achieving Weight Goals

If fitness is a goal, using scrum to achieve your vision is one of the best ways that you can succeed. The struggle many people have with weight loss and fitness is the oft-named "yo-yo" effect. It's easy to start a new year or a new time with a fitness-and-diet regimen — achieve your result and then slowly but surely slide back to exactly where you began. It happens to many people. In 2007, a study at University of California Los Angeles analyzed 31 long-term studies on dieting and found that participants in weight-loss programs were consistently more likely to gain more weight in the following two years than participants in the study who had not.

One of the reasons this happens is focus! And focus, as I have mentioned in prior chapters, can be an amazing thing. But the drawback here is that often in weight loss, this focus is on an extreme and regimented situation. After you fall off the wagon, so to speak, you immediately begin unraveling your hard-earned work. Scrum does allow for focus, but scrum focuses in small, measurable, and achievable segments. In other words, scrum is about taking steps toward your goal and achieving it sustainably, not just jumping on an extreme roller coaster and then burning out.

This is done by working through the roadmap to value, just like with any other major project. The following examples can be tailored by you to adapt to your own vision and goals:

- **Set a vision:** I want to be back to my physical shape in college, which was 185 pounds, 32-inch waste, running a mile in seven minutes, and bench-pressing 200 pounds.

- **Create a product roadmap:** Initial roadmap items to get started may include things such as lose 10 pounds (you may have multiples of these, because incremental improvement is the goal), run three miles without stopping, or reduce cholesterol level to below 120.

- **Create a product backlog:** This includes making new recipes to cook, joining a gym, and having diet and exercise plans.

- **Set your first release goal:** In two months, I want to have lost three pounds and be able to run one mile.

- **Determine sprint lengths:** One week, for example.

- **Choose what to bring into the first sprint:** Cut soda volume by 50 percent, eat dessert only three times a week, walk one mile three times a week, and do cardio-aerobic activity at least once a week.

At the end of each sprint, review your progress on the goals, update your product backlog with what you have learned throughout the sprint, and adapt the next steps to be in line with achieving your release goal.

Even after just one sprint, you should use the sprint retrospective to inspect and adapt. Ask yourself the three sprint retrospective questions:

- **What went well?** The cooking website I used has good recipes. I should keep using it. The mobile calorie tracking app is easy to use. My family is being really supportive.

- **What do I want to change?** I don't like to do cardio on days that I eat sweets. Nighttime workouts are hard to stick to. My lunch group gives me a hard time about my new health goals, which is discouraging.

- **How can I achieve that change?** I will establish set days of the week for sweets, which will not be "cardio days." Try morning workouts this sprint to see whether that time of day is easier to be consistent. Cut down lunch groups to once per week, or maybe not at all. Find a new lunch group.

You would then run your next sprint incorporating both what you want to improve and the new items from your backlog. At the two-month mark, you will do a review for the whole release to examine whether you have achieved your goal and to determine your next release goal.

The key in using scrum to move forward on your weight-loss goal is that each step is a small, but truly incremental, step. At any time, not meeting your goal isn't a failure on your behalf but a learning opportunity to find a new way to move forward. Even if, like in other diet methods, you do fall back on bad habits, getting back on track isn't a massive commitment because the sprint cycles are so short.

Consider a high-visibility task board for items that have the specific status of done. From the preceding example, you could have three workout tasks, each of which gets moved over each time you have completed your exercise. Giving yourself a visual depiction of completing can also help you to identify opportunities (exercises that you enjoy) and bottlenecks (exercises that you avoid) and gives you intelligence for what to consider for your next sprint.

Keeping Life Balance

One of the biggest challenges in life is managing our emotional and mental well-being. Life can be a roller coaster of ups and downs, and it's our personal responsibility to find a way to minimize the volatility and maximize enjoyment and fulfillment.

I want to acknowledge first that when talking about mental and emotional health, a wide umbrella falls under that category. Everything from a temporary increase in life stress to diagnosable mental health issues can create ups and downs in life and cover a broad range of intensity. Using scrum is a framework to address goals and prioritize issues; it's not a substitution for mental or emotional health services, if needed. In fact, you'll probably want to team up with someone who you trust to provide ongoing support and accountability as you build your vision, roadmap, and backlog and work through each of the scrum events. Don't go it alone.

If life becomes overwhelming, it can come from a variety of places (some of which I address in Chapter 16, as well as those in the previous examples in this chapter). Building blocks of our lives constantly get moved and shifted as time requires. With stress, everyone has a breaking point. For one person, a bad breakup might be the building block that makes the other stressors in life feel like too much. For another person, financial hardship or the loss of a job is the building block that along with other life factors, ends up feeling like too much.

When stressors are becoming burdensome, use scrum to find solutions. Here are some beginner questions to ask yourself to start defining your vision, roadmap, and backlog:

- ✔ What are my stressors? Why are these causing such high stress right now?
- ✔ Of that list of stressors, what is the stressor that really puts me in the place where I feel overwhelmed?

Asking yourself these two questions allows you to identify both the source of the issues and also the factor that is currently creating the most "weight." From this identification, you begin to move through the roadmap to value.

Using the current highest stressor as the priority, you build a vision of what you would like to see in your life. From this point you break down your first release, then identify sprint goals and tasks that you can take toward achieving that release.

Just like sprints in any other life goal endeavor, you will consistently return to inspect and adapt. In this situation, you may also ask yourself, "Is this still the highest stressor and the one that I need to focus on solving to feel more balanced?" If so, keep at it until the release goal is achieved. If not (AC + OC > V — see Chapter 5), finish that release and set a new release goal.

As you move through sprints, addressing one issue at a time, you may find to your own surprise that you do feel less stress, but now another "life" item has taken priority, and it is time to focus on that item to feel more mentally and emotionally stable.

Thrashing between projects not only increases time by at least 30 percent, but it is also overwhelming. With your mental and emotional well-being, focusing on one thing at a time is, again, your best bet.

As you progress through the roadmap to value, use the following types of questions to help define your vision, release goals, and sprint goals:

- ✔ **Vision:** What do I ultimately want my situation to look like?
- ✔ **Release goal:** What is a smaller milestone that would progress me toward that vision?
- ✔ **Sprint goals:** What items can I bring in from the product backlog to do that would mean I am taking steps toward achieving that release goal *right now?*

Even though learning about this topic is extremely individual, I'll examine a fictional person, just to talk through an example. John is in his early 30s and currently struggling with feeling overwhelmed and not knowing how to address the many frustrations in his life. First he examines his stressors and discovers the following:

- ✔ Work is very stressful and a negative environment; additionally, it does not pay well, causing financial stress.

- ✔ His current apartment is a stressful and unsafe place to live, but he feels that he cannot move because he doesn't earn enough from work.

- ✔ John also frequently feels alone, and although he wants a relationship, he has not found the right person to be with, and doesn't feel that he has it "together" enough to be in a relationship. His friends and family feel distant because of how stressed he is both at work and home.

John decides that his bad work situation is the worst of these factors (priority decision). He writes a vision statement that reflects what he would like to move himself into: "I want a job that pays at least $80,000 a year, with full benefits and a steady work schedule, not the long and unpredictable hours that I currently work." (Clear and specific vision.)

His first release goal may be to begin searching for new jobs. His first sprint may include dedicating one hour per night to correcting his resume and applying to five new jobs during the sprint. He may also include tasks such as reconnecting with acquaintances and looking for job leads, or searching for positions starting at $80,000 and with specific working hours.

After several sprints of focusing on applying to new jobs, John moves into the interviewing phase. After each sprint (that is, each interview), he holds a review and uses inspect and adapt to adjust his job search or reexamine what stressor now needs focus.

The key from this hypothetical example is that at any point during any given sprint review, John could decide that he has reduced his stress enough to "release" that goal and focus on a new stressor. The point of using scrum to keep mental and emotional balance is that it combines the concept of taking measurable steps to address a need and also uses the sprint review to inspect and adapt those steps or, if necessary, address another issue from the product backlog of stressors.

Planning Travel

Vacations are amazing opportunities for relaxation, exploration, and connection as a "team." Even travel for business can accomplish similar objectives. All too often, however, teams, families, and friends struggle with frustrations over financing and finding time for travel, as well as having differing opinions on what to do and how to relax. Plus, circumstances can change at any time with travel, both before and during. Scrum is a major planning tool that is perfect for this kind of project! Think about it: You have an exact date and often a fixed budget; everything else is prioritization of the scope of the trip. Instead of one person calling all the shots and hoping that everyone likes the decisions made, working together as a team will bring about engagement and satisfaction from everyone:

- ✔ Create a vision plan of the trip or vacation.
- ✔ Set calendar dates.
- ✔ Know your budget.
- ✔ Create a vacation backlog of items from the stakeholders (for example, family members and travel companions).
- ✔ Prioritize the backlog to achieve the best result possible.

With family travel, every member in the family can and should participate in what an ideal vacation would look like to them. Keep in mind that if this becomes a family habit, this year's vacation vision may not have the same "ideal" qualities as last year or next year, and that is the point. Reviewing this as a family will provide insight on how to focus the budget.

As in any scrum project, the vacation budget is the factor that you want to fix first. For example, if the members are focused on activities that cost a higher value, the family can examine more budget-friendly places to do them. On the reverse, if a specific location is the highest priority as a family, the vacation can be planned around more budget-friendly options in an ideal location.

Don't be afraid to include kids in discussing priorities according to budgeting. While they may or may not have the responsibility of saving the money in the bank or setting the total budget, they absolutely should be involved in a trade-off decision as a team. For example, we can either snorkel in Hawaii or go zip-lining but not both; which would we like to do? It's important to teach kids that setting financial priorities and sticking to a budget are major family life skills. Scrum thrives when everyone involved has ownership of decisions.

Rather than a simple "vote" structure, where each member only says yes or no, try fist of five (see Chapter 4), followed by dot voting. In fist of five, you visually show your support for an idea. Putting up one finger means total resistance to the idea whereas displaying five fingers means thinking it's a great idea. For a decision to pass, everyone in the family should at least have three fingers up, meaning that even though they may not love it, they don't hate it either and are willing to support the decision. Using fist of five voting first will allow narrowing a pool of options that no one in the family hates. You then follow with dot voting for a final decision. In "dot voting," all family members have five votes each. They put dots on the choice they would like to vote for, and they can put all dots on the same option or one on different options, indicating a preference for certain decisions.

Items from the product backlog need to be executed by each family member. Reservations need to be set, but changes based on the reality of availability or price, or perhaps changes in expected weather, need to be addressed on an ongoing basis. This allows for the major items with higher risk to be done early, with risk declining as the date gets closer. As dates for vacation grow closer, fewer large decisions will be in progress, and vacation planning will evolve into tasks needed to be accomplished prior to departure. Keep an eye on the calendar and establish short sprints to accomplish any remaining items. Break the product backlog items down so that they are easily moved to the Done column. For example, shopping for the appropriate clothing and also packing for the trip can't all be done in the same week without causing stress and chaos! Place shopping in a sprint that's early enough prior to the trip so that when it is time to pack, items are available. In fact, in an earlier sprint, do a mock packing activity to help you identify things that you'll need to shop for so that no surprises occur during the real packing the night before you leave.

Travel — both business and pleasure — can be very unpredictable. One of my coaches took an anniversary vacation to Hawaii a few years ago using scrum. He scored some last-minute (less than two weeks in advance) travel deals and so did not have much time to plan the trip out in detail. He and his wife had never been to Hawaii, so he asked around quickly for ideas from friends and family on such basics as what to do and where to eat. So with luggage, plane tickets, hotel and car reservation, and a list of potential things to do (road-map) in hand with a general budget amount in mind, they boarded the plane. The vision was simple: Relax with no pressure to see or do everything.

On the plane ride, finally catching their breath from busy life, he and his wife took out their trip backlog of activities and places to eat. They planned out the first day and estimated about how much of the budget it would take. Then they enjoyed the rest of the flight.

At the start of the next day, he and his wife crossed off the things they did from the list and identified a few other things that sounded interesting. One of those things involved making a tour reservation, so they called ahead and scheduled that for three days out.

Each day, they did the same thing, adding to the list, crossing off completed items, and adjusting the priority based on their interests. Some items never reached the top of the list or got thrown out as their interest in the item decreased. It hardly felt like planning.

They were fortunate to have had an open-ended return date (which is not a prerequisite for being able to use scrum). They found that after eight days instead of their projected ten days, they had had enough, accomplished their vision for the trip, did the things they wanted to do, and ate where they wanted to eat. They returned home fully satisfied (AC + OC > V).

Studying

Learning is a necessary part of our lives from birth until death. The theoretical physicist Albert Einstein is quoted as saying, "Once you stop learning, you start dying." Human curiosity is what propels us forward toward the life we want to lead. Primary school is our structured format of learning from the age of five (or lower for some pre-K learners) until the 12th grade, but often formal learning goes beyond primary school through trade certifications, to undergraduate or graduate studies, and into professional education.

The school system is meant to unify basic competency skills for children and help children to identify potential areas of interest for further exploration. As I examine in Chapter 9, scrum can be used to help schools at administrative levels and teachers at the classroom level. While schools and teachers respectively work to improve things at those levels, students themselves can use scrum to enhance their personal experiences with their own education. That is what I will examine in the following sections.

Just like in every other section, students will use the roadmap to value to work toward their goal. They will develop a vision, generate a backlog of items from an overall roadmap, identify a first release, run short sprints against that release, and use a sprint review to inspect and adapt their product (for example, homework) for the next sprint. They will then run a sprint retrospective to inspect and adapt their processes and tools to help them optimize progress with their education. This process will allow students at every step to refine their product backlog, or adapt their study sessions as needed (discussed in the following age-appropriate sections).

Early learning

As shown in Chapter 16, even young children can easily use scrum. Scrum is simply three roles, three artifacts, and five events. In fact, it empowers them and makes it fun to get through their own backlog of items. In this section, I will address early learners as students in grades kindergarten through grade 8. If you are a parent or a teacher, you will see kids struggle with learning in some form or another. Depending on their age, it can be hard for kids to feel like they "need" to learn something difficult because they don't always have the sense of how it applies to their future. If they don't see a connection between their learning and what they want, just like adults, it is hard to want to fight through the difficulty of it.

Helping young learners identify a vision and correlating that vision to their own life are keys to getting them to engage. This can be done by helping them to correlate things they are interested in and like to do with the details of what they are studying. I have a friend whose six-year-old will wake up in the morning and pull out all the supplies to "bake a cake," as she tells her mother. But the same daughter will get frustrated when learning numbers and counting. Her mom saw an opportunity and helped her see that baking a cake needs numbers! After that small lesson, her daughter was much more willing to put in the work to learn numbers.

Early learners can benefit from using task boards to work through their homework on many levels because task boards are easily adaptable as the homework changes and the student grows.

I've talked a lot about thrashing already in just about every chapter, especially in Chapters 6, 12, and 14. Multitasking reduces quality and effectiveness, and scrum helps reduce that error margin by focusing on one project at a time. Students of all ages (but it begins in elementary school) are consistently thrashed across many subjects at once. The key to using scrum for students is to run short sprints against certain topics or projects. Perhaps sprints are several days, or even a single day, to enable a structure for focusing on one item at a time.

Regardless of sprint length, however, after a sprint length has been decided, a student can try using the Pomodoro technique (see Chapter 2) to shift tasks more easily. The Pomodoro technique is used to create a natural resting point, and provides an easy opportunity for task switching. When using the Pomodoro method, a student can easily see whether the task needs to be continued after a break or whether it is time for a new task to begin.

The Pomodoro technique is one in which the student will set a timer for a specific period of time, commonly 25 minutes, and focus on just that activity during the period. When the timer goes off, the student takes a five-minute break, to get up, stretch, move, or listen to one song — whatever is helpful, but not "working." After the five-minute break is up, the student can either return to the task for 25 more minutes or switch to another necessary task. After four cycles of 25 minutes with five-minute breaks has gone by, a longer break of 15 to 30 minutes is taken. This is perfect for any student who knows focus is hard to maintain for hours on end. Again, cycle time and breaks are tailored to individual needs.

Teaching children early how to inspect and adapt is crucial. One of my coaches has a third-grade daughter. She came home and showed her dad her spelling test grade for the week. She was normally a perfect speller, so when he noticed that she had missed four words, he was surprised. He first acknowledged that she still got a relatively good score, but asked why she missed more than usual. After attempting to blame other students for distracting her at first, she admitted that she'd been rushing through her tests and hadn't been practicing as much as she could have each day between the pretest and the final test. Instead of treating her as having done something wrong, he asked her how she thought she could do better on next week's test and avoid rushing through it. She remembered how, at the beginning of the year, she was doing short practice tests every day of the week, not just at the beginning and the night before the test. They agreed it would be good to try that again, and she implemented her new plan the following week. She was able to learn from her own experiences and own the solution for improvement.

Graduating from high school

High school students have a specific set of needs geared around what their vision is for after high school. Up until graduation, most students focus on grade by grade or school-level movement, but at the high school level, they are introduced to taking electives and beginning to steer themselves toward their own vision. High school is an opportunity for students to begin to take hold of the reigns and guide themselves. A student in high school might have many kinds of vision statements, from wanting to go to a four-year university, to wanting to work right away, and everything in between. The best way to achieve that vision is to use each year as a stepping stone toward it.

I want to focus on the popular goal of getting into college. If your vision is to attend college, a specific backlog geared toward college requirements needs to be set. Items on this list should also include all the nonscholarly work that needs to be done. For example, researching schools takes longer than you might expect and should be done as early as possible so that future sprints can include activities tailored toward meeting admission requirements. Just like with early learners, task boards are an effective tool toward progressing on important product backlog items.

Prioritization for high schoolers is key. Few, if any, can take every academic subject, play every sport, score perfectly on the SATs, and participate in every activity — and definitely not all at the same time. By using prioritization, you can edit out items that do not directly support your vision and focus on release goals that are important both personally and for getting in to the right college. Using these release goals in working toward your vision will help create milestones. Having release goals will allow you to organize decomposed requirements into sprints. Here is a specific example of how this breakdown might look for a high school student:

- ✔ **Vision:** To get into a four-year university.

- ✔ **Release goal supporting vision:** Score above 2200 on the SAT.

- ✔ **Sprint goal supporting release goal:** Score over 720 on five practice SAT math tests.

> ✔ **Requirement level supporting sprint:** Find an SAT tutor, spend three hours studying the SAT book this week, focus on SAT math concepts, and ask tutor about SAT-level geometry.

Expectations are high and students are expected to become knowledgeable in a broad base of subjects. Added to that, competition to be someone who can stand out in many ways to make it into college or receive scholarships is extremely high. Students have various mixtures of teachers and classes, so workloads vary from student to student and from term to term.

Also, teachers frequently do not tie together their lesson plans and assignments across the whole school. In fact, a 2007 MetLife study found that teachers with zero to five years of experience were almost twice as likely (14 percent of teachers) as their more experienced counterparts (6 to 8 percent of teachers) to assign more than an hour of homework each day. This leaves the importance of evaluating the highest-priority assignments to the students, which though challenging is a perfect opportunity for ownership of the process.

The sprint cycle of inspecting and adapting provides the framework that students need to adjust to varying loads and situations from term to term as they work through their roadmap.

In 2014, a guest blog post written by Alexis Wiggins went viral detailing the challenges she noticed as she shadowed first a tenth-grade student and then a twelfth-grade student for one day. Of primary concern to her were the constant strain of sitting all day and the passivity expected from learning. In incorporating scrum into at-home study, this is where a student can take charge of learning in another way. While students can't control in-class lectures, they can find alternative ways aside from sit and memorize when at home. This is also where a student's product backlog can heavily influence progression. If extracurricular activities are an important factor in your vision, try choosing one that allows for physicality such as sports or a tactile club such as art to allow different methods of learning into goal progression. If, for some reason, physical extracurricular activities aren't appropriate or available, try incorporating physically active breaks when using the Pomodoro technique for studying.

 A student's vision may change throughout the course of their educational career. Consider the following vision set by a student as a freshman, just starting out with the scrum process, and notice how it evolves as they inspect and adapt along the way. At of the start of ninth grade, they know they want the following:

> Graduate from high school with a minimum 3.8 GPA to qualify to attend an Ivy League school.

This is a start and is based on what they know at the time. They may or may not have done much research on what is required of Ivy League schools. They may also not know that more than just GPA will be needed to get into college. Notice, also, that they may not know exactly what they want to be when they grow up yet. However, this is still a fine start.

By the end of their ninth grade year, they now know that a 3.8 GPA probably won't be enough. They learn what SAT or ACT scores they'll need for entrance, and that they'll also need to achieve extracurricular leadership, service, and activity requirements. They also really enjoyed a couple of social science classes they took that gave them some insights into what they want to be when they grow up. To start off tenth grade, they have an updated vision:

> Qualify to attend Yale, Stanford, or Harvard after high school.

Her roadmap and backlog would include things such as earn a minimum 4.2 GPA, score at least a 30 on my ACT and a 2200 on my SAT, and save enough money to pay for half of a trip to South America (Mom and Dad will pay for the other half) for humanitarian work before the end of my junior year.

At the end of each year, this student's vision and roadmap will probably evolve because they know more than they did when they started. Regularly inspecting and adapting at logical intervals allow them to seek guidance from trusted parents and advisers to make informed decisions.

Achieving in college

College is the perfect opportunity for a student to use scrum. Not only does it help make consistent progression for the student, but more and more businesses are also incorporating agile practices in the real world. For any college student whose vision includes employability after graduation, implementing scrum practices will help prepare them for the current business market.

You have already read about using task boards when I spoke about early learners and prioritization for high school students. Both of these things should continue to be put to use for a college student. Now, the student is fully in charge of his or her own education.

The curriculum for each class may be decided by a teacher, but the overall educational content is totally up to the student. Deciding what to major in is often a huge task for a student, regardless of the decision being made prior to or during college. Inspect and adapt will still influence you on the sprint level to improve learning, but with college, inspect and adapt has the opportunity to be brought to the release or even vision level. The choice of study is up to you. You may find at the end of a semester (release level), for example, that biology is not a study that you want to continue to pursue, while another subject has become a high-priority interest. As your interests evolve, make sure to keep your vision and roadmap adjusted accordingly so that your vision and roadmap are providing the outer boundaries and direction for each release (for example, term) and sprint (for example, week).

College is also a time to pursue team building within a scrum framework. College group projects are an opportunity to use scrum for planning, reviewing, coordinating, establishing team agreements, and responding to changes. Holding scrum events and utilizing a task board bring immediate visibility to who is working on each portion of the project and where the project is in overall progression. Keep group meetings as short as possible by using the daily scrum and discovering whether you have impediments and what items are in progress. If the group needs to address an impediment or swarm on a sprint backlog item that has lagged, the visibility will allow for the project to progress quickly.

In addition, you can also tailor successful completion of projects to your own learning style. College-level projects are frequently defined specifically by a definition of done (the rubric provided by the professor), but getting to done is left up to the learner.

Team building and pair programming techniques apply in collegiate study. It doesn't have to require a group project to work together to review one another's work prior to completion. Use sprint reviews to elevate your work prior to final submission (for example, the release to customer, who is the teacher).

Subsets of release and sprint goals will also include outside work just as it did at the high school level, but in the collegiate atmosphere, this might include building relationships with professors who can refer you for scholarships or jobs or seeking specific internships to gain job skills. Build a strong working relationship with professors by including their feedback and using it to continuously improve your work.

Credit hours, like velocity (see Chapter 4), may only tell part of the story. Just because you took 12 credits last term doesn't mean that 12 credits is the right number next term. A three-credit class last term may not require the same amount of effort outside of class as a totally different three-credit class next term. Doing an internship next term may require taking fewer credits than last term. Or, perhaps you can take on more credits if you take more online credits next term than you did last term. Make informed decisions based on knowing more next term than you did last term.

Sprint cycle for a college student

Just like with scrum for families, scrum for students logically breaks down sprints to one week each. Students review the roadmap and focus on the current release, selecting backlog items for the sprint, which are broken down into activities that can be done in a day or less. So, if 30 pages need to be read for class B, it might be broken down to ten pages per day for three of the seven days of the sprint. At the end of the first day of reading, the student will know whether ten pages is the right amount for the remaining days. Another requirement for the sprint might be to research a specific topic for an upcoming writing assignment.

Some of these activities may need to be time-boxed. For instance, the research might need to be done in two hours or less. Because of work and class schedules, you might only have enough time for 60 minutes of reading. Based on time available and work left to be done, each day a student has to make decisions of how that time will be best used.

At the roadmap, release, sprint, and daily levels, students prioritize and order their work to be done and make adjustments as needed.

At the end of each sprint, a student reviews her work completed against what the goal was, and adjusts the remaining product backlog accordingly. She also reviews her process and identifies impediments that keep her from attaining goals. Perhaps reading is taking too long, and a student explores options for improving speed, like a speed-reading course. Note-taking workshops are probably offered through the school, or perhaps a tutor is needed for one subject. This review of goals and processes for attaining those goals happens every week, and tweaks and adjustments can be made against a limited amount of work — quickly, rather than the typical cramming required to make up for procrastination.

The truth is that your pursuit of learning will always have a next phase, even after you're in the job field. Lifelong learning can be achieved easily with a vision and following the roadmap to value to success.

Part VI
The Part of Tens

 Visit www.dummies.com for great Dummies content online.

In this part . . .

- ✔ Transitioning successfully to scrum.
- ✔ Measuring the right things.
- ✔ Enjoying the benefits of scrum.
- ✔ Joining the scrum community.
- ✔ Visit www.dummies.com for great Dummies content online.

Chapter 18

Ten Steps to Transition to Scrum

In This Chapter

▶ Capitalizing on lessons from successful implementations

▶ Planning for success

Throughout this book, I highlight the fact that scrum is very different from traditional project management. Moving an organization from waterfall to scrum is a significant change. Through my experience guiding all types of companies through this kind of change, I've identified the following important steps to take in order to become a more agile organization and successfully implement scrum.

Step 1: Conduct an Audit

Before you plan where you want to go, you first need to know where you currently stand. A third-party audit of your current processes, methods, practices, and structures will not only tell you some things you don't know about how you currently operate, but it will also validate some things that you already know, with added insights you may not have considered.

Implementation strategy

An *implementation strategy* is the output of an audit and is a plan that outlines how your organization will transition to scrum from where you are today. A thorough implementation of scrum will include analysis and recommendations for

- **Current processes:** How does your organization run projects today? What does it do well? What are its challenges?

- **Future processes:** How can your company benefit from scrum? What additional agile practices can enhance scrum in your organization?

What key changes will your organization need to make, and what are the organizational and personnel implications of those challenges that you'll need to consider? What will your transformed company look like from a team and process perspective?

✔ **Step-by-step plan:** How will you move from existing processes to scrum? What will change immediately? In six months? In a year or longer? This plan should be a road map of successive steps getting the company to a sustainable state of scrum maturity.

✔ **Benefits:** What advantages will scrum provide for the people and groups in your organization and the organization as a whole? This will be a valuable resource as you promote the transition to senior management and the organization as a whole.

✔ **Potential challenges:** What will be the most difficult changes? What departments or people will have the biggest trouble with scrum? Whose fiefdom is being disrupted? What are your potential roadblocks? How will you overcome these challenges?

✔ **Success factors:** What organizational factors will help you while switching to scrum? How will the company commit to a new approach? Which people or departments will be champions of scrum?

Your implementation strategy will serve as your road map to carrying out a successful transformation.

Step 2: Identify and Recruit Talent

Author of the best-selling book *Good to Great* (published by HarperBusiness), Jim Collins teaches:

> *"You are a bus driver. The bus, your company, is at a standstill, and it's your job to get it going. You have to decide where you're going, how you're going to get there, and who's going with you.*
>
> *"Most people assume that great bus drivers (read: business leaders) immediately start the journey by announcing to the people on the bus where they're going — by setting a new direction or by articulating a fresh corporate vision.*
>
> *"In fact, leaders of companies that go from good to great start not with "where" but with "who." They start by getting the right people on the bus, the wrong people off the bus, and the right people in the right seats."*

Scrum roles, although unique, are becoming more and more common, but not all recruiters know how to find people who can fill them. Getting people who really know what they are doing requires working with recruiters to understand the scrum knowledge necessary to separate the fabulous from the fakers.

Cross-functional developers continue to learn new skills and are starting to recognize the need to expand their skill sets rather than restrict their knowledge to a single area. The talent is there. For your transition to scrum to be effective, you need to get the right people in the seats.

Step 3: Ensure Proper Training

Training is a critical step when adopting scrum. The combination of face-to-face communication with a scrum expert and the ability to work through exercises actually using scrum is the best way to help people to absorb and retain the skills needed to successfully run a scrum project.

Training works best when the members of the project team can train and learn together. As a scrum trainer and mentor, I've had the opportunity to overhear conversations between project team members that start with, "Remember when Mark showed us how to . . . ? That worked when we did it in class. Let's try that and see what happens." If the development team, product owner, scrum master, and project stakeholders can attend the same class, they can apply lessons to their work as a team.

Yes, even stakeholders will benefit from training. See Chapter 12 on portfolio management to understand how crucial senior management priority decisions are in making scrum successful. Some of my clients have seen the value of this training with their scrum masters, product owners, and developers to the point of sending their entire executive team and creative, sales, marketing, finance, and HR personnel so that the entire company could be on the same page and speak the same language.

As a result, in follow up, I've heard executives speak to product owners in terms of ". . . at the next sprint review . . ." and ". . . do we have a user story in the backlog for that idea . . ." and ". . . so, with current velocity I could expect . . ."

Step 4: Mobilize a Transition Team

Identify a team of decision makers within your company that can be responsible for the scrum transformation at the organization level (the "transition team"). This team is made up of company executives who have the ability and clout to systematically improve processes and report requirements and performance measurements across the organization.

The transition team will create changes by running their transition efforts using scrum, just like the development team creates product features within sprints. The implementation strategy from the audit is the transition team's road map and outlines what needs to be done for a successful transformation. The transformation team will focus on the highest-priority changes in each sprint and will demonstrate its implementation, when possible, during a sprint review.

Figure 18-1 illustrates how a transition team's sprints align in cadence with the pilot scrum team's sprints (see the following Step 5), and how the impediments identified in the sprint retrospective of the pilot team become backlog items for the transition team to resolve as process improvements for the pilot team.

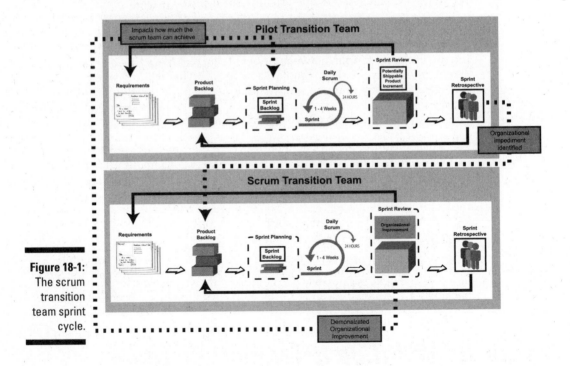

Figure 18-1:
The scrum transition team sprint cycle.

Step 5: Identify Pilot Project

Starting your transition to scrum with just one pilot project is a great idea. Having one initial project allows you to figure out how to work with scrum with little disruption to your organization's overall business. Concentrating on one project to start also lets you work out some of the kinks that inevitably follow change.

When selecting your first scrum project, look for an endeavor that has these qualities:

- **Appropriately important:** Make sure that the project you choose is important enough to merit interest within your company. However, avoid the most important project coming up; you want to have room to make and learn from mistakes. See the note on the "blame game" in Chapter 19.

- **Sufficiently visible:** Your pilot project should be visible to your organization's key influencers, but don't make it the most high-profile item on their agenda. You will need the freedom to adjust to new processes; critical projects may not allow for that freedom.

- **Clear and containable:** Look for a product with clear requirements and a business group that can commit to defining and prioritizing those requirements. Try to pick a project that has a distinct end point, rather than one that can expand indefinitely.

- **Not too large:** Select a project that you can complete with no more than two scrum teams working simultaneously to prevent too many moving parts at once.

- **Tangibly measurable:** Pick a project that you know can show measurable value within sprints.

People need time to adjust to organizational changes of any type, not just scrum transitions. Studies have found that with large changes, companies and teams will see dips in performance before they see improvements. *Satir's Curve,* shown in Figure 18-2, illustrates the process of teams' excitement, chaos, and finally adjustment to new processes.

After you've successfully run one scrum project, you'll have a foundation for future successes, expanding to more and more projects and teams.

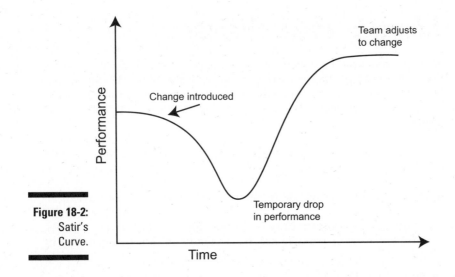

Figure 18-2:
Satir's
Curve.

Step 6: Maximize Environment Efficiency

Having identified a pilot project, make sure that the work environment is one that will set it up for success. Your implementation strategy from your audit will likely outline the things to address, which may include

- **Colocation:** If you're putting together a new team, put one together that is colocated, including the product owner and scrum master. Even if your organization typically has dislocated teams, this is an opportunity to step back and evaluate whether that is the optimal solution.

- **Workspaces:** Make sure that the pilot team has a workspace that promotes collaboration and face-to-face communication. Team members will need an area that not only allows them to focus uninterrupted on tasks, but also makes collaboration and swarming convenient and effective. Cubicle walls may not be ideal. Tables with shared monitors or other shared workspaces may be better. Whiteboards and plenty of tools like sticky notes, 3x5 cards, pens, and markers facilitate collaboration very effectively.

- **Technology:** For improved collaboration with any stakeholder or other project team member not colocated with the scrum team, technology exists to minimize the productivity loss due to communication that is not face-to-face. Videoconferencing, recording, screen sharing, and virtual whiteboard equipment will be key factors in supporting a pilot scrum team to develop a quality product with the efficiency needed to demonstrate success. Consider investments in the technology that suits your team's needs, which may include monitors, cameras, virtual meeting room software, microphones, headsets, and so on.

Step 7: Reduce Single Points of Failure

Your pilot scrum team will need to be as cross-functional as possible to be successful. Identify skill gaps with each team member where a single point of failure exists on any given skill. Make immediate plans for training so that everyone on the team can do more than one thing, and no required skill is possessed by only one team member.

Training may include formal training or may simply require pairing or shadowing with another developer for a certain amount of time. This can be done during the first sprint(s) and doesn't need to delay the pilot team kickoff (see the following Step 9).

You won't have a completely cross-functional team on day one. But the goal should be to get started on day one, and inspect and adapt along the way.

Step 8: Establish Definition of Done

No doubt, you'll be excited to get the project team started right away. But before diving in head first, make sure that the team's definition of done is, well, defined. It won't be perfect at first. The team will revise it often at first until they find what makes sense. It will be important to make this a topic of conversation at each sprint retrospective.

Make sure that the team is clear about what "done" means for each requirement at the sprint and release levels. Make sure that it's always visible and referred to by all team members for every requirement. Having this step in order will avoid many problems down the road.

Step 9: Kick Off Pilot Project

When you've chosen your pilot project, don't fall into the trap of using a plan from an old methodology. Instead, use scrum and other common practices from the road map to value that I introduce in Chapter 1. These include

- ✔ Project planning
- ✔ Vision
- ✔ Road map with estimations

Although you'll have a long-range view of the product through the product road map, you don't need to define all the product or project scope up front to get started. Don't worry about gathering exhaustive requirements at the beginning of your project; just add the features that the project team currently knows. You can always add more requirements later.

✔ Release planning.

✔ Identify major minimum viable product (MVP) releases.

✔ Plan first release.

✔ Sprint planning: Plan the first sprint and go to work.

You cannot plan away uncertainty. Don't fall victim to analysis paralysis; set a direction and go!

Throughout the first sprint, be sure to consciously stick with scrum events. Think about the following during your first sprint:

✔ Have your daily scrum every day, even if you feel like you didn't make any progress. Remember to identify roadblocks and communicate them promptly to the transition team.

✔ The development team may need to remember to manage itself and not look to the product owner, the scrum master, or anywhere besides the sprint backlog for task assignments.

✔ The scrum master may have to remember to protect the development team from outside work and distractions, especially while other members of the organization get used to having a dedicated scrum team.

✔ The product owner may have to become accustomed to working directly with the development team, being available for questions, and reviewing and accepting completed requirements immediately.

In the first sprint, expect the road to be a little bumpy. That's okay; empiricism is about learning and adapting.

See Chapter 5 for planning releases and sprints.

Step 10: Inspect, Adapt, Mature, and Scale

This step is really about moving forward, taking what you've learned to new heights. If you follow the previous steps, you'll start out right with a solid foundation. Beyond that, empiricism will drive your continued adoption of scrum and transformation to scrum using the implementation strategy that you establish at the beginning.

Inspect and adapt sprint 1

At the end of your first sprint, you'll gather feedback and improve with two very important meetings: the sprint review (see Chapter 5) and the sprint retrospective (see Chapter 6).

The sprint review and sprint retrospective will be critical events. The product owner will want to spend time making sure that the development team is clear on what it means to demonstrate working software for the stakeholders, and should prepare questions to ask the stakeholder to draw out feedback and show him the value of attending this review. It may also take several invitations and reminders to the stakeholders to ensure their attendance.

The scrum master should take time studying resources like *Agile Retrospectives,* by Esther Derby and Diana Larsen (published by Pragmatic Bookshelf), to make sure that he establishes the right atmosphere and facilitates a retrospective that avoids venting and rehashing, but promotes celebrating successes and identifying plans of action for improvement.

Maturity

Inspecting and adapting enable scrum teams to grow as a team and to mature with each sprint.

Agile practitioners sometimes compare the process of maturing with the martial arts learning technique of *Shu Ha Ri.* Shu Ha Ri is a Japanese term that can translate to mean "maintain, detach, transcend." The term describes three stages in which people learn new skills:

- **In the *Shu* stage,** students follow a new skill as they were taught, without deviation, to commit that skill to memory and make it automatic.

  New scrum teams can benefit from making a habit of closely following scrum until those processes become familiar. During the Shu stage, scrum teams may work closely with a scrum coach or mentor to follow processes correctly.

- **In the *Ha* stage,** students start to improvise as they understand more about how their new skill works. Sometimes the improvisations will work, and sometimes they won't; the students will learn more about the skill from these successes and failures.

As scrum teams understand more about how scrum works, they may try variations on processes for their own project.

During the Ha stage, the sprint retrospective will be a valuable tool for scrum teams to talk about how their improvisations worked or did not work. In this stage, scrum team members may still learn from a scrum mentor, but they may also learn from one another, from other agile professionals, and from starting to teach agile skills to others.

✔ **In the *Ri* stage,** the skill comes naturally to the former student, who will know what works and what doesn't. The former student can now innovate with confidence.

With practice, scrum teams will get to the point where scrum is easy and comfortable, like riding a bicycle or driving a car. In the Ri stage, scrum teams can customize processes, knowing what works in the spirit of the Agile Manifesto and Principles.

Scale virally

Completing a successful project is an important step in moving an organization to scrum. With metrics that prove the success of your project and the value of scrum, you can garner commitment from your company to support new scrum projects.

To scale scrum across an organization, start with the following:

✔ **Seed new teams.** A scrum team that has reached maturity — the people who worked on the first scrum project — should now have the expertise and enthusiasm to become scrum ambassadors within the organization. These people can join new scrum project teams and help those teams learn and grow.

✔ **Redefine metrics.** Review, identify, and unify measurements for success (see Chapter 21 on metrics), across the organization, with the creation of each new scrum team and with each new project.

✔ **Scale methodically.** It can be exciting to produce great results, but company-wide improvements can require wide process changes. Don't move faster than the organization can handle.

✔ **Identify new challenges.** Your first scrum project may have uncovered roadblocks that you didn't consider in your original implementation strategy. Update your strategy (that is, your transition team road map) as needed.

✔ **Continue learning.** As you roll out new processes, make sure that new scrum team members and stakeholders have the proper training, mentorship, and resources to effectively participate in scrum projects.

Also, to support your long-term effort to improve and mature with scrum, engage with an experienced scrum coach to jump-start mentoring leadership and teams in making the recommended changes from your audit. Also, begin searching for CSP+ talent — Certified Scrum Professional (CSP), Certified Scrum Coach (CSC), or Certified Scrum Trainer (CST) — to internally sustain long-term transformation. Establish this internal role as a source for clarification, ongoing training, and development, and embed this talent to work one on one with teams.

The preceding steps work for successful scrum transformations. Use these steps and return to them as you scale, and you can make scrum thrive in your organization.

Chapter 19

Ten Pitfalls to Avoid

In This Chapter

▶ Avoiding common mistakes

▶ Implementing sound practices

Scrum teams can make a number of common but serious mistakes when implementing scrum. This chapter provides an overview of some typical problems and ways for scrum teams to turn them around.

As you may notice, many of these pitfalls are related to lack of organizational support, lack of training, and falling back on old project management practices. If your company invests in transition support and supports positive changes, if the project team is trained, and if scrum teams make an active commitment to upholding the scrum framework and agile values, you'll have a successful transition.

Faux Scrum (Cargo Cult Agile and Double Work Agile)

Sometimes organizations will say that they are "doing scrum." They may go through some of the scrum events, but they haven't embraced the principles of agile and are ultimately creating waterfall deliverables and products under the false scrum titles. This is sometimes called *cargo cult agile* and is a sure path to avoiding the benefits of scrum.

Trying to use scrum in addition to waterfall processes, documents, and meetings is another faux scrum approach.

Double work agile results in quick project team burnout. If you're doing twice the work, you aren't doing scrum, nor adhering to agile principles.

Solution: Insist on following scrum. Garner support from management to avoid nonagile principles and practices.

Lack of Training

Investment in a hands-on training class will provide a quicker, better learning environment than even the best book, blog, or white paper. Lack of training often indicates an overall lack of organizational commitment to scrum.

Training can help scrum teams avoid many of the mistakes on this list.

Solution: Build training into your implementation strategy. Giving teams the right foundation of skills is critical to success and is necessary at the start of your scrum transition.

Ineffective Product Owner

No scrum role is more different than traditional roles than that of the product owner. Scrum teams need a product owner who is an expert on business needs and priorities and can work well with the rest of the scrum team on a daily basis. An absent or indecisive product owner will quickly sink a scrum project.

Solution: Start the project with a person who has the time, expertise, and temperament to be a good product owner. Ensure that the product owner has proper training. The scrum master can help coach the product owner and may try to clear roadblocks preventing the product owner from being effective. If removing impediments doesn't work, the scrum team should insist on replacing the ineffective product owner with a product owner who can make product decisions and help the scrum team be successful.

Lack of Automated Testing

Without automated testing, it may be impossible to fully complete and test work within a sprint. Most manual testing is a waste of time that fast-moving scrum teams don't have.

Solution: You can find many low-cost, open-source testing tools on the market today. Look into the right tools and make a commitment as a development team to using those tools.

Lack of Transition Support

Without the support of professionals and executives who can help guide scrum teams through new approaches, new scrum teams may find themselves falling back into old habits.

Solution: Enlist the help of an agile mentor — either internally from your organization or externally from a consulting firm — who can support your transition. Implementing process is easy, but changing people is hard. It pays to invest in professional transition support with an experienced partner who understands behavioral science and organizational change.

Inappropriate Physical Environment

When scrum teams are not colocated, they lose the advantage of face-to-face communication. Being in the same building isn't enough; scrum teams need to sit together in the same area.

Solution: Take action to colocate the team:

- ✔ If your scrum team is in the same building but not sitting in the same area, move the team together.
- ✔ Consider creating a room or annex for the scrum team.
- ✔ Try to keep the scrum team area away from distracters, such as the guy who can talk forever or the manager who needs just one small favor.
- ✔ Before starting a project with a dislocated scrum team, do what you can to enlist local talent.

See Chapter 4 for more on colocating.

Poor Team Selection

Scrum team members who don't support scrum, who don't work well with others, or who don't have the capacity for self-management will sabotage a new scrum project from within.

Solution: When creating a scrum team, consider how well potential team members will enact agile principles. The key is versatility and willingness to learn.

Discipline Slips

Remember that scrum projects still need requirements, design, development, testing, and releases. Doing that work in sprints requires discipline.

Solution: Build in the habits of creating working functionality with the definition of done from the project start. You need more, not less discipline to deliver working products in a short iteration. Progress needs to be consistent and constant:

- ✔ The daily scrum helps ensure that progress is occurring throughout the sprint.
- ✔ Use the sprint retrospective as an opportunity to reset approaches to discipline.
- ✔ Review and refine the team's definition of done regularly.

Lack of Support for Learning

Scrum teams succeed as teams and fail as teams; calling out one person's mistakes (known as the *blame game*) destroys the learning environment and destroys innovation.

Solution: Scrum teams can make a commitment at the project start to leave room for learning and to accept success and failures as a group.

Diluting until Dead

Watering down scrum roles, artifacts, and events with old waterfall habits erodes the benefits of agile processes until those benefits no longer exist.

Solution: When making process changes, stop and consider whether those changes support the scrum framework, Agile Manifesto, and agile principles. Resist changes that don't work with the manifesto and principles. Remember to reduce waste by maximizing the amount of work not done.

Chapter 20

Ten Key Benefits of Scrum

*H*ere are ten important benefits that scrum provides to organizations, teams, products, and individuals.

REMEMBER

To take advantage of scrum benefits, you need to trust in empiricism, find out more about the scrum framework by using it, and continually inspect and adapt your implementation of scrum.

Better Quality

Projects exist to accomplish a vision or goal. Scrum provides the framework for continual feedback and exposure to make sure that quality is as high as possible. Scrum helps ensure quality by the following practices:

✔ Defining and elaborating on requirements just in time so that knowledge of product features is as relevant as possible

✔ Incorporating daily testing and product owner feedback into the development process, allowing the development team to address issues while they're fresh

✔ Regular and continuous improvement of scrum team output (product or service) through sprint reviews with stakeholders

✔ Conducting sprint retrospectives, allowing the scrum team to continuously improve such team-specific factors as processes, tools, relationships, and work environments

✔ Completing work using the definition of done that addresses development, testing, integration, and documentation

Decreased Time to Market

Scrum has been proven to deliver value to the end customer 30 to 40 percent faster than traditional methods. This decrease in time is due to the following factors:

- Earlier initiation of development due to the fact the upfront documentation phases of waterfall projects (which typically take months) are foregone by having a dedicated product owner embedded within the scrum team to progressively elaborate requirements "just in time" and provide real-time clarification.

- Highest-priority requirements are separated from lower-priority items. Incrementally delivering value to the end customer means that the highest-value and -risk requirements (MVP — see Chapters 5 and 6) can be delivered before the lower-value and -risk requirements. No need to wait until the entire project is complete before releasing anything into the market.

- Functionality is swarmed to completion each sprint. At the end of every sprint, scrum teams produce working product and service increments that are shippable.

Increased Return on Investment

The decrease in time to market is one key reason that scrum projects realize a higher return on investment (ROI). Because revenue and other targeted benefits start coming in sooner, earlier accumulation means higher total return over time. This is a basic tenet of net present value (NPV) calculations (see Chapter 13 for more on NPV). In addition to time-to-market benefits, ROI with scrum also increases by

- Regular feedback through sprint reviews directly from stakeholders, including customers, enables course corrections early, which is less costly and time-consuming than later in the process.

- Fewer costly defects due to automation and up-front testing means less wasted work and faster deployments.

- Reducing costs of failure. If a scrum project is going to fail, it fails earlier and faster than waterfall projects.

Higher Customer Satisfaction

Scrum teams are committed to producing products and services that satisfy customers. Scrum enables happier project sponsors through the following:

- Collaborating with customers as partners and keeping customers involved and engaged throughout projects.

- Having a product owner who is an expert on product requirements and customer needs. (Check out Chapters 2 through 6 for more about the product owner role with requirements.)

- Keeping the product backlog updated and prioritized to respond quickly to change. (You can find out about the product backlog in Chapter 3.)

- Demonstrating working functionality to internal stakeholders and customers in every sprint review. (Chapter 6 shows you how to conduct a sprint review.)

- Delivering product to end customers faster and more often with every release rather than all at once at the very end.

- Incrementally funding projects instead of requiring large up-front commitments. (Chapter 13 tells you about incremental funding of projects.)

Higher Team Morale

Working with happy people who enjoy their jobs can be satisfying and rewarding. Self-management puts decisions that would normally be made by a manager or the organization into scrum team members' hands. Scrum improves the morale of team members in these ways:

- Being part of a self-managing and self-organizing team allows people to be creative, innovative, and acknowledged for their expertise.

- Development teams may organize their team structure around people with specific work styles and personalities. Organization around work styles provides these benefits:

  - Allows team members to work the way they want to work

  - Encourages team members to expand their skills to fit into teams that they like

  - Helps increase team performance because people who do good work like to work together and naturally gravitate toward one another

- Scrum teams can make decisions tailored to provide balance between team members' professional and personal lives.

✔ Having a peer relationship with a business representative (product owner) on the same team aligns technical and business priorities and breaks down organizational barriers.

✔ Having a scrum master, who serves the scrum team, removes impediments and shields the development team from external interferences.

✔ Focusing on sustainable work practices and cadence ensures that people don't burn out from stress or overwork.

✔ Working cross-functionally allows development team members to learn new skills and to grow by teaching others.

✔ Encouraging a servant-leader approach assists scrum teams in self-management and actively avoiding command-and-control methods.

✔ Providing an environment of support and trust increases people's overall motivation and morale.

✔ Having face-to-face conversations helps reduce the frustration of miscommunication.

✔ Ultimately, scrum teams can agree on rules about how they work to get the job done.

The idea of team customization allows scrum workplaces to have more diversity. Organizations with traditional management styles tend to have monolithic teams where everyone follows the same rules. Scrum work environments are much like the old salad bowl analogy. Just like salads can have ingredients with wildly different tastes that fit in to make a delicious dish, scrum projects can have people on teams with very diverse strengths that fit in to make great products.

Increased Collaboration and Ownership

When scrum teams take responsibility for projects and products, they can produce great results. Scrum teams collaborate and take ownership of quality and project performance through the following practices:

✔ Having the development team, the product owner, and the scrum master work closely together on a daily basis

✔ Conducting sprint planning meetings, allowing the development team to organize its work around informed business priorities

✔ Having daily scrum meetings where development team members organize around work completed, future work, and roadblocks

✔ Conducting sprint reviews, where the product owner outlines his prioritization decisions and the development team can demonstrate and discuss the product directly with stakeholders

✔ Conducting sprint retrospectives, allowing scrum team members to review past work and recommend better practices with every sprint

✔ Working in a colocated environment, allowing for instant communication and collaboration among development team members, the product owner, and the scrum master

✔ Making decisions by consensus, using techniques such as estimation poker and the fist of five

You can find out how development teams estimate effort for requirements, decompose requirements, and gain team consensus in Chapter 4. You can discover more about sprint planning and daily scrum meetings in Chapter 5. For more information about sprint reviews and retrospectives, check out Chapter 6.

More Relevant Metrics

The metrics that scrum teams use to estimate time and cost, measure project performance, and make project decisions are often more relevant and more accurate than metrics on traditional projects. On scrum projects, metrics are more relevant because

✔ Those who will be doing the work, and no one else, provide effort estimates for project requirements.

✔ Timelines and budgets are based on each development team's actual performance and capabilities.

✔ Using relative estimates, rather than hours or days, tailors estimated effort to an individual development team's knowledge and capabilities.

✔ In less than one minute a day, developers can update the burndown chart, providing daily visibility of how the development team is progressing toward a sprint goal.

✔ At the end of every sprint, a product owner can compare the project's actual cost (AC) plus the opportunity cost of future projects (OC) against the value that the current project is returning (V) to know when to terminate a project and begin a new one. You don't need to wait until the end of a project to know what its value is. (See Chapter 5 for more on AC + OC > V as a termination trigger.)

You might notice that velocity is missing from this list. *Velocity* (a measure of development speed, as detailed in Chapter 4) is a postsprint fact, not a goal. It's a metric but only for the individual scrum team. It is one input that scrum teams can use to help them determine the amount of work that they can accomplish in future sprints, but it works only when tailored to an individual team. The velocity of Team A has no bearing on the velocity of Team B. Also, velocity is great for measurement and trending, but it doesn't work as a control mechanism. Trying to make a development team meet a certain velocity number only disrupts team performance and thwarts self-management.

If you're interested in finding out more about relative estimating, be sure to check out Chapter 4. Chapter 20 shows you ten key metrics for scrum projects.

Improved Progress Visibility and Exposure

On scrum projects, every member of the project team (which includes the scrum team and stakeholders) has the opportunity to know how the project is going at any given time. Transparency and visibility make scrum an exposure model to help the project team accurately identify issues and more accurately predict how things will go as the project progresses. Scrum projects can provide a high level of progress visibility by

✔ Placing a high value on open, honest communication among the scrum team, stakeholders, customers, and anyone else within an organization who wants to know about a project.

✔ Daily scrums that provide daily insight into the development team's immediate progress and roadblocks.

✔ Daily scrums around task boards enable developers to self-organize and identify the highest-priority tasks for the day.

✔ Using the information from daily scrum meetings, sprint burndown charts, and task boards allows the project team to track progress for individual sprints.

✔ Sprint retrospectives allow scrum team members to identify what's working well and what's not to make action plans for improvement.

✔ Demonstrating accomplishments in sprint reviews. Anyone within an organization may attend a sprint review, even members of other scrum teams.

Improved project visibility can lead to greater project control and predictability, as described in the following sections.

Increased Project Control

Scrum teams have numerous opportunities to control project performance and make corrections as needed because of the following practices:

✔ Adjusting priorities throughout the project at each sprint interval rather than at major milestones allows the organization to have fixed-time and fixed-price projects while accommodating change.

✔ Embracing change allows the project team to react to outside factors like market demand.

✔ Daily scrum coordination allows the scrum team to quickly address issues as they arise, and swarm together to get requirements to done.

✔ Daily updates to sprint backlogs mean that sprint burndown charts accurately reflect sprint progress, giving the scrum team the opportunity to make changes the moment it sees problems.

✔ Face-to-face conversations remove roadblocks to communication and issue resolution.

✔ Sprint reviews let project stakeholders see working products and provide product owners the feedback they need to ensure that the project stays on track.

✔ Sprint retrospectives enable the scrum team to make informed course adjustments at the end of every sprint to enhance product quality, increase development team performance, and refine project processes.

The many opportunities to inspect and adapt throughout scrum projects allow all members of the project team — the development team, product owner, scrum master, and stakeholders — to exercise control and ultimately create better products.

Reduced Risk

Scrum helps mitigate the risk of absolute project failure — spending large amounts of time and money with no return on investment — by delivering tangible product early and forcing scrum teams to fail early if they're going to fail at all through the following practices:

✔ Having the highest-risk items done first provides the longest runway to work through issues or fail early and inexpensively.

✔ Developing in sprints, ensuring a short time between initial project investment and either failing fast or validating that a product or an approach will work.

✔ Having a working product increment starting with the very first sprint, so that even if a project gets terminated, the highest-value and -risk requirements have been developed and could be delivered to the customer if desired.

✔ Developing requirements to the definition of done in each sprint so that project sponsors have completed, usable features, regardless of what may happen with the project in the future.

✔ Providing constant feedback on products and processes through

- Daily scrum meetings and constant development team communication through colocation

- Regular clarification about requirements and review and acceptance of features by the product owner

- Sprint reviews, with stakeholder and customer input, about completed product features

- Sprint retrospectives, where the development team discusses process improvement

- Releases, where the end user can see and react to new features on a regular basis

Chapter 21

Ten Key Metrics for Scrum

*W*ith scrum, metrics can be powerful tools for planning, inspecting, adapting, and understanding progress over time. Rates of success or failure can let a scrum team know whether it needs to make positive changes or keep up its good work. Time and cost numbers can highlight the benefits of agile projects and provide support for an organization's financial activities. Metrics that quantify people's satisfaction can help a scrum team identify areas for improvement with customers and with the team itself.

Double work agile is the practice of management expecting to see traditional status reports and meetings in addition to scrum artifacts, events, and appropriate metrics. This is one of the top pitfalls of scrum projects. Management is looking for one thing while teams are trying to do another. As a result, decisions are made based on the wrong information, teams burn out from doing double the work, and the benefits of scrum become minimized.

This chapter describes ten key metrics to help guide scrum project teams.

Sprint Goal Success Rates

One way to measure scrum project performance is with the rate of sprint success. The sprint may not need all the requirements and tasks in the sprint backlog to be complete to minimally realize the sprint goal. However, a successful sprint should have a working product increment that fulfills the sprint goal and meets the scrum team's definition of done: developed, tested, integrated, and documented.

Throughout the project, the scrum team can track how frequently it succeeds in reaching the sprint goal and use success rates to see whether the team is maturing or needs to correct its course. Teams should always be stretching themselves, so 100 percent of the sprint backlog is not necessarily the goal. Making sure that individual requirements started get 100 percent "done" is important, but teams should always be stretching themselves, so success rates less than 100 percent sprint backlog completion should be considered an opportunity to learn and improve. Scrum masters should always be looking for ways to reduce drag on the team so that the team can set and accomplish higher and higher goals as they continue to accomplish more and more in each sprint. Sprint success rates are a useful launching point for inspection and adaptation.

Velocity is not a goal; it is a postsprint fact. An increasing velocity and an increasing sprint goal completion rate are both key indicators that a scrum team is continually improving efficiency.

You can find out more about setting sprint goals in Chapter 5, and reviewing them in Chapter 6.

Defects

To be truly agile, scrum teams need to implement agile practices like test-driven development (TDD) and continuous integration (CI). (See Chapter 12 for TDD and CI definitions.) Without quality practices like these, scrum teams will be ineffective at delivering quality as fast as the market demands because of the overhead of manual testing before each release and the amount of defects introduced that automation could easily catch.

It's unlikely that any scrum team will be able to accomplish perfection in these areas, so any project is likely to have some defects. Agile techniques combined with the scrum framework help development teams proactively minimize defects.

Tracking defect metrics can let the development team know how well it's preventing issues and when to refine its processes. To track defects, it helps to look at the following numbers:

- **Defects during development:** If the development team uses practices like automated testing and continuous integration, it can track the number of defects at the build level in each sprint.

  By understanding the number of build defects, the development team can know whether to adjust development processes and environmental factors.

- **User acceptance testing (UAT) defects:** The development team can track the number of defects that the product owner finds when accepting requirements in each sprint.

By tracking UAT defects, the development team and the product owner can identify the need to refine processes for understanding requirements. The development team can also determine whether adjustments to automated testing tools are necessary.

✔ **Release defects:** The development team can track the number of defects that make it past the release to the marketplace.

By tracking release defects, the development team and the product owner can know whether changes to the UAT process, automated testing, or the development process are necessary. Large numbers of defects at the release level can be indicative of bigger problems within the scrum team.

The number of defects and whether defects are increasing, decreasing, or staying the same are good metrics to spark discussions on project processes and development techniques at sprint retrospectives.

Time to Market

Time to market is the amount of time that a project takes to provide value by releasing working products and features to users. Organizations may perceive value in a couple of ways:

✔ When a product directly generates income, its value is the money it can make.

✔ When a product is for an organization's internal use, its value will be the employees' ability to use the product and will contain subjective factors based on what the product can do.

When measuring time to market, consider the following values:

✔ Measure the time from the project start until you first show value to the customer.

✔ Some scrum teams deploy new product features for use at the end of each sprint. For scrum teams with a release with every sprint, the time to market is simply the sprint length, measured in days.

✔ Other scrum teams plan releases after multiple sprints and deploy product features in groups. For scrum teams that use longer release times, the time to market is the number of days between the start of development of a feature and the next release.

Time to market helps organizations recognize and quantify the ongoing value of scrum projects. Time to market is especially important for companies with revenue-generating products, because it aids in budgeting throughout the year.

Return on Investment

Return on investment (ROI) is income generated by the product, less project costs: money in versus money out. On scrum projects, ROI is fundamentally different from ROI on traditional projects. Scrum projects have the potential to generate income with the very first release (which can potentially be as soon as the end of the first sprint) and can increase revenue with each new release.

To fully appreciate the difference between ROI on traditional and scrum projects, consider two scenarios with the same project costs that take the same amount of time to complete. I'm ignoring the additional documentation, meetings, and other expenses of a waterfall project and assuming that they could be kept at the scrum level to simplify the comparison. Both scenarios begin on January 1 and have the potential to generate $100,000 in income every month when all the requirements are finished:

- ✔ Scenario A is waterfall and releases when all requirements are finished on June 30 of the same year, and enjoys monthly revenue of $100,000 per month for each month thereafter through the end of the year (six months, $600,000 revenue).

- ✔ Scenario B begins releasing the highest-value and -risk features incrementally on January 31 after four one-week sprints, five months earlier than Project A. Monthly revenue is less as it builds up each month from the first release (that is, $50,000 in February, $60,000 in March, $70,000 in April, $80,000 in May, and $90,000 in June) until the entire project is complete.

  This extra revenue in each of the five months from February through June gives the project $950,000 in revenue for the year, $350,000 more than scenario A.

 Like time to market, ROI metrics are a great way for an organization to appreciate the ongoing value of a scrum project. ROI metrics help justify projects from the start because companies may fund projects based on ROI potential. Organizations may track ROI for individual projects as well as for the organization as a whole.

Total project duration and cost

To calculate ROI, duration and cost must first be calculated. These can both, in and of themselves, be effective inputs and metrics for scrum projects. Scrum projects should get done faster and be less costly than traditional projects.

A higher ROI as a result of decreasing project durations and costs should be a good indicator that scrum teams are increasing swarming, reducing thrashing, and improving overall efficiency.

New requests within ROI budgets

The ability to quickly generate higher ROI provides organizations using scrum with a unique way to fund additional product development. New product features may translate to higher product income.

Suppose that in the preceding example, the project team identified a new feature at the beginning of June that would take four one-week sprints to complete and would boost the product income from $100,000 a month to $120,000 a month. That would increase revenue by $120,000 for the year in both scenarios. In scenario B, if the new feature had been identified earlier, ROI would have increased even more.

If a project is already generating income, it can make sense for an organization to roll that income back into new development and see higher revenue. Tracking ROI provides the intelligence required to make that decision.

Capital Redeployment

When the cost of future development is higher than the value of that future development, it's time for the project to end.

The product owner prioritizes requirements, in part, by their ability to generate revenue. If only low-revenue requirements remain in the backlog, a project may need to end before the scrum team has used its entire budget. The organization may then use the remaining budget from the old project to start a new, more valuable project. The practice of moving a budget from one project to another is called *capital redeployment*.

To determine a project's end, you need the following metrics:

  ✔ The value (V) of the remaining requirements in the product backlog
  ✔ The actual cost (AC) for the work to complete the requirements in the product backlog
  ✔ The opportunity cost (OC), or the value of having the scrum team work on a new project

When V < AC + OC (or AC + OC > V, as described in Chapter 5), the project can stop. The cost you will sink into the project will be more than the value you will receive from either continuing the project or starting the next project.

Capital redeployment allows an organization to spend efficiently on valuable product development and maximize the organization's overall ROI.

Satisfaction Surveys

A scrum team's highest priority is to satisfy the customer, both early and often, by delivering value. At the same time, the scrum team strives to motivate individual team members and promote sustainable development practices.

A scrum team can benefit from digging deeper into customer and team member experiences. One way to get measurable information about how well a scrum team is fulfilling its purpose is through satisfaction surveys:

✔ **Customer satisfaction surveys** measure the customer's experience with the project, the process, and the scrum team.

The scrum team may want to use customer surveys multiple times during a project, including at the very beginning to establish a benchmark for future comparisons. The scrum team can use customer survey results to examine processes, continue positive practices, and adjust behavior as necessary.

✔ **Team satisfaction surveys** measure the scrum team members' experience with the organization, the work environment, processes, other project team members, and their work. Everyone on the scrum team can take team surveys.

As with the customer survey, the scrum team may choose to give team surveys throughout a project. Scrum team members can use team survey results to regularly fine-tune and adjust personal and team behaviors. The scrum team can also use results to address organizational issues. Customer survey results over time can provide a quantitative look at how the scrum team is maturing as a team.

You can put together informal paper surveys or use one of the many online survey tools. Some companies even have survey software available through their human resources department.

Team Member Turnover

Scrum projects tend to have higher team member morale. One way of quantifying morale is by measuring turnover. You can look at the following metrics:

✔ **Scrum team turnover:** Low scrum team turnover can be one sign of a healthy team environment. High scrum team turnover (resulting from things like burnout, ineffective product owners who force development team commitments, personality incompatibilities, or a scrum master who fails to remove impediments, making the development team look bad in sprint reviews) can indicate problems with the project, the organization, the work, individual scrum team members, or overall team dynamics.

Team members might be quitting, or managers might be stealing team members away to other projects. Either way, the result is increased thrashing and helps to expose organizational issues that should be addressed.

✓ **Company turnover:** High company turnover, even if it doesn't include the scrum team, can impact morale and effectiveness. High company turnover can be a sign of problems within the organization. As a company adopts scrum, it should see turnover decrease.

When the scrum team knows turnover metrics and understands the reasons behind those metrics, it may be able to take actions to maintain morale and improve the work environment.

Project Attrition

Organizations with any size project portfolios should look at the rate of projects being cut short. Capital redeployment should not be confused with thrashing teams between projects at the whim of senior managers. Tracking project durations against capital redeployment analyses may expose trends of either ending projects prematurely or letting them run longer than needed, but most likely the former.

From these trends, portfolio managers can begin to look into reasons why they are getting cut short. High attrition may indicate such issues as thrashing, planning, prioritization, impediments, or cross-functionality.

For more on how scrum improves portfolio management, see Chapter 12.

Skill Versatility

Strong scrum teams are typically more cross-functional than weaker scrum teams. By eliminating single points of failure in a scrum team, you increase its ability to move faster and produce higher quality. Tracking skill versatility allows scrum teams and functional managers to gauge *growth* of cross-functionality. Chapter 13 talks about incentivizing and encouraging skill development for scrum teams.

When starting out, capture the existing skills and levels contained at each of the following organizational structures:

✔ Per-person skills and levels

✔ Per-team skills and levels

✔ Per-organization skills and levels

Over time, as each person increases the quantity and level of skills, each team and the organization will increase. It's not about how many managers or directors you have by title in the organization that will deliver quality products and services to your customers. It's about having team members who can all contribute to the sprint goal each day without the risk of single points of failure.

Manager:Creator Ratio

Typically, the larger the organization, the more likely a heavy middle layer of managers exists. Many organizations haven't figured out how to function well without managers to handle personnel and training and development issues. However, you need to strike the right balance of managers and individuals who produce product.

Every dollar spent on someone who manages organizational processes is a dollar not spent on a product creator.

Track your manager:creator ratio to help you identify bloat and ways to minimize the investment that you're making in people who don't create product.

Chapter 22

Ten Key Resources for Scrum

Many organizations, websites, blogs, and companies exist to provide information about and support for scrum. To help you get started, I've compiled a list of key resources that you can use to support your journey with scrum.

Scrum For Dummies Cheat Sheet

www.dummies.com/cheatsheet/scrum

You can use my online Cheat Sheet as a companion to this book as you start implementing the scrum framework outlined in the previous chapters. You'll find helpful resources there for staying on track with scrum.

Scrum Alliance®

http://scrumalliance.org

The Scrum Alliance is a nonprofit professional membership organization that promotes the understanding and usage of scrum. The alliance achieves this goal by promoting scrum training and certification classes, hosting international and regional scrum gatherings, and supporting scrum user groups. The Scrum Alliance site is rich in blog entries, white papers, case studies, and other tools for learning and working with scrum. Scrum Alliance certifications include

- ✔ Certified ScrumMaster® (CSM)
- ✔ Certified Scrum Product Owner® (CSPO)
- ✔ Certified Scrum Developer® (CSD)
- ✔ Certified Scrum Professional® (CSP)
- ✔ Certified Scrum Coach® (CSC)
- ✔ Certified Scrum Trainer® (CST)

Scrumguides.org

http://scrumguides.org

Jeff Sutherland and Ken Schwaber, the cocreators of scrum, publish *The Scrum Guide™, the Definitive Guide to Scrum: The Rules of the Game* in over 30 languages, all accessible at scrumguides.org. The Scrum Guide is available in both online and PDF formats available for download and is free to use. In less than 20 pages, they have outlined scrum theory and the definitions of each scrum role, artifact, and event.

Scrum.org

http://scrum.org

Scrum.org provides tools and resources for scrum practitioners to deliver value using scrum through assessments and certifications, including

- ✔ Professional Scrum Master™ (PSM)
- ✔ Professional Scrum ProductOwner (PSPO)
- ✔ Professional Scrum Developer™ (PSD)

ScrumPLoP

http://scrumplop.org

Pattern Languages of Programs (PLoP) are methods of describing design practices within fields of expertise, and often have conferences organized around them for shared learning. ScrumPLoP publishes patterns authored by scrum professionals, many of which have been authored by Jeff Sutherland, cocreator of scrum. These are practical patterns that have been used successfully with organizations to get started with and become successful with scrum.

Scaled Agile Framework® (SAFe®)

http://scaledagileframework.com

The Scaled Agile Framework® (SAFe®) is a knowledge base for implementing agile practices and scrum at scale. Its "Big Picture" graphic is its primary interface that you can click through to see highlights of the roles, teams, activities, and artifacts.

SAFe is a registered trademark of Scaled Agile Inc.

LeSS

http://less.works

Large-Scale Scrum (or LeSS) is a scrum-scaling method that provides two different frameworks, known as LeSS and LeSS Huge. Like SAFe, LeSS also provides a graphic that is the interface for clicking through to learn about the highlights of the frameworks.

InfoQ

www.infoq.com/scrum

InfoQ is an independent online community with a prominent scrum section offering news, articles, video interviews, video presentations, and minibooks, all written by scrum domain experts. The resources at InfoQ tend to be very high quality, and the content is both unique and relevant to the issues facing scrum teams.

Scrum Development Yahoo! Group

http://groups.yahoo.com/group/scrumdevelopment

Started in 2000, the Scrum Development Yahoo! Group has thousands of members, including several signatories of the Agile Manifesto. The Scrum Development Yahoo! Group is a good source for staying in tune with the global scrum community.

Platinum Edge

http://platinumedge.com

Since 2001, my team at Platinum Edge has been helping companies maximize organizational return on investment (ROI). Visit our blog to get the latest insights on practices, tools, and innovative solutions emerging from our work with Global 1000 companies and the dynamic agile community.

We also provide the following services:

- **Agile audits:** Auditing of your current organizational structure and processes to create an agile implementation strategy that delivers bottom-line results.
- **Recruiting:** With access to the best agile and scrum talent — because we've personally trained them — we help you find the best fit for your needs to bootstrap your scrum projects, including scrum masters, scrum product owners, and scrum developers.
- **Training:** Public and private customized corporate agile and scrum training and certification, regardless of your level of knowledge:
  - Certified ScrumMaster® classes (CSM)
  - Certified Scrum Product Owner® classes (CSPO)
  - Certified Scrum Developer® classes (CSD)
  - SAFe Scaled Agile training and implementations
- **Transformation:** Follow up on agile coaching and training with agile mentoring to ensure that the right practices occur in the real world.

Index

About the Authors

Mark C. Layton, known globally as Mr. Agile™, is an organizational strategist and PMI certification instructor with over 20 years in the project/program management field. He is the Los Angeles chair for the Agile Leadership Network and is the founder of Platinum Edge, Inc. — an organizational improvement company that supports businesses making the waterfall-to-agile transition.

Prior to founding Platinum Edge in 2001, Mark developed his expertise as a consulting firm executive, program management coach, and in-the-trenches project leader. He also spent 11 years as a cryptographic specialist for the U.S. Air Force, where he earned both Commendation and Achievement medals for his accomplishments.

Mark holds MBAs from the University of California, Los Angeles, and the National University of Singapore; a B.Sc. (*summa cum laude*) in behavioral science from University of La Verne; and an A.S. in Electronic Systems from the Air Force's Air College. He is also a distinguished graduate of the Air Force's Leadership School, a Certified Scrum Trainer (CST), a certified scaled agile program consultant (SAFe SPC), a certified Project Management Professional (PMP), and a recipient of Stanford University's advanced project management certification (SCPM).

When he isn't overseeing client engagements, Mark is a frequent speaker on Scrum, eXtreme Programming (XP), Lean, and other agile solutions. He lives in Las Vegas, Nevada.

Additional information can be found at www.platinumedge.com.

Dedication

To the knockout of my life. Thanks.

Authors' Acknowledgments

I'd like to thank the numerous people who contributed to this book and helped make it a reality. Steve Ostermiller, your thought leadership, diplomacy, and relentless work ethic in helping make this book a reality are inspirational. Renee Jumper, your flexibility and "can-do" attitude make all the difference in projects like this one. I'm so appreciative to have you both on the bus and in the direction we're going. Caroline Patchen, your ongoing support and ability to make concepts come alive visually were instrumental. Thank you.

Additionally, I'd like to thank the industry advisors whose input helped make several chapters of the book better: Amber Allen (LAUSD) and Renee Jumper on education; Anna Kennedy (author of *Business Development For Dummies* [published by John Wiley & Sons, Inc.]) on business development and sales; Brian Dreyer on video game and business development; Adi Ekowibowo, Farid Kazimi, Charles Park, and Scot Karmarich on video game development; Sean Dunn, Benjamin Saville, and Doc Dochtermann on military and law enforcement; Kelly Anderson on talent management (HR); Melani Chacon on customer service; Hiren Vashi, Lisa White, Doc Dochtermann, and Sunil Bhandari on healthcare; Lowell Feil, Rob Carstons, and Steffanie Duchér for enterprise resource planning (ERP); Brady Mortensen on publishing; Mogenns Gilmour on hardware development; Elana Gould-Davies on manufacturing; and Dean Leffingwell, Alex Yakyma, Bas Vodde, and Craig Larman on enterprise scaling models. I'd like to extend a special thank you to Rob Carstons for helping us facilitate and organize the feedback from the various industry experts as we brought everything together.

I'd also like to say thank you to the amazing team at Wiley & Sons: Connie Santisteban, who originated the idea of a second book; Andy Cummings for his relentless support throughout the process; Pat O'Brien for his guidance and ongoing refinements; and the many, many others who contributed their time and expertise to making this book the anytime, any-situation, guide I hoped it would be.

Publisher's Acknowledgments

Project Editor: Pat O'Brien

Copy Editor: John Edwards

Technical Editor: Steve Ostermiller

Editorial Assistant: Claire Brock

Sr. Editorial Assistant: Cherie Case

Project Coordinator: R Kinson Raja

Cover Image: ©iStock.com/Sylverarts

2015
9/16: 6x lad 4/16 A1 F10
19/18: 10x " 1/18

Apple & Mac

iPad For Dummies,
6th Edition
978-1-118-72306-7

iPhone For Dummies,
7th Edition
978-1-118-69083-3

Macs All-in-One
For Dummies, 4th Edition
978-1-118-82210-4

OS X Mavericks
For Dummies
978-1-118-69188-5

Blogging & Social Media

Facebook For Dummies,
5th Edition
978-1-118-63312-0

Social Media Engagement
For Dummies
978-1-118-53019-1

WordPress For Dummies,
6th Edition
978-1-118-79161-5

Business

Stock Investing
For Dummies, 4th Edition
978-1-118-37678-2

Investing For Dummies,
6th Edition
978-0-470-90545-6

Personal Finance
For Dummies, 7th Edition
978-1-118-11785-9

QuickBooks 2014
For Dummies
978-1-118-72005-9

Small Business Marketing
Kit For Dummies,
3rd Edition
978-1-118-31183-7

Careers

Job Interviews
For Dummies, 4th Edition
978-1-118-11290-8

Job Searching with Social
Media For Dummies,
2nd Edition
978-1-118-67856-5

Personal Branding
For Dummies
978-1-118-11792-7

Resumes For Dummies,
6th Edition
978-0-470-87361-8

Starting an Etsy Business
For Dummies, 2nd Edition
978-1-118-59024-9

Diet & Nutrition

Belly Fat Diet For Dummies
978-1-118-34585-6

Mediterranean Diet
For Dummies
978-1-118-71525-3

Nutrition For Dummies,
5th Edition
978-0-470-93231-5

Digital Photography

Digital SLR Photography
All-in-One For Dummies,
2nd Edition
978-1-118-59082-9

Digital SLR Video &
Filmmaking For Dummies
978-1-118-36598-4

Photoshop Elements 12
For Dummies
978-1-118-72714-0

Gardening

Herb Gardening
For Dummies, 2nd Edition
978-0-470-61778-6

Gardening with Free-Range
Chickens For Dummies
978-1-118-54754-0

Health

Boosting Your Immunity
For Dummies
978-1-118-40200-9

Diabetes For Dummies,
4th Edition
978-1-118-29447-5

Living Paleo For Dummies
978-1-118-29405-5

Big Data

Big Data For Dummies
978-1-118-50422-2

Data Visualization
For Dummies
978-1-118-50289-1

Hadoop For Dummies
978-1-118-60755-8

Language &
Foreign Language

500 Spanish Verbs
For Dummies
978-1-118-02382-2

English Grammar
For Dummies, 2nd Edition
978-0-470-54664-2

French All-in-One
For Dummies
978-1-118-22815-9

German Essentials
For Dummies
978-1-118-18422-6

Italian For Dummies,
2nd Edition
978-1-118-00465-4

Available in print and e-book formats.

Available wherever books are sold. **For more information or to order direct visit www.dummies.com**

Math & Science

Algebra I For Dummies,
2nd Edition
978-0-470-55964-2

Anatomy and Physiology
For Dummies, 2nd Edition
978-0-470-92326-9

Astronomy For Dummies,
3rd Edition
978-1-118-37697-3

Biology For Dummies,
2nd Edition
978-0-470-59875-7

Chemistry For Dummies,
2nd Edition
978-1-118-00730-3

1001 Algebra II Practice
Problems For Dummies
978-1-118-44662-1

Microsoft Office

Excel 2013 For Dummies
978-1-118-51012-4

Office 2013 All-in-One
For Dummies
978-1-118-51636-2

PowerPoint 2013
For Dummies
978-1-118-50253-2

Word 2013 For Dummies
978-1-118-49123-2

Music

Blues Harmonica
For Dummies
978-1-118-25269-7

Guitar For Dummies,
3rd Edition
978-1-118-11554-1

iPod & iTunes
For Dummies, 10th Edition
978-1-118-50864-0

Programming

Beginning Programming
with C For Dummies
978-1-118-73763-7

Excel VBA Programming
For Dummies, 3rd Edition
978-1-118-49037-2

Java For Dummies,
6th Edition
978-1-118-40780-6

Religion & Inspiration

The Bible For Dummies
978-0-7645-5296-0

Buddhism For Dummies,
2nd Edition
978-1-118-02379-2

Catholicism For Dummies,
2nd Edition
978-1-118-07778-8

Self-Help & Relationships

Beating Sugar Addiction
For Dummies
978-1-118-54645-1

Meditation For Dummies,
3rd Edition
978-1-118-29144-3

Seniors

Laptops For Seniors
For Dummies, 3rd Edition
978-1-118-71105-7

Computers For Seniors
For Dummies, 3rd Edition
978-1-118-11553-4

iPad For Seniors
For Dummies, 6th Edition
978-1-118-72826-0

Social Security
For Dummies
978-1-118-20573-0

Smartphones & Tablets

Android Phones
For Dummies, 2nd Edition
978-1-118-72030-1

Nexus Tablets
For Dummies
978-1-118-77243-0

Samsung Galaxy S 4
For Dummies
978-1-118-64222-1

Samsung Galaxy Tabs
For Dummies
978-1-118-77294-2

Test Prep

ACT For Dummies,
5th Edition
978-1-118-01259-8

ASVAB For Dummies,
3rd Edition
978-0-470-63760-9

GRE For Dummies,
7th Edition
978-0-470-88921-3

Officer Candidate Tests
For Dummies
978-0-470-59876-4

Physician's Assistant Exam
For Dummies
978-1-118-11556-5

Series 7 Exam For Dumm
978-0-470-09932-2

Windows 8

Windows 8.1 All-in-One
For Dummies
978-1-118-82087-2

Windows 8.1 For Dummi
978-1-118-82121-3

Windows 8.1 For Dummi
Book + DVD Bundle
978-1-118-82107-7

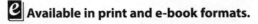

Available in print and e-book formats.

Available wherever books are sold. **For more information or to order direct visit www.dummies.com**